DOCUMENTARY IN AMERICAN TELEVISION

DOCUMENTARY
in American Television

FORM · FUNCTION · METHOD

By A. WILLIAM BLUEM

Newhouse Communications Center

Syracuse University

COMMUNICATION ARTS BOOKS

HASTINGS HOUSE, PUBLISHERS

New York

This book is for Toni
— who could not wait
to see it done.

Second Printing, December 1968
Third Printing, October 1969
Fourth Printing, March 1971
Fifth Printing, September 1972

COPYRIGHT © 1965 by A. William Bluem

Published simultaneously in Canada
by Saunders of Toronto, Ltd., Don Mills, Ontario
ISBN: 8038-1527-1
Library of Congress Catalog Card Number: 64-8111
Printed in the United States of America

CONTENTS

FOREWORD

TELEVISION has as much to do with *Documentary in American Television* as the book itself has to do with television. Were it not for the voracious, time-eating, all-consuming, mesmerizing video screen, I seriously doubt that this book would have been written, or even needed.

Television has given the documentary film its greatest impetus; it has all but rescued an ailing patient *in extremis*. It took an established art form, whose roots lay in the works of such talents as Flaherty, Grierson, Rotha, Wright, Legg, Lorentz, Van Dyke, Cavalcanti, Ruttman, and Eisenstein, and infused it with the two essentials it was lacking — a vast audience and enough money to produce. It also gave it a good deal of artistic freedom, often under the reasonably sacrosanct umbrella of the network news divisions.

The motion-picture exhibitors just about buried the documentary rather insolently referred to as "shorts." As Bosley Crowther of the New York *Times* pointed out not long ago, [The exhibitors] . . . "were loath to pay much money for shorts. They would cough up all kinds of money to get a premium feature film, but no matter how good a short was, they'd scream at the top of their lungs at paying much money for it. . . . When block-booking was eliminated and shorts distributors were left to their own resources in making deals, they were pretty well beat."

While there are still documentaries being made other than for television, some of considerable merit, the main thrust has been for the video screen. This is not the first book written on the documentary as such. *Grierson on Documentary* and Rotha's *The Documentary Film* are still valuable sources in the field. The time is particularly propitious, however, for this

7

book by Dr. A. William Bluem of Syracuse University. The documentary
has been revived, and it is right that this vital subject be re-explored.

Dr. Bluem has avoided one pitfall occurring in some of the recent
literature on the subject, and for this we can be grateful. He is frank to
admit that television has revived the documentary form. He does not suggest that television gave it birth. So pronounced has been this paternal
temptation in television that not long ago a frenetic word game was launched
to try and rename the documentary, which was considered to be archaic,
derivative, *infra dig* — or, to put it more honestly, simply not box office.
After going on a semantic jag with "telementaries," "docudramas," "fact-
dramas," "actuality dramas with a hard spine," to name a few, the game
was abandoned. Documentary was accepted for what it was — and had
been for a long time.

Dr. Bluem freely recognizes the documentarian's debt to his predecessors. It is high time some of the practitioners in the field do so. To give one
example, the next producer who cuts a rousing war sequence and does not
admit some small debt to Frank Capra and *Why We Fight* is probably not
playing fair. His World War II series has been an inspiration to creative
people, particularly film editors, ever since. Dr. Bluem also acknowledges
what I believe to be an important truth: that while television has profited
enormously from the past, it also has materially advanced the art of the
documentary, creatively and in technique.

The important contributions that this book makes, in my judgment,
are these: it treats the subject historically, which gives the documentary a
needed perspective. It treats it seriously, as a creative endeavor and not
merely as a peripheral aspect of the "entertainment" business to mollify
the FCC. It manages to collate, organize, and give clarity to a new, evolving,
and highly volatile subject. The documentary has moved so swiftly that this
book is almost as much current affairs as it is recent history.

The opinions and judgments are all Dr. Bluem's, of course, as is the
factual research and everything else in this book. This reader, who has been
involved in the documentary for the cinema and for television, is grateful
to him for undertaking a study of this magnitude in a field so important to
so many of us.

BURTON BENJAMIN

Scarborough-on-Hudson, N. Y.
July, 1964

PREFACE

AT SOME POINT in time between 1947 and 1950 American television emerged from its technical and experimental stages to become the major communications force in all recorded history. In roughly a decade and a half television has come to dominate our existence by shaping values and attitudes, by influencing the social structures of our civilization, and by setting new standards and goals for the vast populations of a world society which draws ever closer together.

The intention here is not to declare the weaknesses of the medium — a task in which both the sincere and insincere from all walks of life, including those in the television profession, are steadily engaged. Rather, I have attempted to set into some limited context that aspect of television in America which has properly and honorably reached beyond the easy and the merely enjoyable. Television's function to entertain is both right and necessary; but to communicate is also to inform, to stimulate, to make aware. Of TV's power to inform we have been given an impressive measure. In so many ways it has brought to Americans a greater sense of life, of human experience, and of those issues and events which determine the course of our civilization. Television has done so in a variety of program contexts, of which none is more serious in implication than the "documentary."

Since John Grierson first brought documentary into modern usage by adapting it from the word *documentaire* and employing it to describe a certain idea and concept in human communication, many have borrowed the term and applied it to their own efforts. Its use has often become so broad that many sincere students of documentary evolution in the cinema have abandoned all hope of firm definition. Yet there are certain guidelines which are helpful in establishing the meaning of documentary, and since the early 1950's there has been an abundance of work in television which makes definition possible.

The purpose of this book is to offer a detailed record of this work, to describe the major sources which informed and inspired it, to point out achievements, to identify the people instrumental in shaping it, and finally, to consider the problems and possibilities of the uses of documentary in a free civilization. Between purposes and realization always lie obstacles. The sheer number of such offerings over a 15-year period presents an overwhelming detail, and has resulted in a concentration of my discussion toward efforts which were given national or near-national exposure. Such stress does not preclude the possibility that I may have overlooked significant experiments in form and technique at local and regional levels. On the other hand, there is little doubt that documentary in television received its first and most continuing encouragement and experimentation at the national level, and mainly by American networks.

More troublesome are the difficulties of bringing the idea of documentary, as it has been carried across all of the public media in this century, within some reasonably controlled definition. Here one must accept the fact that theorists in the documentary film have already trod rocky paths in attempts to clarify our understanding of this unique 20th-century communications phenomenon. I have relied heavily upon their insights and opinions as I traveled less frequented paths through still photography, radio, and finally into television itself.

In the long history of documentary before television, emphasis had been placed upon its cinematic expressions. I have tried not to neglect or underestimate the contribution of the documentary film, although my discussion of this work is severely limited in length, and largely dependent upon the availability of classic films for study. Yet I also believe that the role of formal drama and dramaturgical structure in relation to documentary has been insufficiently noted, as have been the special conditions of documentary production and distribution introduced by broadcast communication. To these I have given the greater emphasis.

*   *   *   *

Ideas and inspiration were derived from many sources, and I am obliged to credit those colleagues upon whom I have placed reliance in writing certain sections of this book. It was their labor of research which provided the initial studies in non-television areas of the documentary movement as well as in seminal television series.

For the historical evolution of *March of Time* I am grateful to Raymond Fielding, of the University of California at Los Angeles, who has written an authoritative thesis on this film series.

Murray Yeager has contributed an important University of Iowa doctoral dissertation on the *See It Now* series, and Myron Berkely Shaw has performed the same service for *Armstrong Circle Theatre,* on which a thesis was completed at the University of Michigan. These works were useful to me.

For the section dealing with the documentary idea in still photography I am grateful chiefly to Beaumont Newhall, of Eastman House in Rochester, whose several scholarly treatises on the art of photography were consulted.

At Eastman House I also owe a particular debt to James Card, Vice-director, who made it possible for me to view many rare films, and who provided invaluable advice and comment as the project got under way. Since those days when Mr. Card was my teacher in the public schools of Cleveland, he has exerted a strong influence over my professional interest in communication, and the research for this work provided wonderful opportunities for reminiscence and renewed exchange of ideas.

Among the colleagues who read and evaluated the manuscript-in-progress, I am especially indebted to Professor Ernest Rose, of the University of California at Berkeley, and Professor John Driscoll of Syracuse University. Their comments and criticisms were of significant help to me in shaping various sections of this work.

Professor Richard Averson of Syracuse, my loyal associate in the *Television Quarterly* office and a good friend, deserves thanks for his contribution — one not easily measured or described.

Burton Benjamin is acknowledged for his generous Foreword and his kind interest in this project — and for his work, which may be the best of all reasons for gratitude.

Russell Neale, of Hastings House, is thanked for being tough when needed — and gentle when required.

At the networks sincere appreciation is extended to May Dowell of CBS-TV; Sydney H. Eiges and Milton Brown at NBC-TV; John Secondari and John Lynch at ABC-TV; James Nolan, Nancy Astor, Richard Hanser and Silvio D'Alisera at NBC-TV Special Projects; Leonard Spinrad and Robert Chandler at CBS-TV; Richard Krolik and Lillian Owens at Time-Life Broadcasting; Richard Sarno at ABC; Robert Rubin, now at CBS; William Quinn at NBC News Creative Projects; Isaac Kleinermann, John Gilligan, Barbara Sapinsley, and the staff at *The Twentieth Century*; Walter Cronkite at CBS; Lou Hazam at NBC in Washington; Reuven Frank at NBC News; and Don Hewitt at CBS News.

I offer thanks also to David Wolper; Robert Drew; Richard M. Pack, and a number of other helpful people in the Group W organization; Jo-Ann Ordano at Time-Life Broadcasting; Kay Campbell at Granada TV in New York; Marian Moss, Sue Goldman, and Denis Scuse at BBC in New York; Thom Benson, Tony Partridge, and Jack Pascoe at CBC-TV in Toronto.

Nearer home, special appreciation is due Syracuse University staff personnel, including Fern Greenfield of the *Television Quarterly* office and

James Smith and Nancy Laidlaw at Audio-Visual Services. I must add my
appreciation of the efforts by Mrs. Charlotte Pryzchocki and Mrs. Lillian
Lieberman, who were of great assistance in the preparation of the manu-
script.

I also owe a debt to Janet Griffin, a Syracuse student assigned to me
for a senior honors project in documentary broadcasting, who lost none of
her dedication while viewing nearly 300 films and enduring my endless, if
not always instructive, comment thereon.

At home, simple thanks to Janet, Tom, and John — for everything.

Finally, I would extend warmest gratitude to the Trustees of the
Kaltenborn Foundation. In the practical sense their generous grant made
possible the many trips to production centers, innumerable hours of film
viewing, and precious time for reflection. But in a deeper sense I am mind-
ful of that moment on *Portrait,* a nationally televised CBS series carried in
the summer of 1963, when Mr. Kaltenborn leaned forward and corrected
Charles Collingwood's reference to "our business" by saying, quite firmly,
"You mean our *profession.*" That single statement reflected the pride of a
long and distinguished career spent in gathering and communicating the
news of our time, revealing the zeal and enthusiasm of a man who believed
not only in his work, but — above all — in the potential greatness and
dignity of the media in which he performed it.

This book tells of many things, but it deals mostly with the men and
women who share with Hans Kaltenborn that commitment to broadcasting;
and it is their work which honors him.

A. WILLIAM BLUEM

Syracuse, New York
   August, 1964

The Documentary Idea: A Frame of Reference

TECHNOLOGY has afforded us a number of remarkable ways by which to reproduce the sights and sounds of the world, to make accurate and authentic records of human beings and of the events and circumstances in which they involve themselves. It has given us the powers to transmit such records and documents to great segments of the public at incredible speed. Never in history has such an outpouring of recorded fact, a flood of aural and visual detail, washed over a citizenry. Never has such an intense concentration of information been carried to people with such immediacy.

Yet men do not live by, or act upon, facts in themselves. The *documents* of life become meaningful only when they have been invested with significance, first by those who transmit them, and again by those who receive them. The words, sounds, and pictures which transmit us some aspect of reality are still only symbols, the connotative meanings of which move men first to feel, then to ponder, and finally to summon their energies toward controlling the direction of life.

Those kinds of communication which are informed by the *documentary* idea are founded upon the conviction that the events and circumstances which shape man's life must not only be recorded and reported, but that such reporting must be made in as compelling a fashion as possible. The function of documentary communication is to *make drama from life*. For John Grierson the purpose of such communication was to make observation a little richer than it was[1] by creative interpretation of actuality. This precondition must be acknowledged before the very idea of documentary can exist.

13

Yet such easy phrases as "dramatization of fact" or "creative treatment of actuality" are tautologies. They do not define except in terms of themselves. Communication among human beings involves aural and visual expression of reality observed. This implies an observer who, in the act of perceiving that reality, has already begun some process of interpretation. In the transmission of his felt experience, he employs communication techniques which still further interpret and dramatize, giving, in Walt Whitman's terms, "poetic vivification to fact." For sensations do not exist apart from meanings, values, and motives. Only when we accept the role of the symbol in experience can we understand, as Lewis Mumford notes, "the limitations of science and technic, since they are by intention an expression of that part of the personality from which emotion and feeling and desire and sympathy — the stuff of life and art — have been eliminated."[2]

Since man interprets experience in the very act of perception, he must create symbolic equivalents, and consequently prestructure the nature and arrangements of the aural and visual symbols with which he shares his experience. And those to whom he communicates must, in turn, structure the communication in terms of their own experience. In its ultimate sense, then, all communication involves a creative, interpretative process.

With this in mind, the problem of describing the documentary idea begins to take shape. It is not merely by chance that the documentary concept has been characterized as existing in a "gray area" between *art* and *journalism*. The selecting and arranging process which takes place during perception and transmission of experience is fundamental to both subjective (artistic) and objective (journalistic) communication. The unwillingness to accept this condition has led men — perhaps to preserve their sanity — to invent and revere concepts such as "objectivity," and yet, at the same time, seriously propose to make "truth" from facts. On this dichotomy rests the documentary idea.

But documentary is more than an idea. It is an undeniable form of public communication, functioning within certain ascertainable conditions. Valid documentary must involve more than presentation of the records of life. There must be a social purpose in its conception and the use of a technology which permits a significant impact in its dissemination.

Almost all kinds of human communication have some social purpose. The element as stated implies, however, something more specific: *the presentation of socially useful information to a public*. From such information comes knowledge, and from knowledge is derived the understanding which can lead to societal action. Documentary communication seeks to initiate a process which culminates in public action by presenting information, and to complete the process by making this presentation persuasive. Documentary seeks to inform but, above all, it seeks to influence.

These basically didactic purposes — to inform and to persuade — need not be equated with dullness. As Grierson has suggested, the documentary film promised us the power of making "drama from our daily lives and poetry from our problems."[3] And Margaret R. Weiss, speaking of the special medium of the still photograph, observed that "in the broadest sense, a documentary is created whenever 'things as they are' are depicted."[4] Within such views of documentary, dullness does not seem a corollary to didacticism. A dedication to making observation richer than it was surely leaves wide the documentary path.

In the matter of social utility, it may also be noted that much of documentary was born in bitterness and nurtured on human crisis. Before and since television, it has too often been inspired by man's misery and informed by his despair. Social evils and those violent struggles of both men and societies to survive have constituted the bulk of documentary's subject matter for the past half century, and documentarists have not always managed to penetrate the grimness of events to elicit the more hopeful statement.

But these are conjectures upon the direction of content in communication, not a reflection on the unchangeable condition which makes it "documentary," whatever its approach or medium. Communication is valid as documentary only when it is designed to further and advance individual and social causes, values, conditions, and institutions by inspiring man to consider their significance and relationship to himself as a social being. Dullness at one extreme and despair at another do not detract from the validity of documentary itself.

Social value is served in a variety of specialized contexts. Social utility may be realized in instructional communications which deal with a limited area of human knowledge and are designed for relatively small segments of the public. Or it may work itself out as the record of change — that measuring of conflict in a civilization which we have come to call journalism — which is aimed at the largest possible public. Lastly, it may be realized in the many expressions of themes about man as an individual and as a social being: how he lives, how he gets and spends, and how he endeavors to prevail.

It is in the latter two areas of informational communication that the techniques of making drama from fact find the greatest freedom of range in application. While it is impossible to ignore the vast quantity of instructional or formally "educational" communications — all of which may or may not involve documentary's interpretative processes — the nonspecialized informational communications directed toward the broadest public are of more urgent concern.

Granting that some kind of social usefulness is an outcome sought by all documentary presentation, it follows that the dissemination of such information is purposeful and meaningful in direct proportion to the numbers of people reached and influenced. And because of this, documentary does not truly exist without the technology of mass communication. Unless great numbers of men are reached, and to such a degree of immediacy that the information presented is relevant to their condition of life, documentary is denied much of its independent character.

It is not so much the technology of visual and aural recording of reality which undergirds documentary's existence as the technology by which records can be reproduced and disseminated to masses of human beings. The more private and individual the nature of the communication, the less is it related to the very idea of documentary. And this, inevitably, leads to television, the ultimate medium for transmission of documentary communication. Television *is* mass communication, and in this lies its strength as a documentary instrument.

How television documentary has made social drama from the raw material of life is our chief concern. But television has many debts to the media which preceded it and which continue to nourish it. The forms, techniques, approaches, and ideals of documentary all came out of the past, which is where we ought to begin.

1 / Photography: The Fixed Moment

. . . Historical, realistic, factual. While each of these qualities is contained within documentary, none of them conveys the deep respect for fact and the desire to create active interpretations of the world in which we live that mark documentary photography at its best apart from bald camera record.

— BEAUMONT NEWHALL[1]

TELEVISION's long heritage of systems and approaches by which to document life for the world's watching millions began over a century ago when Joseph-Nicéphore Niépce succeeded in his efforts to fix permanently a camera's image upon a metal plate. His work was advanced and refined by Louis Daguerre, who achieved the first practical process for duplicating and preserving a moment of true visual experience. The process was described by England's John Herschel as "photography." With light, camera, and chemicals, it became possible for men to fix in exact detail the actuality of life. What had heretofore been only a dim memory of things once seen, or impressions of life painted by artists, now became the immutable record of life, exercising, in Maya Deren's terms, "an authority comparable in weight only to the authority of reality itself."[2]

PHOTOGRAPHY AS RECORD

As photographic technology advanced, men found new uses for this authority. For Niépce, the simple function of his invention was to "copy nature with the greatest fidelity," and in the 1850's an Englishman named Roger Fenton went to the Crimea. At Balaklava, in 1855, Fenton documented the Crimean War, returning with over 300 negatives taken of battlefields and the men who fought upon them. His documentation was the first important journalistic use of photography. This work was soon complemented in America, where Mathew Brady also learned the secrets of photography in time to record the Civil War. With his aides, Timothy

THE GENOESE FORT AT THE ENTRANCE TO BALAKLAVA HARBOR
Roger Fenton (1855)

. . . to copy nature with the greatest fidelity.

O'Sullivan and Alexander Gardner, Brady directed the work of 22 teams of assistants in the pictorial reproduction of the conflict; and in such remarkable pictures as Gardner's *Home of a Rebel Sharpshooter* and O'Sullivan's *Harvest of Death,* taken at Gettysburg in 1863, it was demonstrated that the photograph could not only record events, but penetrate the surface details of reality to make strong and dramatic commentary.

Out of the early work by growing numbers of photographers grew the understanding that their documents might be used to inform and influence those who could not be present at the scenes of social change, conflict, and discovery. Gardner took his camera west in 1867 to record the life of work gangs laying tracks for the Union Pacific Railroad. The driving of the golden spike at Promontory Point, Utah, was photographed in 1869 by Charles Savage. O'Sullivan accompanied an expedition along the 40th parallel in 1867, and in 1870 recorded the building of the Panama Canal. In 1872 William Henry Jackson, "the frontier photographer," toured the West, sending back the first picture of "Old Faithful," as well as a series of photographs which were submitted as evidence in a successful fight to establish Yellowstone National Park. This was the first important demonstration of the photographer's role in influencing social change.

GEORGE EASTMAN HOUSE

HOME OF A REBEL SHARPSHOOTER — Alexander Gardner. (1863)

GEORGE EASTMAN HOUSE

A HARVEST OF DEATH — T. H. O'Sullivan. (1863)

. . . not only to record events, but to make strong and dramatic commentary.

Photography As Art

The work of these photographers led to the rise of modern photo-journalism, and informed a documentary movement in photography. Other experiments, however, were equally relevant to the emergence of the kind of later still photography which became documentary in name as well as in fact. In Paris during the 1850's a portraitist named Gaspard-Felixe Tournachon earned fame (as Nadar) by photographing people with a new sense of intimacy and penetration, taking his work far beyond the stiff portraiture of the period. In his pictures of such famous people as Baudelaire and Sarah Bernhardt, he added a dimension to portrait photography by seeking to create an impression beyond mere formal records. His were among the initial ventures into creative use of the camera. Arising from such early innovation came a growing interest in photography as a visual art. Pioneered in Europe by such photographers as Oscar Rylander, Henry Peach Robinson, Antony Samuel Adam-Solomon, and Julia Margaret Cameron, the pictorial movement in photography was given additional impetus in America by Alfred Stieglitz.

In 1890 the young Stieglitz began to make a series of photographs in which attention was given to composition, the use of light and shadow, and stress upon purely pictorial impression as well as upon a given content. Moving beyond Nadar's efforts to reveal personality in the portrait, Stieglitz created beautiful, yet natural, studies in form and composition, as represented by such photographs as *The Terminal* (1893), *The Steerage* (1907), and *Georgia O'Keefe* (1932). In his work Stieglitz minimized earlier European controversies over manipulation of the negative in attempts to emulate painting, and demonstrated that what earlier pictorialists had done during the developing process could also be achieved by applying careful photographic method at the outset.

In Stieglitz's path followed such photographic artists as Edward Steichen, Clarence H. White, Alvin Coburn, and others who had found in photography a means of expressing creatively the reality about them. Again, their work went beyond photography merely for the sake of a record. Steichen worked with deliberately and carefully posed picture elements, seeking clarity and precision in the revelation of natural objects. Others sought an expression of pure form with stress upon the interplay of light and design for its own sake; and by so doing, found ways of creating mood and feeling in a strongly subjective treatment of commonplace material.

It is not by accident, however, that many of those whose early interest lay in the pictorial value of photography moved on to work in photo-journalism and the documentary movement. Both approaches required an instinctive and effective sense of composition, combined with an innate capacity to understand the human significance of what was being pictured.

From Stieglitz, as well as from the work of Paul Strand, Edward Weston, Ansel Adams, and others who revealed that photographic art could exist because of, and not despite, the clarity and integrity of the unretouched negative and print, emerged this second great photographic movement which influenced both journalistic and documentary still photography.

PHOTOJOURNALISM

Wilbur Schramm has observed that *"news* exists in the minds of men," that news is not the event itself but something perceived after the event has occurred, "an attempt to reconstruct the essential framework of the event — essential being defined against a frame of reference which is calculated to make the event meaningful to the reader."[3] This function, wrote Arthur Rothstein, is carried on by the photojournalists, "observers of people and events who report what is happening in photographs; interpreters of facts and occurrences who write with a camera."[4]

As early as 1842 such journals as the *Illustrated London News, L'Illustration,* and *Harper's Weekly* carried, in addition to war photographs, the visual records of such minor crises and tumults of history as train wrecks and fires. But the early processes of reproduction left something to be desired, and for reasons of economy, even *Harper's Weekly* found it simpler to have artists base sketches upon actual Brady photos — an odd and ironic corruption of the very quality in the photograph which its invention promised, the "true" record. But advances in the technology of reproducing the tonal range of photographs with greater speed and efficiency were soon forthcoming, and within two decades after the first newspaper "halftone" appeared in the New York *Daily Graphic* in 1880, photographic news illustration became an accepted, and expected, function of the press.

Now the work of the news photographer could be widely disseminated, and as the capacities of his equipment increased, he came to introduce new conditions and principles to photography. He learned that he must work quickly as well as skillfully in order to record events as they occur, and that the reporting camera "does what no other medium can do. It opens up new vistas and bares the relations of people to their environments with unequalled precision."[5]

In many ways, photojournalism closely parallels the documentary movement in still photography. The photograph, in conjunction with print, served a distinct social purpose in that it involved a growing public in matters of vital concern, a necessary condition if the ideal of the democratic process was to have meaning. If the journalist was committed to record what he saw — to let the nature of his subject guide and control the nature of his communication — he could, with clarity and insight, also express universal principles, pictorial records to which witnesses could respond with hearts as well as minds. Social purpose, which is documentary's intent, could also be advanced by the photojournalist. In the tradition of William Henry Jackson the news photographer could record scenes which underscored the need for better social conditions, better laws — and better people — within community and nation.

Finally, the journalist's graphic portrayals of error, evil, and injustice often reflected the purpose and scope of photographic documentary — to make drama from life. No one who has seen the work of Robert Capa, who lived and died on the battlefields of our times, can come away with the feeling of having seen mere "fact." It is in the overtones of his work — perhaps best illustrated in his classic *Death of a Loyalist Soldier* — that identity with life and pictorial instinct combine to make a powerful statement about humanity. In this photo we sense the violence and brutality of war and the strange and furious power of irrational men. Having witnessed it, we come away awed, possessed of an insight which no record of "fact" can give us.

Such revelation of the deep forces which control men in their struggle to prevail is also evident in Joseph Costa's photographs of veterans battling police in Washington during the 1930's, in the terrifying INS shot of the Chinese baby screaming amid the rubble of a gutted Shanghai in the wake of the Japanese bombings, in Sam Caldwell's shot of the relatives of trapped coal-miners waiting at the mine entrance after the 1947 Centralia explosion, and in the study of England's three queens in mourning for George VI. These photographs give us that expression of life's deepest significance which extends beyond events themselves. They give us "theme" as well as "subject." They involve our emotions and, to the extent that they do, are documentary photographs. Yet these were the products of "spot" news photographers, thinking only of the most efficient and rapid way to record an event and, by chance or design, defining and characterizing it in a dramatic way.

For many observers, however, such news photographs could achieve documentary quality only by accident, and only in rare moments when the content was immediate and overwhelmingly dramatic. From a purist's viewpoint, documentary has validity only if it involves a strong effort to move an audience, if not to overt action, then at least to positive expressions of attitude. This helps us to understand why documentary has at one time or another turned to social poverty and despair for its subject matter.

FORMAL DOCUMENTARY

With didacticism as its *raison d'être,* a movement within still photography which may more truly be labeled documentary was founded in the 1880's by a Danish immigrant, Jacob A. Riis, who went to the tenements and slums of New York to photograph the poverty of the immigrant.

ITALIAN FAMILY LOOKING FOR LOST BAGGAGE — Lewis W. Hine (1905)

ITALIAN MOTHER AND CHILD, JERSEY STREET
Jacob A. Riis (About 1889)

*. . . not simply to register events and circumstances,
but to find the most moving examples of them.*

In 1888 Riis published a series of drawings based upon his documents, which included such records of despair as *Italian Mother and Her Baby in Jersey Street* and *Bandit's Roost, 59½ Mulberry Street*. The first photographer in America to use flash powder, Riis created faithful portraits of conditions under which some men lived, fixing in his image the melancholy and longing of humans deprived of all hope.

Then, beginning in 1905, a sociologist named Lewis W. Hine took the camera along as he did his field research. Trained to observe the larger social context within which people live and work, Hine first went to the factories, where he produced such documents as *Carolina Cotton Mill* and other photographs revealing the prevalence of child-labor practices in America. He went next to Ellis Island to record newly arrived immigrants and, in such stills as *Italian Family Seeking Lost Baggage,* pictured with compassion the pitiful lot of the uprooted entering a strange land. It was Hine who first began to publish his works in series that were recognizable as complete photo stories, the most vivid of which included his treatment of the men who built the Empire State Building, included in his 1932 collection, *Americans at Work*.

For Riis and Hine the immediate objective was to reflect life as faithfully as possible; but their ultimate purpose was more humane: they wished that viewers might share the adventure and despair of other men's lives, and commiserate with the downtrodden and underprivileged. This kind of documentary photography offered a new experience for multitudes as it sought to reveal human beings in such a way that would elicit sympathy and understanding.

The work of these early documentarists shows us that at the heart of documentary is the idea of *preformed* purpose. The documentarist sets forth not simply to register events and circumstances, but to find the most moving examples of them. His larger plan is to reveal and document whatever social and political conditions influence human existence. He soon finds that the most convincing way to actively involve others in his purpose is to picture the faces and the environments of people.

As the depression settled over America in the early 1930's, there were many faces and an overwhelming array of environments to record. So desperate were social and economic conditions that the United States Government encouraged still and motion-picture photographers to document the plight of millions of Americans. Their function was to delineate economic ruin in terms of its effect upon a whole society. Roy E. Stryker was named to lead a still photography unit within the Rural Resettlement Administration. Not a photographer himself, Stryker charted a course of action for his camera-recorders when he defined the spirit which would guide them: "Documentary is an approach, not a technic, an affirmation, not a negation. . . . The documentary attitude is not a denial of the plastic elements which must remain essential criteria in any work. It merely gives

BEN SPIEGEL

STRYKER *". . . an approach, not a technic, an affirmation, not a negation."*

these elements limitations and direction."[6] Such an approach precluded recording detail for its own sake, and suggested that pictorial art be used for broader purposes of persuasion. Stryker found the photographers who could assist him, and brought to his unit such talents as Carl Mydans, Gordon Parks, Ben Shahn, Arthur Rothstein, and John Vachon.

Two RRA photographers, Dorothea Lange and Walker Evans, had attracted attention by earlier work which revealed sympathy with this task. In such photographs as *Maine Pump* (1933) and *South Street* (1932), Evans had created the reality of American life in terms of strong social overtones. For the RRA, Evans went to the American south to photograph the squalid lives of sharecroppers. Dorothea Lange, working with Paul Taylor, an economics professor, had been hired earlier by the State of California to document the ugly story of the Okies, California's migratory workers, and here gained the insight and experience which resulted in such photographs as *In a Camp of Migratory Pea-Pickers* (1936). Her portraits of the lives of the migrants inspired two later motion pictures — Lorentz's documentary film, *The Plow That Broke the Plains,* and a fiction film based upon John Steinbeck's novel, *The Grapes of Wrath.*

BOURKE-WHITE . . . *a sociological as well as journalistic instrument.*

The RRA (later named Farm Security Administration) photographic unit continued its work until the outbreak of World War II, and in its seven years of existence produced a collection of still photos documenting all phases of American life. Many of its photographers moved freely between documentary and photo-magazine or industrial photography, where the social documentary was also finding outlets. Numerous workers went directly into motion pictures, bringing their talents to a medium in which social documentary had perhaps its greatest public impact in this era. Among the most distinguished of those who worked in both photo-journalistic and formal documentary was Margaret Bourke-White, who produced her classic study of the south in 1937, *You Have Seen Their Faces,* and continued to create pictorial delineations of social conditions in her impressive later work for *Life* Magazine.

Documentary still photography thus became a sociological as well as journalistic instrument during the 1930's. Despite this activity, however, the impact of documentary was perhaps least realized in still photography. Motion pictures and radio were joined to the documentary movement, and these were to have greater social effect. For still photography is in many ways the most subtle of documentary media — the most limited in its ability to dictate a course of action or articulate a sought-for attitude. The photograph too often required an enlargement and explanation which its fixed visual character could not provide. For this quality it had to turn to the word, which could amplify, enlarge, and direct response along intellectual lines, thus complementing the emotional impact of the photograph and placing it in a context of time and place.

This argument is most clearly advanced by Beaumont Newhall, who reminds us that documentary still photographers often included printed words and wall-scrawls in their images. "More than one photographer in the bitterness of the thirties," he observed, "chose to contrast billboard slogans with the contrary evidence of the camera. A sign, photographed as an object, carries much more impact than the literal transcription of the words it bears."[7] Newhall notes the publication of documentary stills in collections, where the printed word placed each picture in time and space and broadened the significance of the photograph itself. Typical of such studies was Dorothea Lange and Paul Taylor's *American Exodus* (1937), in which bits of conversation heard while the pictures were being taken were printed in accompanying captions. Still later an entire collection of photos taken from the FSA files was published in *Land of the Free* (1939), where the poetry of Archibald MacLeish supplied, in Newhall's significant descriptive phrase, a "sound-track" for the stills.[8] The accuracy of his observation leads us to consideration of the growth of a new approach to documentary in print media — an approach which further evolved out of still photography.

THE PHOTO ESSAY

Those lines of demarcation between the spot-news photograph, or series of photographs, and the picture story are not always distinguishable, nor is their relationship to documentary photography always clear. Yet a photographic approach which afforded time to plan and develop a line of attack in the chronicling of an event moves closer to documentary purpose, not only in still photography, but in film, radio, and television as well. This was made possible by the evolution of the modern picture magazine, wherein the concept of a spot-photo sequence gradually was supplemented by the photo essay. The distinction between them is in many ways vital to a documentary concept in the print media.

The photo sequence, of course, is hardly a recent development. As early equipment was improved, it became possible to record a number of photographs of any single event or incident. In its earliest uses sequential photography was employed to trace an event in time or place, as exemplified by the *Illustrated London News'* series of eight pictures of Queen Victoria's masked ball. The Brady photographers recorded some Civil War scenes in this fashion, and other attempts to give the sense of unfolding-in-time to an event, or even some primitive sense of motion, dotted the 19th

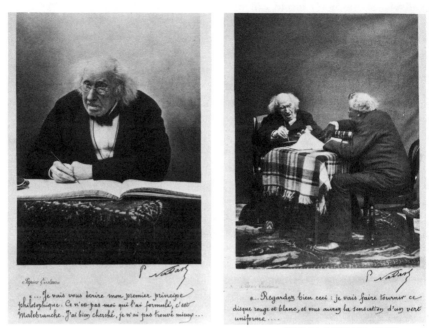

« ...Je vais vous écrire mon premier principe
philosophique. Ce n'est-pas moi qui l'ai formulé, c'est
Malebranche. J'ai bien cherché, je n'ai pas trouvé mieux ...

« ...Regardez bien ceci : je vais faire tourner ce
disque rouge et blanc, et vous aurez la sensation d'un vert
uniforme ....

GEORGE EASTMAN HOUSE

THE ART OF LIVING A HUNDRED YEARS

century. An early demonstration of how the photo sequence could be used to reveal character was made by Paul Nadar, son of the famous French portraitist, who made a series of exposures of the scientist Marie-Eugene Chevreul on his 101st birthday. The words spoken by Chevreul were recorded by a stenographer, and used as captions for the published series of photographs. This could be regarded as the pioneer photo interview, for in the series we see, and in a sense hear, the words of the man as he speaks them.

The contribution of the photo sequence to documentary, however, is less significant than later developments it inspired. The step beyond documentation of an event-in-time came with the photo essay, and its distinction from the photo sequence is largely one of method. In the latter the photographer went out to record material for purposes of illustrating a need and significance which had been established in advance. The "story" had been planned first, and then pictorially supplemented. It may have been refined in concept once the actual taking of photos was in progress.

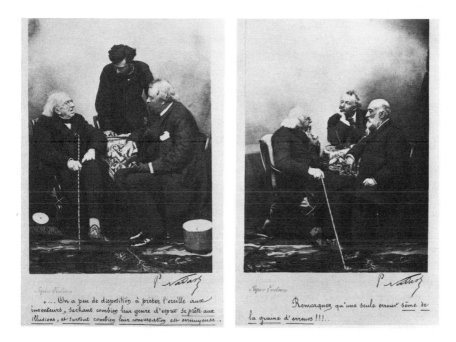

Photographic interview with M. Chevreul by Paul Nadar (1886)
The first photo-interview.

But in whatever order it happened, the "story" — with its inherent elements of a structured narrative, a subject, and a theme — began to emerge, and this marks the crucial distinction between mere reportage and documentary in any medium.

The formation of *Life* Magazine in 1936 offered the first larger opportunities for a print documentary through the photo essay. *Life* began, however, only after three other significant "story" approaches to journalism had already been launched, all by Time, Inc. In the 1920's the Luce organization initiated *Time,* a weekly news-magazine dedicated to reviewing the major events of the week in a sharp and distinctive "in-depth" style. *Time* established itself as a compelling news source by providing a progressing analytical commentary upon the news of the week. It was then, and is now, designed to review and interpret as much as to report and record. Although *Time* used occasional photographs of events or personalities, the printed word was its prime method of reportage. By 1931 radio had also begun to have full impact upon the nation, and the

Time interpretative approach was extended to the newer medium. *March of Time* was introduced to the American public in that year by the Columbia Broadcasting System, and it gained popularity with an insistent, urgent style which combined narration and the recorded or re-enacted voices of those who made the news.

The relationships of the radio *March of Time* to current TV documentaries may be deferred to a later context, along with the introduction in 1935 of the motion-picture version of this dynamic approach to journalism. It is sufficient to note that these three distinct approaches to modern journalism — *Time* Magazine and the radio and motion picture versions of *March of Time* — were making significant contributions to an emerging journalistic documentary form when, in November of 1936, Time, Inc. introduced *Life* Magazine. Within a few months still another photographic news-magazine, *Look,* appeared. In these magazines still photography came closest to documentary.

There were technical problems to be resolved before the kind of documentary represented by the journalistic photo essay could be achieved. *Life*'s editors defined their major problem by seeking the "mind-guided" camera. Following, perhaps, upon Newhall's observations of the weakness of still photography as a documentary medium, or perhaps upon the belief of many thoughtful men that significant ideas cannot be conveyed by visual means alone, the photo-essay documentary could evolve only when journalists recognized, as did press photographer Joseph Costa, that "today's journalists are really two hemispheres of one world — the men of words and the men of pictures. The work of both must be combined to tell the most complete and accurate story."[9]

Life published spot-news photographs and photo sequences with short captions, but it also advanced the form of essay in which not only photographers, but editors, staff writers, and researchers were involved. The amount of printed text became more extensive as all of these talents were brought together in the planning and execution of assignments which may or may not have involved the immediacy of a news story. The great picture essays of *Life* and *Look* often sought merely to develop understanding and an increased awareness of life in its myriad aspects. If many of *Life*'s choices reflected the immediate conflicts of men and nations, its essays also attempted to reveal the wondrous world about us. Some were educational or instructional at one level, clearly editorial at another, or simply a record of change.

For the typical story a team of researchers and editors first developed an approach and then prepared a full shooting script which limited the photographer only by stipulating the general kind of pictures required. In most cases his own creative and reporting instinct were left free to work within a broad story. Often a reporter accompanied the cameraman and complemented the visual record with the facts and details which would place photos in their proper context of time and place.

This procedure at *Life* led to such classic photo essays as W. Eugene Smith's on a day in the life of Maude Callen, a Negro nurse-midwife, or the same photographer's dramatic portrayal of life in a small Spanish city. It led to Alfred Eisenstaedt's instructive photographs depicting the rain forest in *Life's The World We Live In* series, where art work, photography, and the word are combined in impressive educational documentation; and it has been effected in a hundred different kinds of journalistic and historical essays over the years.

STILL PHOTOGRAPHY: DOCUMENTARY CONTEXTS

Our understanding of documentary at this point is still far from complete. The role of the still photographer was to provide elements which could add to documentary the vivification of fact. His photographs, however, often suffered from the lack of context which words alone could provide, and approached documentary only when a combination was effected.

Documentary, as it exists within this framework, is achieved in two different ways. A great single photograph can be documentary in its own right. It can report fact, but can make us move beyond the fact to accept the underlying meaning, thereby making us adopt certain emotional attitudes toward it. Such attitudes can be translated into social action, or simply reinforce a view or an understanding which is part of us and which is not easily expressed or measured. Further, such photos can be created within entirely different approaches. They can represent after-the-fact records, conceived as reports of happenings and therefore important as *news*. But these photos can also be part of a deliberate design, conceived with the purpose of stimulating us to think or react in a specific way. At both levels the photograph can be documentary in concept.

Yet the context of the photograph is also of major concern. The single photo informs to the degree that it registers itself upon consciousness, but as documentary it must *stimulate* as well, and its limitations are such that it may make us feel more than it can make us think. It requires, if it is to be documentary, enlargement and direction. To become truly informative and persuasive, it must suggest the origins and the alternative outcomes inherent in its content. For this, the photograph has had to rely upon the printed word.

A visual content of itself can present this sense of origin and outcome only when it possesses the quality of motion. When photography was no longer fixed in time it could develop *visual narrative,* and when the printed word became *spoken* the narrative could be more complete and better able to make its message compelling and dramatic.

CONGRESS OF THE PHOTO SOCIETY OF FRANCE — Lumière (1895)

. . . the mere novelty of motion.

GOING TO THE FIRE (Edison, 1896)

. . . a concern for the newsworthy

2 / Film: The Fluid Moment

> Documentary films are defined as those dealing with significant historical, social, scientific or economic subjects, either photographed in actual occurrence or re-enacted, and where the emphasis is more on factual content than on entertainment. . . .
> — ACADEMY OF MOTION PICTURE ARTS AND SCIENCES[1]

THE APPROACHES to documentary in a sense repeated themselves as a second technology for the visual recording of reality was developed. Beyond still photography were pictures-in-motion, the recording of moving images and the introduction of a new element — time — in the recording process. These dimensions were added by a host of inventors and experimenters, all building upon the basic work of those who pioneered in photography.

THE NEWSREEL

The applications for this new technology were not long in coming. The earliest films were designed to capitalize upon the mere novelty of motion. Among the first reality films were those made by the Lumière brothers in France, who recorded such scenes as workmen leaving a factory at Lyon-Montplaisir, the arrival of a train at LaCiotat station, military exercises, and life in Paris between 1895 and 1900. In America, Thomas A. Edison followed the same course, making motion pictures of such events as McKinley's Inauguration (1896), Dewey at Manila (1898), and a McKinley speech of 1901. These were the precursors of film journalism, for, while Edison recorded lesser events, his choices also reflected a concern for the newsworthy.

The sensitivity to journalistic uses of this new communication medium marked the beginnings of the newsreel, an application comparable to spot-news reportage in still photography. By 1896 this direction was being pursued by the Pathé brothers and Léon Gaumont in France, Oskar Messter in Germany, and Biograph and Vitagraph in America. The first regular

33

newsreel series is credited to Charles Pathé and his *Journal* of 1907, but the form was probably inaugurated in 1909 when *Pathé Gazette* was introduced in London and America.

The outbreak of World War I offered newsreel photographers their first opportunity to record events of vital concern to men everywhere, and technology was sufficiently advanced to permit extensive filming of the conflict. The newsreel grew in scope after the war, and by the late 1920's Metrotone, International Newsreel, Fox Movietone News, the Pathé Newsreel, and other producers had established news-gathering facilities throughout the world. With the coming of talking pictures and the development of the single-system sound camera, the newsreel expanded. Narration was added, along with the authentic sounds and voices of life, and as these capacities for the presentation of reality were added the functions of photojournalism and cinematic recording of reality became more distinct.

But before these new conditions even existed, it was apparent that the quality of motion, and consequent freedom in time, gave the film important narrative powers. Cinematic art developed rapidly. The work of D. W. Griffith, chiefly, established the dominance of story films. For audiences of millions, "the movies" became narratives of human conflict cast in theatrical form. Time and motion offered the possibility of presenting men *in action* — and this meant drama. But it also implied the beginning of a new kind of reality film, for once a conflict of human will could be revealed, the presentation of social crisis and outcome could be made as valid a function of the reality film as the idea of climax and resolution in the story film. Now the spectator could see both beginnings and outcomes, and while pictorialization and cinematic principles of editing were important to the film, they had to share ("co-express," as Erwin Panofsky put it[2]) their artistic contribution with the drama of human action. Cinema, whether dealing with fiction or reality, simply *told* a story, whereas still photography, without accompanying printed text, could at best say, "There is a story here to be told."

This sense of the possibility of a story soon brought the newsreels under critical fire. At first no one disputed their simple function of recording events. But as such records became commonplace, objections were raised: first, to the endless repetition of ship-launchings and bathing beauty contests and then, more significantly, to a lack of completeness in the pointless reels. When Andrew Buchanan suggested that newsreels were "jumpy little postcard collections [which] for some reason or other are never produced — they merely happen,"[3] he was in fact voicing dissatisfaction with the newsreel's failure to actively engage itself in its natural form. As a result of hurried or incomplete rendering of the beginnings and outcomes related to these events, newsreel producers neglected to tell the story which was in their power to tell. In Grierson's view, the newsreel was "just a speedy snip-snap of some utterly unimportant ceremony."[4]

March Of Time

Then, in 1935 — as critics were growing restless over the newsreel and as significant reality films from abroad were beginning to capture attention — Time, Inc. introduced its novel concept in screen journalism, *March of Time*. The first issue of the series was premièred at the Capitol Theatre in New York City on February 1, and subsequently was shown in 70 first-run movie houses throughout the country. A different approach to the factual film had arrived, and for the next 16 years this series was to have a great impact upon the nation, the world, and documentary thinking in all media of public communication. At the height of its achievement, between 1936 and 1942, the series played to weekly audiences of nearly 20,000,000 in over 9,000 American theatres.

Louis de Rochemont was the producer of this motion-picture version of Roy Larsen's successful radio *March of Time*. It was de Rochemont who, after a decade of earlier work with various newsreel companies in every capacity from cameraman to executive, had angrily complained that the newsreels "never get behind the news. . . . What has led up to a given event? What does it portend? . . . Someday I'm going to revolutionize the newsreel."[5] *March of Time* afforded him that opportunity.

NERVE CENTER OF THE MARCH OF TIME IS THE PROJECTION ROOM WHERE ON THE FINAL WEEK OF PRODUCTION IT IS ALMOST CONSTANTLY IN USE. ON ITS SCREEN FLASH THOUSANDS OF FEET OF FILM THAT ARE EVENTUALLY EDITED AND CUT TO THE CONCISE, INTERESTING EPISODES THAT APPEAR IN EACH MONTH'S ISSUE.
(Above) MOT's Producer Louis de Rochemont and TIME Inc.'s Vice-President Roy E. Larsen review the first print of the current release.

DE ROCHEMONT , LARSEN

". . . to revolutionize the newsreel."

At the outset *March of Time* was bound to the newsreel tradition, but from the magazine and radio experience which preceded it came ideas and methods which enabled de Rochemont to establish pictorial journalism in his own unique way. The procedure of *March of Time* was described by Rotha: "Using partly the same naturally shot material which is the stuff of the newsreel, and partly staged scenes with both real people and actors, it tries to present an event in relation to its background — an approach that calls for a considered restatement of fact."[6]

Among the first of its innovations was to probe more deeply into events by allowing time to re-create a news story in the very act of its unfolding. In its first issue *March of Time* covered six stories in 22 minutes, which was not much of an improvement over existing newsreel treatments; but by its second release, it had dropped to five stories and, in its fifth issue, only two. For three years thereafter *March of Time* treated between two and four stories in a time period ranging between 18 and 22 minutes. Then, in January of 1938, it released its first single-story production — "Inside Nazi-Germany, 1938." Running just over 16 minutes, the entire issue was devoted to a study of the menace of Naziism, relating what Hitler had done to Germany and describing the Nazi movement in America. The usefulness of the single-story approach was apparent, and the series then regularly offered single-story features between 15 and 18 minutes in length. This marked its first departure from the "jumpy little postcard collections" which had brought criticism in earlier years.

This expansion of time in the reporting process was important chiefly because it permitted a journalistic style in which emphasis was divided between the inherent drama of an event and a dramatic technique of presentation. *March of Time* sought to establish an ordering, or plotting, of elements within its news presentation, moving toward a dramatic climax which, in turn, dictated a unified continuity. As a journalistic approach, this created some entirely new opportunities which the series moved to exploit.

It is difficult, in this day of transistorized equipment and advanced camera technology, to conceive that any newsworthy event would not be fully recorded, both visually and aurally. But this was not the case in 1935. The need to re-enact missing elements in story continuity was acknowledged by the earlier radio version of *March of Time,* and re-enactment also became the film version's second departure from the entire philosophy of recording fact in the tradition of photojournalism and the newsreel. This technique established, for the first time in factual film, an interpretation of reality which extended beyond the making of the visual records and the selection and arrangement of those elements within an event best suited to a dramatic narrative. For the first time in a visual medium a journalistic record of an event admitted the validity of a *reconstruction of reality*.

March of Time simply avowed that the news story was valid reportage

"INSIDE NAZI GERMANY"
MARCH OF TIME, Volume IV, Issue 6 (January, 1938)

. . . no more jumpy postcards.

"HUEY LONG"
MARCH OF TIME, Volume I, Issue 3 (April, 1935)

. . . the art of the sharp point of view.

even if certain voices and actions were staged. The implications of this admission, and the acceptance of it by critics and audiences alike, supported that school of perceptive criticism which had long insisted that even the records of reality were not "true" — that the very presence of the camera and the microphone changed in subtle ways the situation being recorded, thus making objectivity only a desired condition of journalism, but hardly a fact. In its first issue one of the scenes purporting to show Prince Saionji of Japan was made in New York with a Japanese actor. And even when newsreel material was available, impersonation was sometimes preferred by the film's editors in the interests of dramatic effectiveness.[7]

This was, perhaps, no more a privilege than newspapers enjoyed from the outset. True, the still photographer may have "faked" his pictures but, if detected, a stigma was cast upon the journalistic value of his product. In *March of Time,* however, the means of reportage stretched the limits of journalism by implicitly arguing that the picture as well as the word was, after all, only symbolic of reality. What mattered was not whether pictorial journalism displayed the facts, but whether, within the conscience of the reporter, it faithfully *reflected* the facts. The question of impartial reporting of the news rested, then, upon whether what was purported to be reality had a basis in fact and was the result of a sincere attempt to present it in a compelling fashion. This was an overlooked contribution of *March of Time,* and yet it may have been the most revolutionary change in the history of pictorial journalism.

March of Time's third notable departure from earlier reality films was the introduction of controversy. In its second issue of the first year the series devoted attention to a story of Adolph Hitler's rise to power in Germany, and almost at once it came under censorship. The Ontario Board of Censors deleted the Hitler sequence, as well as a report on the Hauptmann trial. Nevertheless, the series moved to a still more controversial third issue: a satire on Huey P. Long which succeeded in lessening his stature by bringing together certain of his speeches and allowing Long to demolish himself by his own words and actions. There was little doubt thereafter that the art of the sharp "point of view" had been brought to the screens of America. No mere newsreel could have provoked such a continuing battle with local and state censorship boards. Whether *March of Time* dealt with the rise of European dictators, using newsreel footage and specially shot films for the story, or whether it was re-enacting problems of national concern, as in an early staging of a *Reader's Digest* article on auto accidents, the series was creating controversy.

Its purposes in selecting controversial subjects were to stimulate thought, to probe and lay bare the sensitive issues confronting America. Yet it had insisted upon its own journalistic "objectivity" in that it did not offer resolutions but, instead, possible outcomes. For critic George Dangerfield this was an intolerable condition. "I wish," he wrote, "that the editors of *March of Time,* since they have at their disposal these fictions which excite and enrage people, would use them to some purpose — I wish they would say — outright beyond question — that somebody was right or wrong. Then we could attack them or defend them, and they would be exciting their audiences honestly."[8]

It was this inconsistency — this dramatic portrayal of real crises and conflicts — which could not easily be accepted. A crisis which does not resolve itself makes incomplete drama, just as a dramatized reconstruction of reality is not fully compatible with journalism. This was the dilemma of *March of Time,* and it passed on this heritage to all subsequent traditions, no matter the medium, style, or form, which would seek to make fact compelling by means of dramatic narrative.

If *March of Time* became a great journalistic force at a critical period in American life, it was because of the men who created the series. Alistair Cooke, in reviewing its value, suggested that it was not a result of mere bright inspiration. "Behind it," he observed, "is ten years' experience with a magazine of the same general style; an army of correspondents and cameramen scattered throughout the world; a historical film library it took two years to prepare; a newspaper cutting library as exhaustive as anything extant; and in New York and Chicago a vast research staff alert to trace the origins of any family, war, author, statesman, treaty or breath of rumor. With no less than this should any other film company irresponsibly compete."[9]

Between 1935 and 1951 this series gave to the documentary film movement, to print media, to the living theatre, and to television a vital source of ideas, principles, techniques, and inspiration. The idea of a "screen-magazine" soon encouraged imitation. RKO-Pathé produced a similar series, *This Is America;* Canada came forth with *Canada Carries On* and *World in Action,* produced by the National Film Board; and the British began a popular series in similar style, *This Modern Age.* But none had the arrogance of *March of Time.*

Those "jumpy postcard collections," the newsreels, continued to play in the nation's movie houses — bringing to audiences football, bathing beauties, and Lew Lehr's commentary upon the animal world — until television absorbed such trivia along with the more serious records of life in this age, and cast them in its own special mold. Yet it is unfair to dismiss the contribution of the newsreel. If *March of Time* and the screen-magazines introduced more powerful communicative concepts, they were not wholly responsible for the near-demise of a useful and exciting form. The problems created for the newsreel by newer forms of motion-picture journalism were not so serious, perhaps, as the blows dealt it by its own industry. In addition to the double feature, which effectively worked to crowd the newsreel from screens, there was the matter of industry attitude in general. The entrepreneurs who decided the fate of the newsreels were film executives who regarded the newsreel merely as another "short subject" and cared little about journalistic standards. As a result of such indifference the newsreel became a repository for heavy-handed publicity "gimmicks" for star-building and premières, and few discriminating people could retain much respect for them. The entrepreneur's answer to financial hard times was to cut the length of these offerings, still further reducing the opportunity for serious journalistic effort.

Another factor contributed to the decline of this form. During World War II newsreel companies were forced to pool their coverage, and the result was a sameness of film. The advantage of pooling, however, was a lower cost to individual companies, so the practice was retained after the war; and soon all newsreels began to look and sound alike. They lost the vital force of any journalistic medium — competition.

Some summary is necessary at this point. In reviewing major developments in a journalistic approach to print and film documentary, it may be observed that in still photography there came first the camera-reporter, whose instinct was simply to record. Out of his experiments grew a more specific function: to record the scenes and faces which revealed the flow of change in human events. This was photojournalism, the measurement of human confrontation in direct visual terms. In a closely related tradition came the work of the documentarist, and both photojournalism and documentary were modified by a third tradition — the creation of pictorial beauty.

The patterns repeated themselves once photography had been linked with time and motion. Reportage had come with the newsreels, and social argument began to emerge in the journalistic documentary, or story form, of *March of Time.* Time and motion, however, widened the distinction between print and the film, as pictorial value became an ancillary contribution to journalistic documentary film. The dominant artistic characteristics in this kind of film shifted from pictorial communication to the story and to the cinematic art of editing as it was used to advance a narrative.

Once we consider such work as *March of Time,* however, we are chronologically in the midst of equally significant documentary film developments, and must also recognize ways in which film has been used in other approaches to recording reality. The journalistic documentary was designed to inform great audiences of the immediate conflicts and crises of the age, which dictated that the subject of documentary was in control of the communications process — that the internal structure of an event itself was still the *sine qua non* of its reconstruction in narrative form. Film gave the journalist new ways to appeal to sensations, to involve the emotions of an audience. The screen-magazine could document and dramatize an event in its completeness, setting it in time and context. But its major function was still to describe, and in this sense it was related to a second significant application.

INSTRUCTIONAL FILM

Historically, Russian films showing surgical procedures were made as early as 1896, and there had since been growing use of films for specialized educational and instructional purposes. Herbert Ponting's *With Scott in the Antarctic,* made between 1910 and 1913, established the tradition of the educational travelogue; and in 1924 Dr. G. R. Canti filmed the cultivation of living tissues — an early scientific use of film. In 1913 Gaumont-British Instructional Films was founded, and for this organization such producers as Bruce Woolfe, Percy Smith, and Mary Field created the famous *Secrets of Life* series, anticipating Walt Disney and later producers who have since made numerous films on all aspects of the world around us. In the 1930's, in France, Jean Painlève directed and photographed films on marine life, and throughout that decade the German company, UFA, used the talents of Walter Ruttman, Dr. Martin Rikli, and others to produce further series of instructional films. As early as 1926 Pudovkin himself produced a Russian film dealing with the work of Pavlov.

The descriptive documentary of the instructional type, said Rotha, is separated from other documentary forms in that "its function is to report, to describe or delineate a series of events, the nature of a process, or the workings of an organization on the screen."[10] The point at which such instructional films border upon documentary is tenuous. A film which records open-heart surgery might be used to instruct surgeons in advanced techniques, and hence not be "public." Yet the same film might also be used to inform a general audience on new discoveries in medicine, hence answering documentary's claim to presenting public information. *March of Time* released a Forum Edition for use in the classroom, and so films originally made to inform a general audience on current and newsworthy social problems also became instructional tools to be utilized within special social studies or similar educational contexts. Yet most instructional films hold a character of their own in that they do not actively set out to interpret an aspect of life, but to show it as clearly and deliberately as possible. This should not imply that such films must be devoid of creative visual techniques which assist in reinforcing learning or making education enjoyable. The interpretative process is certainly at work in films of this kind, as well as in a variety of films such as travel, or what the British call "interest," films.

Nevertheless, all these instructional approaches to documentary are only half-realized. The film which seeks to instruct must present an impartial record, and for many this restricts the possibility of documentary. For Raymond Spottiswoode such films are "descriptive rather than normative . . . they comment, but they do not correct."[11] To this Rotha would add that the aim of the instructional film is description, and not dramatization, "which is the qualification of the documentary method."[12]

Such qualification introduces related questions. Journalistic documentary claims impartiality too, which suggests that any filmed record of actuality can be purely descriptive only when treating processes or events in which elements of human contention are at a minimum. At that moment when human conflict is involved (and perhaps few events are newsworthy unless it is), the idea of "comment without correction" loses strength. When human struggle is involved, "drama" enters at a different level. Journalistic documentary may be descriptive and impartial, and yet involve some dramatic method, while the instructional film, as Spottiswoode speaks of it, is limited by function.

Yet can the descriptive film be denied documentary status merely because it purports to *teach*? This seems a contradiction. While most "how-to" films are devoid of interpretative emphasis, many can follow an imposed order of events, or offer an impartial presentation of information, and still evoke the viewer's emotional involvement. A case in point is Wilbur Blume's Academy Award-winning *Face of Lincoln* (1956), which might be termed a "lecture" or instructional film since it features sculptor Merrell Gage as he talks while creating a bust of Lincoln. As anyone who has seen the film will testify, there is a deep pull for the viewer in the counterpoint of Gage's narration as the face of Lincoln changes. With only simple sound and routine editing to sustain action, this film is as emotionally moving as any in the so-called dramatic tradition. What distinguishes a documentary approach, therefore, is the involvement of the viewer in the human significance of events. Even those films which merely describe routine processes can have a documentary value under these conditions. This recognition turns us toward a kind of reality film in which human aspiration is the keystone, and it is this approach which has led to what is commonly accepted as "true" documentary.

DOCUMENTARY FILM: THE BEGINNINGS

From the earliest days of the fiction film, men recognized that it was possible to place dramatic stories against natural backgrounds. In 1922 an American film-maker, Robert Flaherty, demonstrated that stories of real men might also constitute drama of the first order. In that year, under commission by a New York fur company, Flaherty went to the Arctic to make his classic film of the life of an Eskimo family, *Nanook of the North*. In this first study of man in his natural environment, the formal documentary film movement began. Living among those he recorded, Flaherty observed their daily activities and managed to photograph these with sympathy and an eye for their essential humanness. By showing man in a struggle against his environment, Flaherty demonstrated that the silent film could forcefully convey the drama of primitive life.

In *Nanook* and such later films as *Moana* (1927),[13] *Man of Aran* (1934), and *Louisiana Story* (1948),[14] Flaherty pursued the great themes

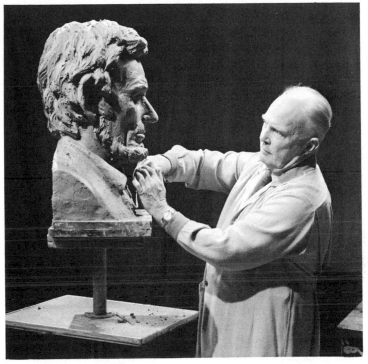

THE FACE OF LINCOLN (1956)

. . . to instruct and to involve.

of man, and revealed his own preoccupation with the idyllic life. Yet the very conditions of civilization which produced the technology enabling him to record the drama of uncomplicated societies served also to make Flaherty's work anachronistic. The "individualistic" documentary found little true purpose in modern industrial societies. The documentary film had other, more demanding, purposes to serve, and would become, in turn, a sociological instrument and then a political weapon.

A false start toward sociological use of documentary was begun with Alberto Cavalcanti's 1926 silent film of a day in the life of Paris, *Rien que les heures,* and Walter Ruttman's *Berlin: Die Sinfonie Der Grosstadt* (1927). What Flaherty had done to portray the life of primitives, these films attempted in behalf of the tortured "civilized" man caught up in the social complex of the modern city. Inspired by Russian developments in cinematic techniques and by the work of Eisenstein in particular, these documentaries sought to reveal their drama of real life in terms of filmic re-creations — sweeping, impressionistic studies of the beauties and horrors of the metropolis.

FLAHERTY AT WORK (Louisiana, 1948)

AND HIS CLASSICS:
NANOOK (1922), *MOANA* (1927), *LOUISIANA STORY* (1948),
MAN OF ARAN (1934)

. . . other, more demanding purposes to serve.

In *Berlin*, Ruttman organized his film records into a jarring study of man in the vise of social structures, systems, and institutions he had himself created but could not now escape. The tumult of a great city offered him opportunity to create rapidly flowing visual impressions, contrasting pace and mood in sequences devoted to the rush of city traffic, to Berlin night-life, to the routine of a harsh business world, and even to the eating habits of men (sharply juxtaposed with animals in the forced comparison technique of Eisenstein). Man, said Ruttman, created his own ugliness, his own despair, and was now atomized within it. But the swirling, flashing appeal to the senses in *Berlin* left men no time to reflect upon what they saw. They could only *feel,* and this could not be the great purpose of documentary.

Documentary film could not move forward from Flaherty, who showed that natural life held compelling drama, but who could not relate this work to the realities of life in changing, restless societies. Nor could it proceed from the impressionists, who preferred to make men feel without thinking and who, by translating subject material into emotion-inspiring symbols, could not provide positive cues for public thought and action in pursuit of common social goals. Documentary, as Flaherty and Ruttman had conceived it, could not serve as a useful social instrument. It required new lines of development, and a documentarist in England showed it the way.

GRIERSON AND THE BRITISH DOCUMENTARY SCHOOL

John Grierson brought two personal interests and two kinds of training to documentary in the late 1920's, and these inspired the most comprehensive and far-ranging of all documentary film movements. Skilled in the social sciences, Grierson had also studied public relations in America under a grant from the Rockefeller Foundation. He sought to establish a use for film which is most efficiently defined by Spottiswoode as a "characterized presentation of man's relation to his institutional life, whether industrial, social, or political; and in technique a subordination of form to content."[15] The final phrase suggests how documentary under Grierson was to evolve. He sensed the need for the poetic quality in reality films which had been advanced by the impressionists, but insisted that poetics be used only to supplement and enhance a descriptive, socially significant film content. Persuasion was his purpose, and he set himself the task of waking both the heart and will of the British public.

Grierson's first important film was his 1929 production of *Drifters*, a silent film commissioned by the Empire Marketing Board, an organization charged with promoting the sale of British products. Now the concept of public relations set a pattern for the use of the reality film in a context of mass communication. *Drifters* showed one part of the British people how

BERLIN (1927)

. . . no positive cues.

another part of the population worked and lived, and by so doing engendered a larger sense of social interdependence.

To tell his story, Grierson followed the daily routine of the herring fishers, beginning as their boats set out to sea and carefully recording the men's activities as they worked their nets, brought in their catch, and returned to sell the herring at day's end. Life aboard ship was presented in sequences distinguished by a constant flow of intercutting between the men, the ship's engines, and the silently swimming fish. The unraveling and casting of the nets were depicted with infinite care and edited in the rhythm of the action itself. At one point Grierson used the superimposition, at another a rapid sequence of cuts, at still another a series of lingering dissolves. At the close of the day the boats returned and the fish were brought to the dock, where the packing and shipping processes were given the same careful depiction. Designed to let men sense the simplicity and beauty in the routines of daily life, these final scenes also carried an important message about Britain's dependence upon international trade.

Among later Empire Marketing Board productions in the 1930's, perhaps the most interesting are such films as *Industrial Britain*, which first brought the talents of Grierson and Flaherty together in the making of a sound film, and Edgar Anstey and Grierson's *Granton Trawler*, almost a short sound version of *Drifters*. Finally released in an abbreviated version by Grierson, *Industrial Britain* reveals the photographic genius of its makers, and yet is also an awkward revelation of what may happen when a filmmaker concerned with great and universal themes of humanity becomes involved in a work which must make specific and clear social points. Although less impressionistic in treatment than *Drifters*, the visual portion of *Industrial Britain* is a sensitive filmic interpretation of manufacturing processes. The film's sound-track, however, almost destroys its pictorial narrative. At best it is often gratuitous — supplying a "message" about the power of average British working men which, backed by strains from Beethoven's Fifth Symphony, strikes us today as clumsy. What we see in *Industrial Britain*, as well as in a number of other sound-film documentaries of this era, is a working-out of entirely new relationships — first between the creative film-maker and sponsoring organization, and next between cinematic narrative and the new possibilities which sound offered to the creative interpretation of reality.[16]

When, as a result of the depression in the 1930's, the Empire Marketing Board was discontinued, Grierson and many of his colleagues joined the film unit created by the British General Post Office. The GPO Film Unit, now possessed of a wide range of techniques and additional expressive means offered by sound, entered an exciting period of documentary production in which its films were designed to interpret the role of communications in the British Commonwealth. This charge resulted in numerous analytical films dealing with all aspects of British life, made by such Grierson protégés

JOHN GRIERSON (1963)

persuasion was his purpose.

and peers as Basil Wright, Edgar Anstey, Arthur Elton, Paul Rotha, Thorold Dickinson, Stuart Legg, Harry Watt, and Alberto Cavalcanti. These documentarists, some with GPO and others with film units of various corporations, government departments, and instructional film companies, created an impressive series of documentary films in a variety of individual styles.

In such subsequent films as *Contact* by Paul Rotha, *Song of Ceylon* by Basil Wright, and *Night Mail* by Harry Watt, Basil Wright and Alberto Cavalcanti, the British documentary of "social analysis" advanced. By 1937 the work of the GPO and the other film-producing units of Britain had attracted world-wide attention. Grierson later went to America and Canada, and in 1939 was appointed Film Commissioner of Canada, where he was instrumental in creating the National Film Board.

THE GROWTH OF DOCUMENTARY FILM IN AMERICA

Apart from the screen-magazine, the American documentary movement was restricted in its quantity of output and decidedly pointed in the social functions it embodied. Its early evolution was sharply political in origin. As early as 1928 the Film and Photo League made newsreel-like films of

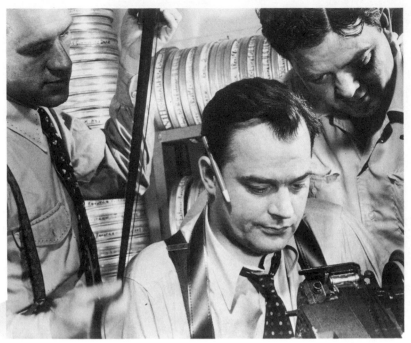

PARE LORENTZ

. . . a vital social statement.

labor conflicts, hunger marches, and other evidences of social unrest. In 1931 Seymour Stern's *Imperial Valley* depicted the exploitation of labor in the California fruit fields, and political overtones were evident in many early treatments of the civil rights struggle and a growing labor movement. To America in this period came Joris Ivens. In his earlier films in Holland, Ivens had brought the propaganda documentary to realization in *New Earth* (1934). In America he worked in the production of *The Spanish Earth*, a highly charged, partly re-enacted treatment of the Loyalist cause in Spain, narrated by Ernest Hemingway. Other strongly pro-Leftist films were turned out during this period. These included *Heart of Spain, China Strikes Back, People of the Cumberland,* and *Native Land*, the latter an angry pro-union film narrated by Paul Robeson.

It was not, however, these films in an *agitprop* vein which found strong support in a restive America. Instead, a more moderate reflection of the liberalizing change sweeping the nation in the form of Franklin Roosevelt's New Deal was in clear evidence. By the mid-1930's, as *March of Time* and the British "social-analysis" documentaries began to be seen in America, the Federal Government commissioned a noted critic, Pare Lorentz, to make a film in which the American farmer could be given a firm understanding of the Government's soil conservation and resettlement programs. Lorentz, with Floyd Crosby,[17] Paul Strand, Ralph Steiner, and Leo Hurwitz as his photographers, wrote and directed *The Plow That Broke the Plains*, a film which suffered many of the limitations of experiment. Partly brilliant photography, partly self-conscious "cinema," and partly blunt verbal explanation, *The Plow* reflected many of the faults of *Industrial Britain*. It tried to be both art and social document — and was neither.

When Lorentz produced *The River* in 1937, many initial weaknesses were overcome. In this study of erosion in the Mississippi River basin a verbal message was again attached, but the film's greatness lay in its lengthy first section, where the visual poetry of falling streams and trees being stripped from the land was accompanied by rhythmic repetition in narration. In this section, perhaps for the first time in American documentary, the great narrative power of film was employed to record natural phenomena in such a way that a vital social statement was advanced.

In the same period the United States Government created a regular film unit, which, along with the Federal Theatre and similar projects where art became associated with political propaganda, eventually was disbanded. At the start of World War II the film service was assigned, with other documentary agencies, to the Office of War Information, and the work it had initiated was undertaken by foundations, educational groups, and private corporations. Such activity resulted in significant films like *The City*, a 1939 production for the American Institute of Planners Through Civic Films.[18] *The City* was the first of many American films devoted to problems of growing communities. It portrayed the ugliness and human inconvenience which result from improper planning, and then contrasted slum areas in overcrowded cities, first with idyllic communities in New England and then with the more realistic goal of a planned urban community. In its scenes depicting human existence in a great metropolis, *The City* revealed a debt to Ruttman's *Berlin*. Traffic sequences and an entire episode on the lunch hour might literally have been snipped out of the earlier film. Yet the narration carried a hopeful note, and an over-all lightness of tone prevailed.

DOCUMENTARY IN WARTIME

As World War II began, interest in the reality film as a propaganda tool was heightened. The way in which such film could be used to promote frenzied national response had been demonstrated by the Nazis as early as 1933, when Dr. Goebbels and his Ministry of Propaganda began using all communications media in the service of *die Partei*. The extent to which documentary film could be used to lead public opinion had been revealed in Leni Riefenstahl's 1937 *Triumph of the Will*. This full-length film was conceived by the Nazis as a means of transmitting to the German people the emotional fervor of the hard Nazi core.

The party staged its 1934 Nuremburg rally specifically for the purpose of making this film, using nearly 100 cameramen to record the Wagnerian spectacle. Its opening scene is a magnificent photographic record of the towering clouds through which Hitler's plane carried him to Nuremburg, accompanied by music befitting the gods. The clouds break and the city waits peacefully below for its god and conqueror to descend. For the next two hours the vision does not dim, as men, women, and children show their obeisance. In these sequences Riefenstahl served notice that the treacherous power of film was something to be reckoned with.

In *Triumph of the Will* and in such propaganda films as *Blütendes Deutschland* (1933), *Für Uns* (1937), *Wir erobern land* (1936), and *Bilddokumente* (1935), the Nazis created a filmic truth of their own, exalting the glory of the German nation. In *Flieger, Funker und Kanonier* (1937), they used documentary to display their growing armed might; and as war began they created *Baptism of Fire*, a document of the brutal and incisive way in which Poland was destroyed — a warning to others in Europe who dared resist the Nazis. Along with such major propaganda efforts the Germans turned out numerous informational and training films, typified by *Männer gegen Panzer,* which sought to train foot soldiers to effectively combat tanks. This film, made under hurried conditions as the Russians began to throw increasing numbers of tanks into the Eastern front, re-enacted combat action with precise realism.

England moved slowly toward the documentary propaganda effort, and it was not until after the first London blitzes that the need for lifting public morale became imperative. The Ministry of Information assumed control of the GPO Film Unit, renamed the Crown Film Unit, which engaged at once in the production of films that would hold broad appeal for the British populace. Early efforts included the 1940 *Men of the Lightship* and *Merchant Seaman.* By 1941 Crown had already achieved a feature-length success in Harry Watt's *Target for Tonight.* In this story of an RAF raid over Germany, a shaken and uncertain England found a rallying point and a touch of courage in a desperate time. The story of the raid and the tense waiting for the return of the planes, coupled with an intimate study of the men of the RAF, gave to large audiences in both England and America their first identification with people at war. Crown followed with similar successful feature-length documentaries such as *Coastal Command, Fires Were Started, Close Quarters,* and *Western Approaches,* all of which portrayed the valor of the British people. Among the triumphs of the unit's work was Ian Dalrymple's 1942 *Listen to Britain,* an impressionistic study of the nation, told in terms of the sights and sounds of daily wartime life.

Of significance to the war effort was the work of various military film units, which produced films intended to show those at home how British forces were carrying the battle to the enemy. In *Tunisian Victory, Burma Victory, Desert Victory,* and *The True Glory* the creative skills of producers who had entered the services from the commercial cinema contributed to

LENI RIEFENSTAHL

. . . something to be reckoned with.

shaping dramatic stories of battle. David McDonald's experience in fiction films was turned to greatest advantage in his 1943 *Desert Victory*, one of the best of the service-made feature documentaries to come from Britain in those years. In this film, gripping portrayals of men in action were combined with a specific record of the facts and circumstances surrounding the battle of North Africa, told with clear and intelligent use of maps and other visual devices. But the importance of this film, as with all films made by service units, lies in the achievement of combat photographers, whose pictures never let us forget the omnipresence of violent death.

Perhaps the finest of many great British films of this period was *The True Glory* (1945). British and American talents were used to create this summary of the battle of Europe, as Carol Reed and Garson Kanin worked together in editing footage shot by countless combat photographers throughout the European war. Produced for both the United States Office of War Information and the British Ministry of Information, the film involved a variety of materials shot at different times and places, and the editing was complicated by the equally difficult task of blending natural sounds, voices, music, and spoken narration into a compilation story. Of all these elements the blank verse, read in a ringing Shakespearian style, provided a single unifying narrative into which battle sounds, the voices of Allied soldiers, and the battle pictures themselves were interwoven.

The outbreak of the war had brought most of America's documentary and fiction film-makers into service. To the Army's Signal Corps Pictorial Service and its Information and Education Section, to the OWI, the OSS, the United States Navy and Marines, and to various civilian and military information offices and departments came America's film-making talents: John Huston, Frank Capra, William Wyler, John Ford, Louis de Rochemont, Edward Steichen, Samuel Spewack, Eric Knight, Darryl Zanuck, Walt Disney, Garson Kanin, Willard Van Dyke, John Houseman, Anatole Litvak, Irving Jacoby, Henwar Rodakiewicz, and Jules Bucher.

The most impressive of the many compilation films developed in the early years of the war was Frank Capra's *Why We Fight* series. Designed to convey to the fighting man America's reasons for entering the war, this series used available newsreel footage, maps, charts, and clips from Nazi films to describe the growth of Naziism and Fascism. In such 1943 films as *Prelude to War, The Nazis Strike,* and *Divide and Conquer*, Capra and his production staff created strong statements which used filmic shock techniques. The series revealed how effective a weapon the compilation film could be, proving again that a film sequence in and of itself has no meaning until a "point of view" has been created and the film strips fitted into proper sequence within the larger concept.

Wartime training films for troops did not always result in unimaginative step-by-step instruction. Dealing with more complex information, Walt Disney produced films such as *Cold Front* and *Fog* for the United States Navy in 1943, which were designed to teach flyers facts about meteorology by the use of animation techniques. The way in which drama and drill could be combined to advance effective instruction was made vividly clear in *Resisting Enemy Interrogation,* a 1944 film made by the Army Air Forces First Motion Picture Unit. This film has the quality of many of the better fiction films of that era. Using such stars as Arthur Kennedy, Kent Smith, and Lloyd Nolan, it told a completely re-enacted story of how a captured bomber crew was betrayed into revealing information to the enemy. In the process a sharp lesson was taught to pilots-in-training.

Along with such films the Army's Information and Education Section began to produce the *Army-Navy Screen Magazine*. Fashioned after newsreels and the journalistic documentary, the series released bimonthly issues which sought to bring the whole scope of war to the serviceman in straight GI language, combining news, information, and lessons to observe.

A number of films were also released to theatres by the Office of War Information. Broader in content, and planned for both soldiers and civilians, these "incentive" films were made in the tradition of the earlier British service unit films. In *To the Shores of Iwo Jima, Memphis Belle,* and *Big Ben* the war was brought to Americans in blunt and personal terms. A fine example of this series of combat records is Louis de Rochemont's *The Fighting Lady*, a story of an aircraft carrier in the Pacific for which Edward

WHY WE FIGHT — "THE BATTLE OF RUSSIA"
(Office of War Information, 1944)

. . . compilation could be a weapon.

THE FIGHTING LADY

"*. . . the faces of men never become obsolete.*"

Steichen supervised the photography. (It was Steichen who had cautioned his photographers to record men rather than machines. The faces of men, he observed, never become obsolete.) Narrated by Robert Taylor, the film included a superb record of bombing and strafing missions during a series of campaigns in the South Pacific, as well as scenes of life aboard the carrier.

Many of the Service Unit films originally made for military use only commanded wider attention, and among them was John Huston's *The Battle of San Pietro*. This 1944 story of the capture of an Italian town is counterpointed by a moving narration by Walter Huston, who describes with irony the city's "scenic beauties" after contesting armies have finally moved on through. The slow, almost dreamlike, pace of an infantry advance in combat has seldom been recorded more truthfully, and a tragic sequence depicting the recovery of an Italian woman from the rubble of a mine explosion remains fixed in memory as one of combat documentary's most moving records.

In addition to these authoritative works a continuous flow of lesser films sponsored by industry and various civilian agencies was released in this era. Many were obviously dull and self-serving, and rang false in their pleas for patriotism. American civil defense films "staged" bombing raids on "Elm Street" with agonizing frequency. Films designed to promote such causes as the support of day-care centers for children of working mothers were turned out in profusion, but few such efforts were saved by the wry inventiveness and drollness of comparable British theatrical "quickies" such as *Mr. Proudfoot Shows a Light*.

POSTWAR DOCUMENTARY FILM

By 1945 the nation had need of films for other purposes. The OWI commissioned a series intended to show American life to other nations. Ranging across such subjects as our Library of Congress, public school systems, the TVA, and profiles of our cities and villages, these films marked the final phase of an inspired documentary effort. The war ended, and the emotional fervor of national causes which had swept the world for over a dozen years began to ebb. The development of the "Cold War" made it clear that the Communist world and the liberal democracies had taken sharply divergent paths in the quest for fulfillment of human destiny. As a political instrument, however, documentary film had lost its impetus. New problems and new social needs would soon arise as civilization was caught up in the struggle to maintain a permanent peace. But few documentary films thereafter would deal with these matters in a manner which reflected the hard-hitting, broad audience appeal of the inspiring and encompassing wartime films.

In Canada the National Film Board continued the tradition begun in

CITY OF GOLD (1957)

LONELY BOY (1962)

. . . still in the first rank.

DONALD L. VELDE

ON THE BOWERY (1954)

. . . the dispassionate analysis.

England in the 1930's. Since its founding in 1939 the NFB has produced some of the world's finest instructional and experimental films, as well as documentary films of the first rank, including *City of Gold* (1957) by Colin Low and the recent portrait of rock-'n'-roll singer Paul Anka, *Lonely Boy*, by Wolfe Koenig and Roman Kroitor. Since that time when Grierson, Stuart Legg, Raymond Spottiswoode, and other documentary producers began work with the National Film Board, Canadian output has grown in quantity as well as quality. Yet its triumphs were seen by comparatively few, and too often reflected personal instincts and sensibilities of film-makers who were not necessarily seeking to move or persuade masses of mankind.

Throughout the 1950's, accompanying television's rapid growth as a mass medium, the Americans and the British have also produced limited numbers of films intended for theatrical audiences. The year 1953 saw the production of such American works as *The Living City*, a film on municipal planning produced by the Twentieth Century Fund and the Encyclopaedia Britannica; Walt Disney's feature-length nature film, *The Living Desert*; and such British "interest" films as *Conquest of Everest* and *A Queen Is Crowned*. In 1954 there was Lionel Rogosin's intimate and dispassionate analysis of skid row, *On The Bowery*. The next year brought forth Dore Schary's *The Battle of Gettysburg*, made for MGM, as well as Wilbur Blume's small classic, produced at the University of Southern California, *The Face of Lincoln*. A year later the USC unit created *Bunker Hill*, a sympathetic study of aging people displaced by "progress' in a downtown section of Los Angeles.

Privately sponsored films have continued to be made throughout the years since World War II. Fred Zinnemann created a poignant study of crippled children in *Benjy*, a 1951 film made to raise money for the Los Angeles Orthopedic Hospital. Sidney Meyers directed *Decision for Chemistry* for the Monsanto Chemical Company to help enlist young people in the profession of chemistry, and then, in 1949, made *The Quiet One*, a sympathetic study of an emotionally disturbed Harlem boy. In England, Guy Brenton made a 1957 study of the epileptic, *People Apart*, for the British Epilepsy Association, and in the same period were produced such films as James Hill's *The New Explorers* (for British Petroleum) and Lindsay Anderson's *Every Day Except Christmas* (for the Ford Motor Company). Among the finest documentary films made in the 1950's was Lindsay Anderson and Guy Brenton's *Thursday's Children*, a beautifully shaped film about deaf children learning to get on in a silent world.

None of these documentaries made since the war is weak in concept or sincerity. All represent genuine dedication and the highest standards of creativity in film-making. Yet all of them, in one important sense, miss the mark of documentary. For despite this great activity (and the listing above is barely representative), the social documentary — the purposive film which strives to do more than merely describe processes and functions, and seeks to reach beyond the specific needs of sponsoring groups or the intensely subjective aim of "experimental" film-makers — is missing. The intent to persuade and influence, to involve great audiences, to make exciting the great issues and causes of our time, lost its force with the end of violence; and by the time the crises of the world loomed large once more, television had arrived and was ready to assume this documentary responsibility.

Yet it must be recognized that television has been influenced by one other important medium for public communication. While its ties to the documentary film are strong and direct, the video documentary has also been shaped — and often dominated — in approach and execution by the reality and semireality forms of radio.

3 / Radio: The Forgotten Art

> Like the biography, the [radio] documentary is a script in which fact is presented dramatically. It is supposed to dramatize life facts, to anatomize the problems of large masses of people, to comment on ideas. The documentary resembles drama, in its manner of presentation; facts in the documentary are not merely stated, but stated in a dramatic manner, as if they were fiction.
>
> — MARTIN MALONEY[1]

As AMERICAN network radio began in 1926, there was little understanding of how the medium could deal with reality in a dramatic way. It was certain that radio could serve important informational functions, and after 1926 a number of news and news-commentary programs took the air. In the first years of network radio such noted news analysts as Lowell Thomas and Hans V. Kaltenborn began distinguished careers which spanned more than three decades. And as early as 1927, radio took on other informational functions. Soon a variety of talk, interview, and general discussion programs dealing with national and international affairs evolved.

RADIO DOCUMENTARY BEGINS

In 1928 the first network experiment in dramatizing instruction was created when "Biblical dramas" were initiated.[2] A year later "informative drama" struck out in another direction when a series of biographical presentations based upon the lives of great historical figures was introduced. It was obvious, after only four years of network program development, that radio's unique communicative powers could well serve its uses as an informational medium. Sound effects, music, and the human voice in combination could create a distinct kind of reality in the mind of the listener. As broadcasters sensed this, the stage was set for the first developments in a documentary tradition.

During the 1932-33 season, Time, Inc. brought the first of its drama-

MARCH OF TIME (RADIO)

. . . not bound by the ultimate authority of the photographic record.

tized *March of Time* news formats to the American public via radio. Setting a general style and approach for the later film version — and perhaps for the bulk of all subsequent journalistic documentaries — the series also sought to dramatize news events, and from the outset it used actors to play the parts and to speak the words of real headline figures. Throughout most of its history it continued to use actors, rather than people actually involved in the described events, but it was not an arbitrary decision which led *March of Time* in this direction. In that period a mild limitation in funds and a severe restriction in equipment prevented broadcasters from moving to actual locations for reality materials. Wire and tape recording was still years away, and the difficulties of obtaining authentic records of events for a regular series were almost insurmountable.

Yet there is another reason for radio's indifference to the use of actual sounds and voices. Radio did not have to deal with the visual presence of a person living his own experience as opposed to an actor playing a role. It was not bound by the ultimate authority of the photographic record. As a result many of the early documentary series did not hesitate to employ the actor so long as the re-creation of an event could be based upon reality and accepted as real by an audience. If some raised the argument which had been debated in the film medium — that documentary can exist only when it reveals "natural man in his natural environment" — the single-sense appeal of radio diminished the force of such argument. There was little agreement throughout radio's early history upon the true nature of documentary, or what its proper technique of presentation should be. Thus, documentary radio in America before World War II was a conglomeration of dramatic, semidramatic, and actuality techniques.

If controversy existed, *March of Time* managed to ignore it. Its general method was to dig some essential truth out of those news events in which human struggle and conflict were inherent elements. As in the film version, Westbrook Van Voorhis set the background, established scenes, conveyed atmosphere and mood, and commented upon the action. In the half-hour format the weekly series continued on the Columbia Broadcasting System until 1935, when it experimented for a year with a 15-minute daily program, and then returned to the half-hour until it went off the air in 1939. Brought back during the war, it made concessions in technique by making use of people who had actually participated in an event. In this instance it was undoubtedly influenced by other series and by one of its own imitators, *We the People,* which had come on the air for CBS during the 1936-37 season and survived until 1951. *We the People* dramatized newsworthy "feature stories" with strong personal conflict elements, telling its stories from the point of view of those who were actually involved. It employed a narrator to set the scene and used some musical and sound effects, but relied upon true "documents" in the form of actual statements rather than re-enactment.

If radio was quick to recognize ways in which journalistic functions could be combined with drama, it also understood the need for a dramatic treatment of general informational materials reflecting domestic issues as well as America's growing involvement in international affairs. In 1937 the United States Office of Education used the dramatic techniques of radio to promote greater understanding of the Central and South American nations. With the assistance of the Pan-American Union and CBS, which carried the programs, it designed and produced a unique series, *Brave New World.* Based upon Latin American history, this series and others like it were the result of an increasing awareness of radio's power as a social force, and a growing educational broadcasting development in America which also served to advance the documentary. Challenged by some as not "true" documentary because they involved actors in the studio, such important series as *Brave New World* nevertheless provided a first step in the evolution from historical drama to a true reality documentary in radio.

Soon radio documentary began to widen its concepts. In 1939 the University of Chicago supervised production of a series called *Human Adventure*, which continued into the 1945 season, relying upon a great deal of narration to dramatize such diverse subjects as the Einstein theory, the causes of Naziism, and the origins of the earth. A typical program, "Typhus," dramatized the conquest of typhus in Naples by using flashback scenes relating the history of the disease. These were followed by re-enacted scenes and narration which brought the story to the present.

The late 1930's saw an increasing number of such works devoted to meeting general social needs. The United States Office of Education produced a CBS series in 1939, *Democracy in Action*, describing governmental processes. The National Broadcasting Company carried a series based upon the Smithsonian Institution, *The World Is Yours*, from 1936 through 1940. The Office of Education, in cooperation with other governmental agencies, offered such additional series as *Roof over America*, dealing with housing, and *Municipal Government*, describing the functions of local government. And of course local commercial and educational stations were now also finding their way to the dramatic treatment of civic problems and issues.

To all such programs the term "documentary" may legitimately be applied, despite the fact that most of them relied heavily upon actors reading from scripts in a studio. Like the film documentaries of that period, they attempted to present to men some idea of the world about them. They sought to change attitudes, broaden philosophies and outlooks; and, for the time being, technique remained a secondary consideration so long as a documentary intent and purpose were in evidence.

TOWARD ACTUALITY DOCUMENTARY

The idea of natural environment, however, was not altogether ignored. Actuality recordings were technically possible by this time, and the uses for them tended to be concentrated in areas of socio-economic conflict. Under a grant from the Rockefeller Foundation, which had figured so importantly in the growth of documentary film in this country, the Library of Congress developed a number of programs dealing with significant social problems. At the same time documentarists attempted programs devoted to transmission of the nation's cultural heritage. Among early experiments in this approach was a series entitled *The Ballad Hunter*, produced by John Lomax, who attempted to duplicate Flaherty's method in sound by going out to the field to secure on-location recordings of folk songs and folklore. Lomax then provided unifying narration.

Using the same approach, Lomax's son, Alan, took equipment into the hills near the Tennessee Valley Authority and there recorded the expressions of people who had been displaced by the various TVA projects. The program which resulted was "Mr. Ledford and the TVA," aired in 1941 under sponsorship of the Library of Congress. In this unusual offering "Mr. Ledford" served as the narrator, commenting upon events and speaking directly to the audience as well as to the "true" people whose voices had been recorded. Such programs carried the same intent as the great film and still photographs in a documentary vein throughout this era — to help the Amer-

MURROW IN LONDON (1940)

. . . the authentic journalistic record.

ican people understand social changes taking place as a prerequisite to accepting new social moves. Yet this "natural" movement in documentaries remained a minor effort, producing some theory but few solid demonstrations of approach.

At the journalistic level, however, the recording of natural sounds and voices had far greater impact after the war in Europe began. Edward R. Murrow, for example, used a number of CBS newsmen to record the sounds of London during a blackout in his 1940 "London After Dark." Such authentic journalistic records would come to dominate radio documentary in later years.[3] As America entered the war, however, radio documentary was still cast largely in semidramatic forms, and a full range of new technology would not be used in actuality documentary until after the war.

Meanwhile, the Columbia Broadcasting System had initiated its revolutionary *CBS Workshop* in 1936 and until April, 1941, the series offered a number of distinguished experiments in drama as well as in semidramatic documentaries. In its 1938 production of Alfred Kreymborg's "The House That Jack Didn't Build," the *Workshop* successfully revealed how actors could be used in a dynamic documentary approach to serious social problems. The characters in the play were passengers on an imaginary trolley, and the conductor served as narrator as he guided them (and the listeners) through America's problem housing areas, all the while expounding facts and figures. In its own way the program was as profound a documentary treatment of this social issue as the film *The City*, released a year later. Significantly, at a time when the term "documentary" was seldom used in radio, CBS was specific in labeling this program as such.

RADIO DOCUMENTARY IN WORLD WAR II

The most significant efforts throughout the war remained in this semidramatic tradition. Less than a week after Pearl Harbor, Norman Corwin, who brought the semidramatic documentary to perhaps its highest level of creative achievement with the *CBS Workshop*, produced "We Hold These Truths." Planned to commemorate the 150th anniversary of the adoption of the Bill of Rights, the program was given an additional impact by the events of a few days earlier. Considered among the best wartime documentaries, the program served as a final definition of one documentary approach. The use of the narrator and the dramatized scene from the studio, as well as natural voices and sounds when they could be obtained, had become radio's dominant technique. Its approach followed the lines of the work of other media before it — to inform, to inspire, to let citizens sense their new roles and functions as America plunged into war.

The United States Office of Emergency Management entered radio documentary on a large scale, producing some 275 programs in the first six months of the war, all designed to inform the populace of the role of the civilian in wartime. In such other programs as "Report to the Nation" and "Dateline" the earlier traditions and techniques of *March of Time* and *We the People* were adapted to the presentation of informational and inspirational news-feature materials.

By mid-1942 the OWI had moved into radio at a different level with its propaganda series, *This Is War!* Norman Corwin served as writer and producer of this series in which the narrator was made central to the action as he interviewed people and spoke directly to the listener on the problems of the war. This series set a tone and style for such offshoots as the CBS *Man behind the Gun,* which won a Peabody award and brought to a state of high perfection the "second-person" style of narration ("you're in the cockpit — you hear the motors begin to warm up"), combined with realistic sound effects.

Other wartime series developed rapidly between 1942 and 1945. The Mutual network introduced *Keep 'Em Rolling,* combining documents — the facts and figures of wartime production — with dramatic segments. In 1942 the Office of Emergency Management arranged for the production of *This Is Our Enemy,* a series carried by Mutual. The United States service forces presented their own series, *America in the Air* (Army Air Forces) and *First Line of Defense*. NBC offered a four-part biographical series, *These Four Men,* based on the lives of Roosevelt, Stalin, Churchill, and Hitler. In 1943 CBS originated one of the best-received single documentary programs of the war, "An Open Letter on Race Hatred," which ended with a postscript delivered by Wendell Willkie. The program involved narrational exchanges between "Mr. Detroit" and "Mr. Reason" and dramatic sequences carrying strong arguments against racial intolerance.

RADIO DOCUMENTARY IN TRANSITION

By war's end radio had mastered the dramatic-documentary approach. In a vast number of programs based on reality, it had developed a rhetorical style of its own, capable of dealing with facts in a swift-moving episodic type of presentation closely paralleling the development of a dramatic plot structure and involving some measure of persuasion. But now the directions which radio could take were more specific. The idea of "news-drama" like *March of Time* lost its importance in the wake of the remarkable expansion in techniques of news reporting — in which Paul White (who is regarded as the leader of the movement to establish news as a dominant function of radio), Edward R. Murrow, and CBS led the way. Throughout the war, Americans became used to hearing the sounds of actuality in a continuing series of news and commentary programs originating at all points of the globe and narrated by newsmen rather than disembodied "voices of God." Radio's "reality" was dominant in news presentation, while the semidramatic technique of re-enactment was confined largely to general informational documentaries.

By 1946 CBS News had established its first documentary unit, which Murrow bluntly described as "an involved, expensive and altogether obvious thing to do."[4] The formation of this unit marked a high point in the growing influence of the journalist in broadcast documentary. Argument would be raised in radio, and later in television, over the role which the journalist had come to play in the movement. Yet the quality of immediacy in the media made it clear that the journalist would have a vital influence.

The significance of Orson Welles's 1938 "Invasion from Mars" broadcast is often overlooked in this regard. Social researchers have by now concluded that a nervous America was conditioned to the point where it was ready to accept such a realistic enactment of a science-fiction piece, but too little emphasis is given to the program's use of *news* techniques — the "on-the-spot" voices of newsmen and the "bulletin" device — in relation to the audience's reaction to this program. Ironically, in media often scored as mere "entertainment" forms the public has had little difficulty in recognizing both radio and television as *reporting* instruments. As early

PAUL WHITE

. . . news is a dominant function of radio.

ROBERT LEWIS SHAYON AT WORK ON "THE EAGLE'S BROOD"

as 1938 American audiences had already come to accept the informational techniques radio had developed. Conditioned by an increasing flow of news bulletins, commentary, and daily hard-news broadcasts in the prewar period, the audience reacted strongly when the techniques of news were employed falsely as in "Invasion from Mars." The power of radio was underscored, and it was to the credit of Paul White that, following this incident, the use of such techniques was prohibited in all fictional broadcasts at CBS. Concomitantly, the use of dramatic techniques was banned from news programs. There is a sharp lesson to be observed in this connection once we consider the TV documentary.

The idea, then, of news documentary as envisioned by the CBS Unit was a natural outcome of this long move toward understanding broadcasting's peculiar qualities and methods in presentation of information. When the time arrived to deal with social issues of newsworthy and controversial dimensions, the journalists were the ones to develop them. Under the direction of Robert Heller, the first chief of the CBS Documentary Unit, this group pioneered a classic series of reality documentaries dealing with major issues of the postwar world. Its initial experimental effort, "The Empty Noose," dealt with the Nuremburg trials, but the official "first" of the unit is considered to be its March 1947 production, "The Eagle's Brood."

The documentary writing and production talent of Robert Lewis Shayon provided the hard thrust of "The Eagle's Brood," which dealt in an incisive way with juvenile delinquency in America, and ended by making clear recommendations on how the nation must deal with the problem. Hailed as a "new documentary," this and subsequent efforts of the CBS Unit represented a final departure from the heavy "stagey" drama of an earlier time. The use of unidentified voices, interrupted by crashing sound and music effects, was regarded as wasted effort in this probing kind of approach, but emotional involvement was still a prime factor in the growing concept, and the idea that a dramatic plot line is a valid documentary tool was confirmed.

More successes followed in this specially scheduled series, including "A Long Life and a Merry One," on national health; "The Sunny Side of the Atom," on peaceful uses of atomic energy; "We Went Back," a review of the world two years after V-J day; "Fear Begins at Forty," on the problems of the aged; and "Among Ourselves," a frank and open approach to the problems of race relations. Such analytical reports on social issues reflected the long tradition of documentary in other media and showed that radio had finally achieved its goal of making documentary a force to influence a vast listening audience.

In the process, radio began to separate its functions. The poetic style of Corwin (exemplified best in his wartime "On a Note of Triumph") and the dramatic instincts of many creative producers and writers were channeled away from this journalistic documentary. If men were to make "truth" from facts they still had to possess a great dramatic instinct, but they had also to be trained observers, researchers, and reporters. If all who engaged in this approach were not journalists in a traditional sense, their work was controlled and influenced by a respect for the demands of objective appraisal, impartial reporting, and a careful and responsible outlook upon their task. Out of the work of the CBS Unit came the clear recognition that news documentary could create an active and moving image of the world — a narrative which involved listeners, which more than covered a story, but did less than editorialize. The technique could be used to reveal honest alternatives, to focus upon things that *mattered* to free men — and for journalisic documentary in radio this was a remarkable step forward.

This successful attempt to break away from the actor and the dramatic script led others to modify their approaches to documentary. The tape recorder had by now become standard equipment. In NBC's *Living* series (1948-51), dedicated to "showing America to itself," extensive use of the taped interview was employed. Under the guidance of Robert Saudek (who later produced one of TV's most successful cultural series, *Omnibus*), the American Broadcasting Company network also created special documentary programs, beginning in 1946 with "Unhappy Birthday" which noted the anniversary of the bombing of Hiroshima. The series included "Schoolteacher 1947," on public schools; "Communist, U.S. Brand," a Morton Wishengrad script based upon the life of an American converted to Communism; "VD — A Conspiracy of Silence," scripted by Erik Barnouw; "From Where We Came," a strong pro-union story again scripted by Wishengrad; and "Berlin Story," a 1949 production dealing with the first of the long series of crises on the divided city. In this series both actuality and dramatic techniques were used.

Saudek, as well as others, was still wrestling with the problem of the legitimacy of re-created studio materials in documentary treatments of political, economic, and social problems. In working out a rationale, Saudek finally concluded that "the most important single objective for a broadcaster or a producer is to maintain the integrity of his subject. Whatever technique is used it must not overbalance the subject itself. . . ."[5] The same argument was used to defend the work of *March of Time* a decade earlier by Alistair Cooke, and would be used by Reuven Frank 15 years later in defending television's documentaries.[6]

For if some documentarists still maintained that "pure" documentary could involve only natural man in his natural environment or in actuality records, the history of radio would still register a more extensive range in documentary technique. The journalistic documentary would grow away from "drama" in the sense of re-enactment, but would continue to regard the creation of dramatic structure — the carefully ordered plotting of events which occurred in reality — as a valid approach to documentary. The control of his subject distinguished the journalist's method, even though interpretation and presentation of a theme might still exist within his work. Indeed, no great journalistic documentary can avoid including such elements, and yet the approach does not undermine the inherent integrity of a fair and honest report.

The postwar effort was characterized, then, by a continuing application of approaches and techniques other than actuality broadcasts. CBS often presented programs using a combination of techniques. Stuart Novins wrote and produced a documentary on medical quackery, "Menace in White," and in 1947 Norman Corwin flew around the world with a recording machine and put the results into a 13-week series titled *One World Flight,* a remarkable work which combined actuality records and the Corwin poetic-narrational style.

Then, in 1947, Robert Lewis Shayon created still another kind of documentary as he assumed production and writing responsibility for radio's exceptional historical documentary series, *CBS Is There.* In this series the journalist's influence broke through once more, informing the entire concept and dictating the style. Instead of conventionally historical "based-in-fact" drama, the concept embraced a pace, tempo, and approach cut out from the fabric of radio news itself. The use of CBS news correspondents as "on-the-spot" narrators of a historical event, to which they reacted as if it were happening at the moment, may seem an anachronism but, as a result of painstaking research by Shayon and his staff, great events of the past were brought with dramatic force to radio's millions for whom history as a formal subject had little appeal.

In one view, to say that the re-creation by actors of scenes from great events removed this series from a documentary spirit or intent would be the equivalent of striking off such a superb film as the National Film Board's *City of Gold* because it used the still photographs of that "demented summer" of the Klondike gold rush rather than living people out of actuality. Yet it can be argued plausibly that even here the photographs were of real people, and we are still confronted with the true distinction of documentary — the creation of dramatic structures out of life's raw material. Still, in re-creating history in the form of a newscast, the series had taken historical drama and given it a form and *éclat* which could capture great audiences where lesser efforts had failed. Within radio documentary, where lines between dramatization and the recording of actuality are by far the most elastic, *CBS Is There* deserves recognition for its contribution.

Meanwhile, a variety of efforts continued to attract attention in pre-television years. In the semidramatic tradition NBC offered a 1950 four-part production on atomic energy, *The Quick and the Dead* — once again an attempt to combine actuality with re-enactment. Bob Hope played the role of a taxpayer, asking questions of a newspaperman who in turn referred them to various experts who had recorded their statements. The production called attention to a young producer whose name would soon become familiar in documentary, Fred W. Friendly. A year later Friendly moved to CBS, where, with Murrow, he developed the short-lived *Hear It Now* in 1951, a series which would move into TV after less than a year.

Another series of that era, *The Nation's Nightmare,* dealt with organized crime in America, making heavy use of taped records gathered from around the country. This 1951 CBS series was produced by still another creative newsman, Irving Gitlin, who would rise to prominence in network television. A year later, out of the TV-Radio Workshop of the Ford Foundation, came CBS's *The People Act* — a vigorous series, also produced by Gitlin, which was devoted to showing communities in action. By now the technique had advanced to the point where much that could be predicted in advance was taped "live," and those segments which needed to be re-enacted were staged with the original people involved. After almost three decades, radio had found a dynamic, completely authentic approach to the "justifiable reconstruction of reality" which characterizes documentary in its most ideal form. And once technology permitted the true records of life to be gathered, the re-enacted documentary was no longer valid or necessary.

In the six years, then, between the end of the war and the final demise of a national radio service which had dominated the American scene for a quarter of a century, the interaction of various forces within radio, together with technological advances and a constant pressure of example from the documentary film movement, had brought the radio documentary to its most faithful expressions in the dramatic interpretation of reality. From experience gained in earlier experiments it had evolved an authentic and dramatic form of journalistic documentary, dealing with the crises of the world as they continued to arise. It had worked forward from dramatic restatement of fact to drama made *with* fact. It had presented information in a compelling form on numberless major and minor issues and problems confronting the American people. It had evolved a special combination of drama, journalism, and education in a successful presentation of history. And as it did all these things, it gave a legacy to television, which had begun, by the early 1950's, to assume radio's role as the dominant mass medium of this nation.

RADIO DOCUMENTARY IN DECLINE

With the advent of television, radio's function altered so drastically that the latter lost much of its significance as a documentary instrument. While sporadic individual efforts in a documentary style are still made by local stations, it is fair to observe that one of the central conditions we have established for documentary — to create a massive impact upon great audiences — has ceased, in radio, to exist. Documentary requires budget, talent, and creative effort, and too few American radio stations have found that they can support this activity.

This situation is regrettable in two respects. First, radio is now freed from many of the sharp restrictions which once influenced its creative ventures. With time unlimited, the documentarist in radio now has a greater opportunity to build thorough and sustained treatments of actuality. The very conditions of time and technological advancement which once hampered the medium are now among its prime advantages. Second, as radio has become less of a "family" medium it has also been possible for it to operate at a more adult level in choice of themes and topics for documentary treatment. Thus Edward R. Murrow has offered a study of the "call-girl" business, and independent "minority-audience" stations have ventured into such areas once-taboo as homosexuality. It is not that television could not treat such problems if it chose to, but that it would have to fight off many more pressures than radio in order to do so. And there is, in addition, the important factor of relative anonymity which radio offers to participants in such sensitive areas as homosexuality. The chances for more candid and spontaneous statements are increased when subjects feel that they are literally not in the public eye.

Despite these new possibilities, there remains one overwhelming reason why documentary no longer belongs in radio. For even when skill, adequate budgets, and new freedoms are available, such efforts remain largely wasted upon the greatest part of an audience which now regards radio as little more than a pleasant diversion, and to which it seldom gives its undivided attention.[7] Television has assumed the documentary, as well as entertainment, functions of radio. Like the motion picture, radio has become more selective in finding its audiences, and the specialized audience cannot be the concern of the documentarist. Many of radio's forms and formalities moved directly to video, to be sure, but the introduction of the visual gave the audience a choice, and it preferred the sight-and-sound form.

Television, particularly in its documentary role, has *absorbed* radio. And by so doing it has left only a shell of a medium which now combines some functions of a hi-fi set and some functions of a newspaper, and little more. But the spoken word, the pacing, the formats, the use of sound and music — all of those exciting elements of a truly "mass" communication which radio had developed — moved into television and were there combined with the visual elements brought from the film to open up a new era in documentary.

4 / Life to Drama: Documentary's Limits

Documentary ends where free will and choice begin.
— NICHOLAS VARDAC[1]

ONCE aural and visual communication was coupled with time and motion, the possibility of relating stories of men in action brought documentary into a series of direct relationships with the intent and purpose of drama in the living theatre, motion pictures, and television. These relationships must be examined, for if the documentary is to make drama from fact it must also distinguish itself from those fictional representations of life which have sought their basis in "life as it is."

The deceptively simple rule of thumb by which the forms of drama and documentary have been kept distinct — actor *versus* natural-man-in-natural-environment — by no means settles the issue. More fundamental principles underlie a separation of these forms, and if we are to understand and appreciate the tenuousness of that thin line between drama and documentary we must also move to examine the efforts of the living theatre and the fiction-film in the past half century.

The phrase *c'est la vie et la verité* — supposedly exclaimed by awed witnesses of the earliest Lumière films — might also have been used to describe the reaction of theatrical audiences at one time or another throughout the past 20 centuries. The instinct toward natural portrayal of life in both the drama and its theatrical execution has informed the theatre's entire history. Theatrical technology for giving added vividness to drama began in ancient Athens, as did the poetic attempt to involve drama with the more immediate concerns of a society. Side by side, drama and its theatre moved toward putting life upon the stage: life enlarged, life made poetic — but life recognizable to audiences. The introduction of artistic principles of perspective in the Renaissance, for example, led stage-designers to create settings which were closer to what the eye beheld as "true." In the 18th century the actor-directors, Macklin and Garrick, sought a greater authenticity in costume and properties, and along with this interest in more realistic environment came a newer drama, rooted in the human interests of the age. Now dramatists created expressions of romantic interest in nature and life, which in turn declined eventually to the use of illusory method in service of the melodramatic and sensational — a "surface realism" steeped in the romantic excess of the 19th century. These extremes finally brought about a reaction in the form of naturalism, or realism, as a dramaturgical method and a theatrical production style.

NATURALISM AND REALISM IN THE THEATRE

The sweeping social change of the modern period worked its influences upon all the arts, particularly upon the living theatre which, Gassner reminds us, was born in the passion for showing things just as they are — for verisimilitude.[2] In that period, then, when literary romanticism was in its decline and novelists like Flaubert and Balzac were creating deeply founded psychological probings of modern civilization, the European theatre and its drama was also in ferment. Émile Zola raised the cry for a new *Naturalisme* in the drama — a psychological dissection of real people in real struggles.

To match this sought-for drama a new theatre was required. In Paris, Antoine turned the *Théatre Libre* into a showcase for reality by setting forth exact environmental details of life itself — to the extent of hanging carcasses of beef in a butcher-shop scene. In Bavaria the Duke of Saxe-Meiningen drilled actors to maintain a constant reality of movement and reaction in ensemble scenes. In Moscow, Stanislavsky asked for a "psychological truth" in performance. The performer sought to create the illusion of life, the apparatus of the theatre was converted into the presentation of authentic environment, and the playwright was exhorted to authenticate his characters in terms of their background and behavior. Now human instincts and social milieu began to dominate the dramatist's construction of character, and audiences saw the approximation of reality not only in setting and costume, but in the way humans behaved in moments of conflict and crisis. This realistic drama turned to social themes as Shaw, Ibsen, Tolstoy, Becque, Gorki, and Chekhov labored to reveal intense and inward struggles of people caught in psychological or social circumstances.

Seemingly, if the drama could be drawn from life itself — and if the technology of the theatre could effectively re-create authentic environment — then documentary as an independent form might be superfluous. This is not the case, and the explanation lies in the drama's inability to escape its own form even while its practitioners sought freedom. In the preface to his

Thérèse Raquin, and in a series of essays entitled *Le Naturalisme au Théatre* (1881), Zola constructed the platform for a drama which would apply science to the study of human nature and behavior — putting characters in drama under control of immutable laws of the universe and making all dramatic action subject to deterministic principles. Quite clearly, Zola insisted, the matter of free will in human choice could not be included within such a system.

Yet Brunetière had already observed that the exertion of the human will is the single essential element of drama. A record of life without ordering and control is not art. A play in which characters are not free to make decisions is a contradiction in terms, for drama demands, Brunetière decreed, the struggle of the human will to overcome obstacles while *conscious of the means it employs.* The art of the dramatist is to frame the struggle, provide for a protagonist the alternatives which face him, and insure that he makes a conscious choice. Unless these functions are executed, no form exists; and thus it is that Zola's desire to present life *precisely* came to naught.

Because drama could not be both life and art at once, *Naturalisme* yielded to a different concept — realism. This is a style in which men can not only portray social and psychological phenomena of human existence, but also control the system of events in which they occur and bring them to ultimate crisis and positive resolution. The details, the background, the motivations of characters, can be both honest and faithful to life. They can be drawn *after* life itself, but not *from* life.

To be sure, *Naturalisme* inspired a variety of reactionary nonrealistic styles in the revolt of the Symbolists, Expressionists, Social Realists, Theatricalists, even Dadaists, who were working away from the "slice of life" and toward freer expressions of the human condition. Nevertheless, realism continued to dominate 20th-century drama and theatre. If many dramatists learned that the control of human will was incompatible with the documentary function of recording natural man, and if many artists of the stage learned that their efforts to create authenticity in environment were doomed to live in the shadow of that ultimate presentation of the natural which film could offer, none of these abandoned the firm idea that the realities of life could still be presented in dramatic form. Realism was the style by which they would reveal the recognizable conditions of our modern world.

The theoretical distinctions, then, which set drama forever apart from documentary are formidable. Even realistic drama, near to documentary in spirit and purpose, could not avoid the theatrical and dramaturgical conventions which made it art. There exist, however, some experiments within the drama which have sought to cross the line from art to life. These have succeeded in giving us some sharper sense of what documentary, as a form, implies.

We begin by observing that the same political fervor and social dedication which led to many documentary films "staged" in the early 1930's — wherein rabid and partisan re-enactments of "truth" seemed entirely devoid of documentary principle — led equally partisan and politically conscious men of the theatre to reverse the process. It is unnecessary to set down in detail here the history of the workers' theatre movement: the *Proletbühne,* labor stages, and "left-wing" theatres here and abroad in the 1920's and 1930's.[3] The New York theatre, left-wing or otherwise, produced its share of worthy dramas, as well as mere *agitprop* vignettes, inspired by the political conditions of the time. Certainly, the work of such playwrights as Clifford Odets, Elmer Rice, Marc Blitzstein, Paul Green, and others has been given its proper recognition and analysis.

Of greater importance in this context are those approaches and styles which went beyond presentation of social theses and actually invaded areas assigned to the documentary, using the technology of public media of communications in staging, and integrating authentic records of reality into script and production. In one sense, such experiments came near to breaking down distinctions between drama and documentary. To the extent that they succeeded, they also underscored the implications of the questions we have posed at the very outset: Where does "art" become distinct from "journalism"? What are the differences between "objective" and "subjective" accounts of life? And when is the documentary idea and spirit to be separated from mere social propaganda in which the authentic is subservient to partisan and untruthful reconstruction?

"THE LIVING NEWSPAPER"

A forceful illustration of these dichotomies can be found in a specific production style evolved during the 1930's, "The Living Newspaper." In 1935 the United States Government had made an unprecedented move in the history of the American arts when, largely to ease the problems of acute unemployment among artists, it established a Federal Theatre. This Works Progress Administration project was headed by Hallie Flanagan, then director of the Vassar College Experimental Theatre. Some of the plays were hardly social in nature, as unemployed actors, writers, directors, stage artists, and technicians, combined talents to offer such New York productions as the morality play *Everyman,* some Gilbert and Sullivan, and T. S. Eliot's *Murder in the Cathedral.* But the Federal Theatre's New York company found it hard to refrain from politically minded production, and there were frequent charges of Communist infiltration into the group. The *Saturday Evening Post* saw fit to condemn the company for producing "undisguisedly revolutionary plays."[4]

Charges and countercharges need not be detailed here in order to examine the evolution of a new dramatic genre which took its style from

TRIPLE-A PLOWED UNDER (THE LIVING NEWSPAPER)

we must look beyond the actor.

the documentaries of radio and film, "The Living Newspaper." Conceived by Elmer Rice, directed by Morris Watson, and sponsored by the Newspaper Guild, it was designed to be operated as a regular newspaper, with an editor-in-chief, managing editor, and a large staff of proofreaders and researchers. Its goal was to bring journalism into the theatre by dramatizing important issues of the day "in terms not of romantic stories, but of the documented facts themselves."[5]

The experiment was short-lived, as was the entire Federal Theatre, but during its brief and stormy life it succeeded in getting two productions on the boards. An account of one of these, *Triple-A Plowed Under,* suggests not only how the style was influenced by other media, but how far the living theatre could move toward a documentary concept. Staged at the Biltmore Theatre in New York, *Triple-A* offered a rapidly paced series of 26 scenes, the substance of each based upon authentic news reports and public statements. The scenes not only sped by in an "edited" style, but involved projected pictures counterpointed by crashing musical effects and narration over a loudspeaker. All of the elements were focused upon the history of the New Deal's Agricultural Adjustment Act, its economic influence, and its ultimate demise by Supreme Court decision.

A scene would include a chanted dialogue by a farmer's family, then abruptly "cut" to the "Voice of Living Newspaper," which offered a leading statement from a speech by then Secretary of Agriculture Wallace, which would in turn "cut" to an actor portraying Wallace, who continued the speech without skipping a beat or a word. As the loudspeaker intoned facts and figures, a projection screen would show graphic illustrations. This kind of driving pace and technique in production borrowed liberally from film and radio documentary types, placing the output of all three media at the documentary level not only in attempting to present actuality or re-create real events as faithfully as possible, but also in following a continuity flow which abridged time and space. In the latter case, real physical space was altered and juxtaposed by lighting techniques — in radio done solely by changing sound stimuli, and in film by picture and sound-track editing. Even spot-news bulletins were broadcast at the end of each performance — bulletins carrying information relating to a farmer-labor political alliance culled from the news of the day and even that very evening.

No detail was spared to give the production the authority and immediacy of journalism. Obviously influenced by the radio version of *March of Time*, "Living Newspaper" shared some of the social urgency and method of *agitprop* plays of the American workers' theatres and was inspired by earlier experiments in "journalistic drama" by the Russians and the German anti-Fascist theatre productions of the 1920's and 1930's.

"Living Newspaper" is gone, as are the political ferments of another age, and yet it marked an interesting departure in theatrical style. The questions it raised with respect to the distinctions between realistic drama and documentary are far more complex and disconcerting. For "Living Newspaper" undoubtedly used "facts." It used spoken and written accounts of unimpeachable authenticity — documents in the form of published speeches, real photographs and film clips. These were welded together in a story and given an urgent political theme. To argue that it put art in control of fact is to dismiss this same phenomenon in many of the finest documentaries of history. To insist that its effort to whip up audience enthusiasm would remove it from documentary is to deny the purpose of the whole wartime documentary movement in America, a fervent plea for America's cause in a world conflict.

Perhaps the only quarrel, then, over whether "Living Newspaper" could be styled as documentary revolves around the use of the actor instead of the natural man. The condition is firm and unyielding; it is also unsatisfying, unless we look beyond the actor to the more fundamental distinction which lies beneath his presence. For the use of the actor implies the existence of a character — a fictional re-creation of life made by a dramatist. And it is the dramatist, the plot-maker, who inevitably produces the true distinction between drama and documentary. So long as characters exist it matters not how closely they are patterned after real people. They are *not* real people, and this makes all the difference. Our understanding of how this principle operates in sustaining this inevitable distinction between documentary and drama is enlarged by consideration of the theory and work of Bertolt Brecht, a dramatist of considerable power who claimed that he created "documentary plays."

EPIC REALISM

Brecht and his stage designer, Erwin Piscator, also sought to express dramatic truth with the help of a technology which served both the recording of reality and the staging of fiction. It is a classic irony that these men saw in films, still photographs, slides bearing printed words, and aural recordings the opportunity to take emotion and subjective appraisal of life *out of the drama* in the same way that others were attempting to use them for the purpose of eliciting emotional response *in the documentary*. It is a paradox of human communication that the documentarist would seek the emotional power of the records of reality while the artist would see in them a capacity for minimization of emotion. This paradox — the "gray area" between art and life — was given its theoretical parameters in Brecht's vaunted theory of *Verfremdung* — alienation.

The pointed didacticism of Brecht could not be served by the conventions of a realistic drama and theatre. Committed to a drama which expressed social significance, even his earliest works were analyses of problems in Germany during the 1920's. He called them *Lehrstücke* — learning plays — and combined in them elements of various nonrealist theatrical styles. In such plays as *The Expedient* (1929) and *Round Heads and Peaked Heads* (1936), Brecht wove music, choral chants, and elements of both realistic and purely theatrical styles into the script. He even turned to the musical comedy for his 1928 adaptation of John Gay's *Beggar's Opera*, renamed *Threepenny Opera*. But Brecht and Piscator finally adopted "Epic Realism," the style which brought them closest to documentary.

The key to success in the "Epic" style, both in dramaturgy and in staging, was unsentimental social analysis in treating reality. Emotionalism for its own sake — particularly an attempt to establish mood and tone by seeking empathic response to a conventional protagonist — were elements of realistic drama which Brecht sought to avoid. The audience, he felt, had too strong a tendency to accept illusion, and he sought to subvert this through the techniques of *Verfremdung*. If he could hold *Einfühlung* — empathy — to lesser proportions, the audience would be forced to think about the social meaning and implications of what they were witnessing. Just as Rotha and others had declared the dangers of "beauty" to documentary film, so Brecht wanted none of Aristotelian catharsis in his "documentary play." Pity was the greatest enemy of his drama, and to minimize its role he insisted upon "distancing" the audience from what was shown — disengaging the emo-

BERTHOLT BRECHT (1942)

. . . to make audiences think.

tions in order that intellectual processes might be stimulated. What was left, in theory, was a broader social and clinical dissection of the kind which Zola had sought in his *Naturalisme*. For the same reasons that Zola failed, Brecht would also fail, but in the process he created a few works which were of important value, not only as enduring drama but in helping us to set once more the limits of documentary.

In his 1944 play, *The Private Life of the Master Race*, Brecht employed his distancing technique to perhaps its best advantage by introducing both reality-recordings and poetic flights of language and theatricality. In episodic construction the play followed a group of Nazi soldiers as they rode across Europe in a Panzer. Brecht thus concentrates upon the common dramatic figure, the *Massenmensch*. With the use of flashback, however, he shows related incidents in the lives of each individual — personal experiences which give him pause to reflect upon his empty glories. Since the single hero is not exploited, a sense of continuing identification is lost, and attendant theatrical devices of suspense and rising action are held to a minimum. Just as one soldier's thoughts are developed — but before he can take hold as a character — Brecht deliberately drops the action and returns to the Panzer.

On it rolls, filling the theatre with its roar. A dispassionate "voice of God" reviews the action and sets new scenes. Title cards flash time and locale to indicate a new action. The stiff rhythm of choral chants fills the air, and finally we are placed into a scene involving human action and struggle again. Certainly there is drama in these — brief moments in which we share the subtle, restrained terror of a Jewish wife who must leave her husband, or sense grim irony in the couple who fear their son has turned informer against them. But none of it lasts. Each time it builds it is summarily dropped and we are returned to the less emotional, less personal, interludes where we can "reflect" upon the larger social issues these scenes suggest.

Despite the actors, despite poetry and theatrical conventions, the documentary idea and spirit is omnipresent here as it struggles to gain control of an independent art form. The whole is as documentary in one sense of its conception as many films and radio plays which were styled as such. But theory and practice are still separable, and the differences between drama and documentary are in effect once more as the execution of Brecht's theories is reviewed. Here we are given full and final understanding of the distinctions between actor and natural subject, and we are led to recognize that not only theatrical technique but dramaturgy is involved in the separation of the two forms.

For what, in the final analysis, can Brecht tell the actor? The creation of illusion — the "feeling into" the role by the Stanislavsky actor — was obviously unsuited to "Epic Realism." If the actor performed in such a manner that the spectator believed in his creation and identified with his character, anti-emotionalism was defeated. To ask an actor to distance himself from the character he represents may be simple enough when he is part of a group, braced with the mechanics of films and slides, or engaged in poetic choral flights. But Brecht also created powerful, realistic characters within *The Private Life of the Master Race* who underwent intense and natural personal struggles against a background of real social and psychological conditions. To demand that the actor stand aside from his character in such cases is quite another matter, and here the schizophrenia of the whole "Epic Realist" style is revealed. To insist that artists working within an artistic form (and with the techniques and conventions of art their only communicative means) produce "non-art" is unintelligible. But Brecht was anything but unintelligible. He made his social points vigorously and lucidly, using realism, and engaging emotions throughout. His "alienation" effect and his somewhat doctrinaire theories, with their implicit challenge to the very source and wellspring of dramatic art — catharsis — created a stir among intellectuals and politically minded critics. But Brecht did not create documentary plays. He created compelling dramas by exercising every prerogative of the artist.

These two experiments in documentary theatre, "Living Newspaper" and "Epic Realism," represent the living theatre's most exciting and far-reaching ventures into that gray area between art and life. In some ways they were farther removed from an imitation of life than many socially conceived realistic dramas; and yet, paradoxically, they seemed closer to documentary, providing a disconcerting demonstration of how the records of life itself could be woven into the larger whole of an emotion-stimulating art form. As they came to view these efforts, men realized that they could never dispense with the ultimate conventions of the stage, and the control of a playwright over depiction of human choice and destiny.

Thus theatre and drama were set apart from documentary at the deepest and most profound level. Documentary's instinct — its thrust — is still to avoid and escape the theatrical. Before any final parameters of documentary can be set down, however, it is necessary to disengage its spirit and intent from dramatic form in the film medium.

DOCUMENTARY AND FICTION FILM

The invasion of the film by the playwright and actor, Maya Deren has observed, brought with it the concept of realism which dominated the stage, and which "in the *a priori* reality of photography, is an absurd redundancy which has served merely to deprive the motion picture medium of its creative dimension."[6] The argument bears weight in light of the early history of the medium, where the theatrical conventions and dramaturgy of the proscenium stage did much to delimit the natural capacities of the film. The documentary movement was inspired precisely by the desire to escape and avoid this inherent redundancy of a convention-ridden theatrical art in a medium where it was no longer necessary to create the *illusion* of men in action.

These conditions at least provided, however, some ease of distinction between documentary and fiction films. So long as fiction film-makers were content to rely upon costume and make-up, studio settings, and the art of the performer, the direction of documentary was clear: it would go to the natural location, it would seek the natural man, it would represent nothing that did not exist in truth, and it would attempt to fashion its story only from these records.

But when the fiction film was inspired to leave the studio and move to the streets, the forms blended once more. When it attempted to present a deeper psychological honesty in character, when it began concerning itself with social purpose rather than entertainment, when it used real people in their natural backgrounds to set off a fictional story — when it did all of this, the discernible identities between the two schools of film-making became more difficult to isolate. Many critics began to share Gavin Lambert's sentiment that the important distinctions no longer lay "between the slick feature and vital reportage, but surely between the living and the dead, the true and the false, in any form or style."[7]

Such a renaissance in the fiction film was dimly perceived in the new realism of Hollywood's gangster cycle of the 1930's, where the brutality of some aspects of American life was delineated with natural detail, but tricked up sufficiently to provide entertainment and escape. The sobering realities of the times were better reflected, however, in later films of the decade and throughout the war. Inspired by *March of Time*'s willingness to use both documentary and fictional techniques, and perhaps by its exposés of threats from abroad, *Confessions of a Nazi Spy* was released in 1939, and raised immediate controversy in a still isolationist nation. In John Ford's 1940 film version of Steinbeck's *The Grapes of Wrath* many documentary themes of the mid-1930's were given final expression. When the war ended, many of these social concerns upon which documentarists had founded their movement were no longer so urgent. But new issues had arisen, and the techniques of the documentarist were further adapted to express them.

In the immediate postwar period, experiment in documentary technique was witnessed in *The Lost Weekend*, where the hidden camera was used to record environment on New York's Third Avenue. In Jules Dassin's *The Naked City* real people on the streets were interwoven into the drama as minor characters, and the adaptation of the newsworthy was seen in such films as Louis de Rochemont's *The House on 92nd Street, Call Northside 777* and Elia Kazan's *Panic in the Streets*. The subjects of social concern also found more frequent expression in the story film, as postwar filmmakers created thematic treatments of lynch law, the Negro question, anti-Semitism, labor racketeering, drug addiction, the inadequacy of schools, juvenile delinquency, and mental illness.

In its explorations of social issues, its increasing use of the natural environment, and its new-found willingness to create more authentic characterization, the story film began to strike down many landmarks which once set separate paths for fact and fiction film. Yet the key markers still stood — the control of character and the use of the actor in those roles which carried the major emotional thrust of story. The removal of the control of a storyteller over the human will could not be made without affecting the final transformation of form. Still, the course of the modern fiction film has shown us some remarkable attempts to provide such a final cross-over, and our most penetrating examples of it were made within the Italian postwar "neo-realist" movement. The film which is often said to have initiated the movement is Luchino Visconti's 1942 *Ossessione*, but perhaps its definitive and enduring achievement was Roberto Rossellini's *Open City*.

Rossellini had worked in the Italian documentary film before turning to fiction films early in the war. Before the Germans even departed from Rome in 1944, he was shaping his classic story of the Italian resistance movement of that period. A terse and accurate reconstruction of reality dominated *Open City*, as the records of hidden cameras caught life unaware in the city. All was authentic, including the records of the streets and the people of Rome. Nazi soldiers were caught, newsreel style, as they completed their preparations for evacuation. The tricks of the studio were gone, and the powerful authority of true visual documents was heightened by the very lack of careful lighting and undue attention to pictorial qualities. Ros-

OPEN CITY

. . . the choices were Rossellini's.

sellini integrated stock actuality footage, showing us moments of the agony in human experience in a way which only actual combat films could reveal, and made these a part of his total design.

All this might still not move drama nearer to documentary in terms of the control of human beings portrayed, were it not for the fact that Rossellini, De Sica, and others who followed them in the neo-realist tradition were working with the ultimate authority of the photograph. Like many before them in the living theatre and in the motion picture, they sought to avoid the non-natural, to minimize convention, and to portray humans as they existed in life, not as heroes or villains who pass through irreversible crises and make strong assertions of will. But they did it with greater authenticity, a deeper respect for human beings and a calm, controlled reliance upon the authority of film. This concatenation of aims and execution brought their work closer to documentary than any fictional form in history — but not *to* documentary, and the difference still lies in the matter of human will and choice, of which the use of the actor is only a technical manifestation.

Nicholas Vardac, in pursuing this point, cites the scene in *Open City* where the mistress of the underground leader, while under the influence of dope, betrays her lover. She is drugged, Vardac suggests, because of Rossellini's desire to minimize her freedom as a "conscious, willful agent." If the decision were made consciously, he argues, "she would immediately become a villain, the piece would fall into melodrama and, hence, fiction." Aside from the point that there is no inherent one-way relationship between melodrama and fiction (fiction may also be non-melodrama) the logic of this argument is unsubstantial when it leads Vardac to conclude that "these characters exist beyond the limits of the script. They are *non-fictional* characters."[8]

The quarrel here is not with Vardac's understanding of what separates documentary from drama, but with his apparent willingness to confuse the *appearance* of Rossellini's work with the fact of it. The assumption that *Open City* is a documentary is in error. The idea of a "nonfictional character" is just as unintelligible as Brecht's insistence that actors should not be allowed to act. A "person" is not a "character." One is real, the other is a fiction, created by a plot-maker for a larger purpose. It is quite true that Rossellini may have created characters who, on the surface, did not have strong commitments — characters caught in the senseless pattern of war who could not carry on in the romantic tradition of "to will and to do." But this suggests only that the techniques by which drama is made true and recognizable have changed, not that drama has become something else.

When the authentic records of life are used, documentary exists and it cannot exist otherwise. But it must be acknowledged that the mere use of authentic records, no matter how extensively they are employed or how realistically they expose life to us, cannot in themselves make documentary. Documentary cannot exist simply because the reality of life is introduced in a situation and environment, or in details of psychological and physical imitation. So long as the plot-maker controls what "characters" do, whether he strives to minimize their exertions of will or not, we are not seeing real persons and witnessing their choices and decisions. "Character" still implies "imitation" of an action, not the true action, and documentary's final concern is with the authority of the record of the true action.

Unless we understand the distinction between documentary and drama in terms of past attempts by one or the other to escape its independent form, we cannot fully comprehend the immense possibilities of documentary work in television. In no other medium in history have the two forms been forced into such close and immediate relationship with each other within a single social and aesthetic context — a framework which suggests the existence of an entirely independent television form.

To be sure, the medium was first applied as a mere transmitting device, capable of simple informational and artistic communications or of conveying the actuality of events themselves. Our only notions of form, however, embrace the various conditions under which a communication is framed and received — conditions that are, if not immutable and unchangeable, relatively stable and continuing. These shape the nature of the communication in terms of what the communicator does when he is functioning at the level of his clearest expression. We can measure form only in terms of the most important and satisfying works created within it; and if this is the case, then the nature of television as a communicative medium was defined in its earliest years.

The television dramatist gave clearest definition to the medium's unique qualities. It was not long before critics followed along in recognition that TV allowed for — and was most meaningfully employed in — a drama which focused upon one or two individuals engaged in that "small crisis" which playwright Paddy Chayefsky argued TV alone was capable of sustaining.

The position had its origins in earlier dramaturgical theory, principally in Maurice Maeterlinck's concept in the late 19th century of a "static" drama. Maeterlinck's hope was for a drama which would express the implicit, and in such plays as *The Intruder* he was more successful in expounding his theories than was Zola. The direction of many of his works was away from the large and obvious dramatic statement toward revelation of moods and intensities of inward, subjective states of mind. If he abandoned his theory of stasis in drama later in his life, it may have been because he sensed that the inward reality of life, like Zola's external reality, could not overcome a central reason for the creation of a play: performance from a public platform. Not until television came into existence was that platform of such a nature that Maeterlinck's theories would have true significance.

In the arguments over technological distinctions between electronic and filmed recording methods and such related matters as the size of studios, the number of people who can "fit" into a TV scene, the number of lenses on cameras, the size of the screen, and other impermanent and perhaps nonessential matters, the point may be lost. Television drama, however it is produced, staged, or edited, achieved its highest expression in a handful of plays produced in New York City between 1947 and 1955 — a brief experimental period comparable, in its own small way, to the golden ages of Pericles, Queen Elizabeth, and the years at the close of the 19th century when the modern drama was born. The products of this experiment, however technically imperfect they may seem now and despite all the varieties of technical recording and transmission which have come along since then, demonstrated a new approach to drama which television, in its intimacy of transmission and reception and in the greater context of actuality itself, alone could create.

The art of small crisis is realized best in those early works of Chayef-sky, Tad Mosel, Horton Foote, J. P. Miller, Reginald Rose, Robert Alan Aurthur, and others who framed dramatic actions which were essentially inward, and often incapable of expression in the larger actions required of stage plays and fiction films. These men created plays in which the action "happened off-stage," and in the process also worked out those devices for revealing inward conflict that were somehow ideally suited to the small scene and the audience in the living room.

Maeterlinck's suggestion that the great drama of mankind — the strongest of dramatic actions — is locked within the mind of an old man, as he calmly sits and rocks in a chair, is vivified in Chayefsky's *The Mother*. In this television play an elderly widow must finally decide whether she will continue to maintain her independence or lose the meaning of her existence by accepting care from an overly possessive daughter. Her decision — the full climax of the play — is revealed in a lengthy scene wherein she sits quietly in a chair, staring out a window. The scene fades as night comes on, and we are returned to the same action the following morning. She rises, her mind made up, and leaves her daughter's apartment. A major dramatic crisis has been met and overcome without a word of dialogue. It is the same kind of crisis which faces Howie and Eunice, the hapless, disenchanted middle-aged couple of Tad Mosel's *The Haven*. They must reorder their existence in light of Howie's act of infidelity — an act committed long before the action begins and which is made clear to Eunice in a series of minor discoveries during a family vacation at their summer cottage. Once again we see "the little people," working out the subtle private problems of their relation-ship to each other in a final act in which the words unspoken are more shat-tering in their implication than those which are.[9]

The same small crisis is found in Chayefsky's *Marty*, Aurthur's *Man on the Mountain Top*, and J. P. Miller's *The Rabbit Trap*. As each of these inward conflicts evolves into a dramatic action we sense a certain kind of technique — the "interior monologue" wherein major characters suddenly express themselves in long speeches of self-analysis, doubt, and confusion. This kind of soliloquy, delivered within a framework of realism, is both old and new in dramaturgy, and holds the subtlety of television at its most powerful level. Self-revelation became the mode not only of that realistic video drama of a decade ago, but the central means by which the entire documentary movement in American television rose to achievement in the creative treatment of actuality.

Control of Subject: The Essential Framework

ANY EXAMINATION of the roots of documentary inevitably draws attention to the eternal dichotomy — the subjective-objective or descriptive-impressionistic split which not only constitutes the major dilemma of human communication but holds the key to understanding of all documentary expression. Television, bursting upon the national scene as a mass medium in the late 1940's and early 1950's, inherited all of the styles, methods, and techniques of earlier media in addition to the great and insoluble problems of the nature of documentary itself. Dealing with the new and penultimate authority of the moving photograph transmitted to the viewer in a context of immediate or near-immediate actuality, television has come to face, as perhaps no documentary medium before it, severe and distinct questions of definition and function.

The limitations inherent in attempting to explain television's documentary purposes and forms are revealed somewhat in recent observations by René Wellek in his discussion of the effects of literary realism in the modern era. Realism, he suggests, has in "its lower reaches constantly declined into journalism, treatise writing, scientific description, in short into non-art . . . [but on its highest levels] with its greatest writers, with Balzac and Dickens, Dostoevsky and Tolstoy, Henry James and Ibsen, and even Zola, it constantly went beyond its theory: it created worlds of imagination."[1] This statement bears directly upon the great issues of public communication with which television has come to grips, for the visual and aural media of "realistic" expression are also subject to the truth of Wellek's assertion.

The assumption upon which television documentary is based is that its journalistic descriptions of the world around us must in one sense be regarded as non-art if they are to have full significance as public information — and yet conversely they must engage in the "world of imagination" if their constant interpretations of the life which flows around us are to create affective responses in watching millions. The application of Wellek's distinctions forces us to take into account a concept of audience involvement in the real events and circumstances of our age, and this demands recognition of the possibility that levels of purpose and function in TV documentary not only exist but must be maintained by deliberate design. As these levels are separated, they must be shaped and directed by the initial choices of the documentarist.

Television documentary divides its purposes into the journalistic, which falls within those "lower reaches" of communication, and the poetic, where the "world of imagination" can be stimulated and represented while firmly anchored in life's realities. The first allows for the precision and impartiality of description, with emphasis upon the detached and dispassionate in techniques of presentation; the other frees its techniques and approaches to advance the subjective purpose of the poet in his presentation of those universal themes of life and humanity which he senses in the documents themselves. The journalistic is controlled by subject, the poetic by theme.

Drawing such a line forces one to accept the consequences. The effort here is to classify the television documentary upon that tenuous basis of whether it is controlled in approach and technique by its subject or by its theme. Control need imply neither dominance nor exclusivity in the documentary creative process. It represents no more than human effort to pay a first obligation to the tenets of either reportage *or* art in the making of documentaries — the giving of proper respect to one *or* the other. To be sure, it cannot represent an either-or alternative. Control must recognize and allow for the possibility that both art and reportage exist to a certain degree in any interpretation of reality, and yet it must represent a willingness to come upon the interpretation in a special way, and with specific methods of presentation.

Such a scheme of classification rests upon the position that some kinds of documentaries are less free to depart from the descriptive — that they can involve the human mind and imagination only when content permits. These documentaries are not so free to engage in flights of imagination, to use certain emotion-arousing devices. They are, in truth, subject-controlled. Primarily they are *News Documentaries*, and their creation is, above all, governed by a human concept which is unrelated to the purpose and function of the artist — objectivity.

It has become easy to argue that objectivity is a myth, but we can never dismiss the meaning which man has assigned to the concept. Objectivity was invented to serve the rational in mankind, and it has become the essential means by which we struggle to escape those convictions which

Nietzsche has called our prisons. To argue that objectivity cannot exist is to pose the frightening possibility that we are hopelessly subject to all that is dark and irrational in human nature. Without the concept of objectivity we abandon all outward meaning of life and events, even reason itself. This concept represents no less than the attitude by which men and societies are enabled both to survive and prevail.

The first objective of news, Wilbur Schramm reminds us, is *to reconstruct the essential framework of an event*, and the subject-controlled News Documentary must observe this first principle. It must set the subject itself as the determinant of interpretation. This should not imply that subjective insights are to be ignored or minimized. The News Documentary, as a broad generic approach, may not only present the subjective and the imaginative, but may actively seek to develop these qualities within the basic function and limits of reportage. In the News Documentary, however, life must always be in control of art.

The origins of the journalistic or News Documentary in television are found in the earliest examples of hard-news presentation. At the outset the nature of the TV medium dictated the addition of the visual element in news presentation, and the idea of news programs which incorporated visual material (as in the weekly picture-news magazines) was effected in earliest efforts. By 1948 both WCBS-TV and WNBT (now WNBC-TV) in New York were carrying short weekly reviews of the news in which the influence of the theatrical newsreel was apparent. Even in daily news programs the addition of film helped further to visualize the day's headlines. This tradition continued, and as late as 1951 NBC was engaged in the production of its own fully scored newsreels, with each short reel covering approximately 40 news stories in a period of seven to eight minutes. These films, intended for distribution to local stations as an adjunct to hard-news programming, were accompanied by full scripts which were revised at the last minute before shipment. In this period both United Press and 20th Century-Fox also completed negotiations to establish news-film services across the nation.

But these developments would play only a partial role in an emerging TV documentary form, for early in its history the medium also moved to exploit its own greatest natural capacity, the presentation of actuality at the moment of occurrence. In January 1947 the existing networks televised the opening session of Congress and, two weeks later, President Truman's address to that body, revealing that television's window on history was almost as clear as the newsreels' and far closer in time.

A combination of these two technologies soon resulted. Enlarged concepts were introduced, and the idea of News Documentary, as begun in the radio and film versions of *March of Time*, moved toward further realization. In 1951 both General MacArthur's return to America and the activities of the UN General Assembly in Paris were covered by the networks, and by November NBC had begun a weekly series of 12 half-hour special reports on the UN, produced by the Ford Foundation. The programs used film and narration as well as extensive interviews.

These were early straws in the wind. At the same time local stations and networks were building upon the concepts of in-depth and hard-news coverage, while evolving techniques of studio presentation held forth the possibility of expanded and detailed explanation and interpretation of events. As reporters in other media had recognized that reporting of the complex news events of the day required greater analysis, so TV's journalists found ways to move the simple news story beyond events and personalities and into more elaborate presentations of origins and outcomes — of what had gone before and what might ensue. The elements of voice, sound, and picture — whether a live or film record — were close at hand, and could now be cast into the more meaningful and compelling journalistic form of the TV documentary. At this point the evolution of the subject-controlled News Documentary in television must be brought within its different contexts.

5 / News Documentary: The Ongoing Crisis

What the American does *not* know can kill him.
— FRED W. FRIENDLY[1]

WITHIN THE RANGE of documentary news presentation in television over the past 15 years, one particular type may quickly be isolated.
This is the major, nationally distributed documentary series which deals
with current and contemporary crises of national and international import.
Treating serious and perennial social, political, economic, cultural, and
philosophical conflicts of this era, programs within this class have been
originated primarily by the American networks, where they are produced
with the kind of facilities, talent, and budget which assure national attention. Such "prestige" series in American television News Documentary actually number only three: the continuing *CBS Reports* and NBC *White Paper*
series and the now defunct ABC *Close-Up!* which, between 1960 and 1963,
instituted a number of vital and dynamic variations in approach to News
Documentary which have had far-reaching impact upon form and function
within the entire category. These series, like all other current News Documentaries in TV, drew their form and inspiration from the work of two
men, Edward R. Murrow and Fred W. Friendly.

SEE IT NOW

In November 1951 Murrow and Friendly initiated the first and definitive News Documentary series in American television, *See It Now*. Its origins were founded in Murrow's earlier radio work, beginning with the
creation of the 1946 CBS Unit as well as *March of Time*; but in many ways

See It Now was a pioneering effort. As Murrow commented on his first program, it was a simple matter of "an old team trying to learn a new trade."[2]

Here were experienced journalists who, believing that television was "in a sense an instrument of transportation," applied film in a way in which it had not heretofore been used on television — to relate a news "story." The TV newsreels and hard-news shows had offered odds and ends of a number of unrelated events, relying for story only on the hurried shots of cameramen and segmented "here you see" narration. But the primary aim of the *See It Now* crew was to report in depth — to tell and show the American audience what was happening in the world by using film as a narrative tool. Reporters came first. They "viewed the stories as competent newsmen and then asked the cameramen to record on film what they had observed."[3] From "story" came film, natural sound, and then a simple, direct editing continuity which preserved journalistic objectivity, but which also condensed, squeezed, and rearranged actuality material to conform to the demands of time and a distinct plot line.

Yet the forthright approach of *See It Now* to the controversial issues of modern life was not immediately achieved, and its earliest efforts repeated the same patterns of those journalistic forms which preceded television, notably the screen-magazine and the photo essay. Like Louis de Rochemont, 17 years earlier, Murrow wanted to move beyond daily news reportage because he felt there is nothing less satisfying than daily newsreel clips. Careful planning was thus directed toward creating a news-magazine — with the important exception that it had to be compiled weeks in advance. To Murrow the program content was news only because they said it was. The first *See It Now* set the pattern for offerings during the initial seasons and followed a general newsreel style, with separate stories about Winston Churchill, Anthony Eden, Senators Dirksen and Smith, and two United States Army Divisions. This composite news format was maintained for more than a year.

The third season was well under way before the December telecast of "Christmas in Korea," a program which marked a departure from earlier formats, and which represented the culmination of Murrow's search for a proper TV News Documentary form. Thenceforth, *See It Now* moved steadily away from all attempts at hard news as its function became one of providing timely and searching reports ranging over the leading edge of history.

"Christmas in Korea" became a milestone in the evolution of TV's journalistic documentary. The recounting of the day's battle losses or the latest word on the progress of armies was left to daily news programs, as Murrow and Friendly took their crew to Korea to record the faces, voices, sounds, and sights of the stalemate there in human terms. The technique was simplicity itself. Led by Murrow, the *See It Now* reporters introduced themselves at the beginning of several scenes, related where they were and

MURROW AND FRIENDLY

". . . it's news because we say it is."

MURROW IN KOREA (1953)

. . . the leading edge of history.

what was happening, and then talked to the troops as the cameras turned. Murrow began the program, then Ed Scott spoke from a hospital ship. After three GI's sang "The Rotation Blues," the action jumped to Joe Wershba in an airplane, then back to Murrow, who pointed to a bridge and spoke briefly of its importance before turning again to the soldiers.

That is how it went: the simple record of a war; a scene-setting, a feel of the place, and the showing of men in action, or in reflection. It was un-complicated reportage, and events were secondary. It was the depth of war's meaning that the *See It Now* crew sought, and — in the drawn and weary faces of GI's fresh off the line, in their cautious smiles, and in their moments of reminiscence — this was what they found.

From this significant beginning, *See It Now* continued for seven years, probing into controversial events and into the minds of the people who, in a sense, made those events happen. Its basic method approximated the radio actuality documentary: to record people with something to say and hold its own narration to a minimum. The approach was not, then, essentially new, but the visual had given it a power and force which radio seldom achieved. It took no liberties with actuality, and its method finally came to incorporate the single story as *March of Time* had done before.

To critical acclaim — and to the consternation and indignation of many throughout the early and mid-1950's — the series progressed, choosing its own subjects and developing conflict-charged treatments of them. It moved to examine burning domestic issues such as civil liberties, Communism, and integration as well as the new problems of America's role in world affairs. By its fifth season *See It Now* had expanded its old half-hour format to a full hour or hour and a half. A number of programs were now devoted to study-portraits of some of the world's great figures as Murrow interviewed Gandhi, Nehru, Carl Sandburg, Winston Churchill, and others whose mere presence before the camera gave viewers a sense of living history. Concern-ing this kind of interview, Murrow noted that most of the good writing was done by nonprofessionals ad-libbing what they knew and believed. "Under the pressure of the moment," he wrote, "and armed with the conviction born of conflict, they composed compelling literature."[4]

The observation points to the true significance of the interview in TV documentary journalism. It has been argued by some in both film and TV that the interview is essentially a weak documentary technique, but Murrow and Friendly had worked their way through to that same understanding of television's unique capacities for revealing inner conflict in human character which their peers in TV drama were also discovering. The interview became, in a sense, a journalistic application of stasis drama, and Maeterlinck's ex-ample of the struggle locked within the mind and heart of an old man sitting in a rocking chair was given its consummate realization in the *See It Now* interview of Carl Sandburg. What was dramatic and subjective was the man himself and the depth of his character and experience as revealed by the

MURROW ON McCARTHY   McCARTHY ANSWERS MURROW

CBS *See It Now* (1954)

. . . Murrow passed him the club.

television camera. What was factual and journalistic was his words and opinions, which had a pertinence and relevancy for all who heard them. No added dramatic values of sound effects, mood music, camera manipulation, or stylized editing were necessary to sustain these programs as documentary in the best tradition.

See It Now built its largest audiences, however, with its deliberate choice of those social conflicts which define the course of a free society, and thereby were of compelling interest to most Americans. It took its cameras to Michigan to record the full cast of characters in the little tragedy of Milo Radulovich, an Air Force officer stripped of his rank as a result of his family's political activities. It moved to Indianapolis, where a momentous conflict on civil liberties was under way, to record both sides of the battle; and to Clinton, Tennessee, to show a community torn by the issue of segregation. It was stirred to the defense of Annie Lee Moss when a triumphant McCarthy grew too careless. It could reveal the scope of these conflicts by letting combatants speak, or it could let one man represent his own wisdom and point of view. And finally, it could make an angry editorial statement of its own, as in the famous "McCarthy episode."

The program on McCarthy, and McCarthy's answer, have suffered from too much heat and too little light in most subsequent analysis. Murrow's treatment of the Senator was far more deadly in the Annie Lee Moss study, where the approach was an impartial journalistic report, than in the program in which he used the Senator's own statements as a weapon of editorial attack. Gilbert Seldes, whose assessments of the impact of the mass media remain the most insightful in American criticism, came nearest to making the point when he suggested that a moral principle was involved — in which one man clubbed another and then passed him the stick, knowing full well he could not use it so effectively. This opinion, of course, was not so much a defense of McCarthy as an attack on the potentially treacherous quality of documentary film.

In point of fact, little of the technique used by Murrow had not already been demonstrated by McCarthy's planners. In selecting film clips taken from McCarthy's speeches and juxtaposing them in a certain manner, Murrow only did what McCarthy had already done in other American media. If the Senator's answer seemed clumsy in comparison, it was in the ineptness of execution, *not* in unawareness of the arts of persuasion and how to invoke them.

Upon reviewing these films at the Museum of Modern Art's retrospect, *Television U.S.A.: 13 Seasons*, one is led to conclude, after almost a decade has blunted the edges of hatred, that McCarthy's response was only too good — better, as sharp one-sided persuasive documentary, than Murrow's first blow. McCarthy never lost the confidence which only fanaticism could breed. His use of maps and charts may have seemed unprofessional, but he did not let these dominate his personality or interfere with what he wished to say. Murrow's superiority of technique in this quarrel did not, then, constitute a moral issue as grave as Seldes may have felt it to be.

The heat of that controversy, however, attracted attention to the purpose of editorial documentary, prompting continuing argument over what constituted valid film technique in this kind of documentary. In this regard the central question is not really one of whether documentary can and should take a stand in dealing with controversial issues — although it is disturbing to find among contemporary critics the tendency to regard favorably those efforts which take points of view in agreement with their own, while dismissing others which aim to be fair and impartial as superficial or "carefully neutralized." Such criticism of the quality of documentary discounts all possibility that the journalist, by giving light, may help people to find their way, and is characteristic of political extremists on both left and right. Thus Murrow's reporting of various civil liberties cases, particularly the Annie Lee Moss episode, provided Americans with a forthright journalistic documentary from which they could draw for themselves the inevitable conclusions one had to reach about the dangers of McCarthyism. In his very selection of these incidents, it could be argued, Murrow was not objective. He said these were bad situations, and even suggested that wrongs had been done. But once the basic decision to do the story was made, he reported the facts without making the record itself an emotional element within the program.

The true question, rather, is whether Murrow's direct editorial attack on McCarthy did not cast suspicion on all similar technique in TV documentary. At that moment when Murrow engaged in an essentially *cinematic* method of dramatizing a point (by juxtaposing film clips of several of McCarthy's own statements), he crossed a line between use of film as an emotion-inspiring aesthetic form, and as a recording instrument of the passing scene governed by less subjective rules of direct expository narrative. He turned from making film *tell* something to making it *will* something (to use Jacques Maritain's concise distinction), and this gives true substance to Seldes' critique of the entire affair. It also raised the main point of argument which will arise again and again as we further consider the evolution of documentary journalism in TV.

For in terms of production, the primary contribution of this series was the "cross-cut" interview — a device which was always available to theatrical film documentarists but seldom used with flair and imagination. Subsequently imitated by many others in television and film, the technique involved the procedure of recording many interviews at great length and in considerable detail — a certain way to achieve the conviction Murrow and Friendly sought — and then fragmenting them into a series of shorter statements to be "shotgunned" throughout a program. The process permitted not only arresting and rapid flow of visual interest, but a bold juxtaposition of different points of view in short and emphatic bursts. The method had its dangers, and producers have been accused of employing statements out of proper context, just as Friendly and Murrow suffered such criticism on more than one occasion. The major distinction, however, between the shotgun-interview technique and juxtaposition of clips as in the McCarthy program is that in the first instance the device served to heighten interest and drama in a clash of opinion between opposing forces, a conflict in which *See It Now* functioned merely as a reportorial instrument. In the McCarthy case a similar if not identical practice was employed to advance a specific editorial statement, and here the use of technique took on new dimensions and therefore required additional responsibilities to an audience.

Despite this debate, *See It Now* remains the generative and seminal force in TV News Documentary. Like *March of Time,* it had achieved independence of form by first breaking away from the television equivalent to the newsreel, the hard-news report. By virtue of its recognition of television's intrinsic characteristics of intimacy and immediacy in presentation, it did what no printed or verbal form of communication could do as well — *involve* people in events at a maximum level of identification. By insisting that the reporter would come first, and that film be used only as an expository supplement, it retained, in most of its programs, a true attempt at impartiality.

See It Now must be given its due as the prototype of a dominant form of television documentary — the factual, timely report in depth on issues of prominent national and international concern. The approaches developed here were borrowed by all subsequent series of this type, and its influence spread throughout the entire field of "depth" documentary news reporting. All of its successors owed some of their working principles to the originality of Murrow and Friendly, who had found television's form for documentary journalism. Their News Documentaries often combined what, in print, was the feature and the background story, but they added the terse, spare narration of the radio style, a visual faithfulness to reality in the best tradition of film documentary, and — at the heart of their success — a probing, controversial treatment of those events and conditions of our existence which, indeed, became news because Murrow and Friendly said it was.

CBS REPORTS

See It Now continued through mid-1958, when CBS announced cancellation of the program for reasons which are not entirely clear. The shift from institutional to consumer advertising by Alcoa (its sponsor) was doubtless involved in the decision to cancel, as was the program's tendency to create friction and difficulties for the network. Murrow, too, grew restless. He sharply criticized television, charging that during peak viewing hours it "insulated us from the realities of the world in which we live." The situation smoldered until February 1959, when Murrow asked for a leave of absence. It was granted, and a 20-year association which had produced some of the most stirring moments in electronic journalism moved toward a conclusion.

During Murrow's leave CBS made ready for a revitalized series of reports on the issues of our time. Conceived by Frank Stanton, *CBS Reports* came on the air in the fall of 1959. The program was seen only 12 times in its first year, was a biweekly during the next, and became a weekly in the 1961-62 season, after which it returned to a less demanding schedule. It might be maintained that *CBS Reports* was not a mere continuation of *See It Now* under a new title, but there were really few distinctions save the essential one of policy control. Where *See It Now* was basically a Murrow package, *CBS Reports* became a "company show" — a total CBS News effort, marked with the stamp of corporate responsibility. But the same intensive approach to critical issues continued and *CBS Reports* was often as challenging and controversial as its forerunner.

Friendly indicated at the outset that he disliked having *CBS Reports* called a "documentary" series and described his efforts as "stories," the success of which depended upon their plots. "Though based on truth," he wrote, "the programs still have to have stories of their own, with the basic outline of beginning, middle and end."[5] This dictum constituted no radical departure from *See It Now,* nor did a shift in policy control mean much basic difference in selection and treatment of subjects. Indeed, when in October 1959 Murrow introduced and narrated the first program in this series, "Biography of a Missile," it seemed there had been no interruption at all in the long sweep of *See It Now*. But Murrow's appearances in this series were only occasional, and after his appointment as director of the United States Information Agency, he left Friendly to carry on alone the work of reporting the recurrent crises of a civilization.

Even if Fred W. Friendly were inclined to avoid perpetuating the outlook and example he established with Murrow, it would have been extremely difficult for him to do so. He had been associated with Murrow for over a decade since their first co-operative venture in producing the *I Can Hear It Now* recordings for Columbia in 1948 and through the short-lived *Hear It Now* on CBS Radio. He had worked with Murrow during the eight years of *See It Now* and the CBS *Small World* series as well. His experience and commitments were shared with the man he replaced as *CBS Reports* got under way.

In its course through the years, then, the new series followed the same approaches to News Documentary that had been developed by its forerunner. There were, first of all, an impressive number of "character documents" and biographical treatments of important newsmakers, relying upon the interview or biographical compilation technique. In these, content reflected the man, and control of story was determined essentially by the interviewee. Second, there were the general studies of events which dominated the current scene. Finally, *CBS Reports* continued to present editorial statements, offering visual and aural evidence in support of attitudes which extended beyond the mere selection of subject and into the treatment itself.

Among the personality interviews were discussions with Walter Lippmann, who shared his thoughts on national and international affairs in each of the years in the series. Carl Sandburg reviewed Lincoln's prairie life, and told the story of Gettysburg as the cameras toured the battlefields. Eisenhower reflected upon the Presidency and returned to the Normandy beaches with Walter Cronkite to make a special 1964 program commemorating the 20th anniversary of D-Day. The lengthy personality documentaries of this kind provided a kind of portraiture which, in the words of critic Jacques Andrès, were "as handsome and serene as a photograph posed for hours in the time of Mrs. Cameron."[6] In one sense, of course, these were purely interview programs, steeped in the tradition of radio interview; and yet one could witness, in most of them, the documentary instrument in use — carried forward from *See It Now*'s "Christmas in Korea." A sense of time and place was provided visually, as when Eisenhower strode the beaches of Normandy once again, or walked about the peaceful countryside of Gettysburg. On other occasions, notably the Sandburg interview at Gettysburg, the battlegrounds were brought to life with exploratory sequences of film.

CBS REPORTS — Lippmann and Sevareid; Truman, Reasoner, Friendly

. . . the control of story was theirs.

In the interviews with Secretary of State Dean Rusk and Defense Secretary Robert McNamara the visual revelation was less, but the sense of journalistic importance remained.

The classic interviews of *CBS Reports* represented journalistic documentary in the truest sense simply by virtue of the compelling nature of each subject's personality and of his essential newsworthiness, as well as by a limited effort to create added involvement by pictorial means. Not all interviews were so easily brought into the true documentary concept. An additional journalistic value of these interview documentaries was most apparent when, after the assassination of President John F. Kennedy, *CBS Reports* brought from its film vaults its recorded interviews with Truman (by Murrow in the original *See It Now*), Eisenhower, and Kennedy, and edited therefrom their personal reflections upon the office of the Presidency. By the mid-1960's television had its own enormous backlog of reality documents with which to make the present meaningful in terms of the past.

The documentary personality interview, somewhat biographical in nature, was complemented by the documentary portrait, which used the direct interview with its subject wherever possible, but also wove the records of his newsworthy actions and statements into a definite story line. Without question, the most effective stories in this group included "The Trials of Charles De Gaulle" and the heroic battle of Dr. Tom Dooley told in "Biography of a Cancer." In both cases one finds an almost perfect dramatic structure, with a line of rising action leading toward climax and resolution — a triumph in the Algerian question for De Gaulle and an ultimate surrender to death by the gallant Dooley. Along with similar portraits of newsmakers — such movers of our time as Dominican dictator Trujillo, Barry Goldwater, and others — *CBS Reports* combined the journalistic and the biographical study in a distinct fashion which let millions witness the men who made news as they were involved in the very process.

Like *See It Now*, *CBS Reports* functioned at its journalistic best in detailing those continuing stories which set contemporary issues squarely before the public — issues in which the element of controversy was inherent. From one of its earliest studies — the population problem — the series moved to detail all sides of argument in American civil rights questions, the courts, education, labor, national defense, the economy, national welfare, politics, and government. The treatments took two basic forms: either the balanced and impartial analysis or, more rarely, the undeniably editorial statement.

The majority of such programs were impartial news-treatments, but *CBS Reports* could not touch upon some issues without engendering controversy and the challenge of "editorializing." It met criticism about two programs in particular — "The Business of Health: Medicine, Money and Politics," which drew accusations of "slanted" and "unfair" treatment from the American Medical Association, and "Harvest of Shame." The latter proved a source of continuing dissent when Murrow was led to change his mind about the effect of the program upon other nations after he had become director of the USIA. It was one thing to present for domestic audiences an angry indictment of a nagging social problem, but quite another to give unfriendly forces abroad such a choice opportunity to foster anti-American opinion. There was no doubt, however, that "Harvest of Shame" went beyond impartial reportage; it stands as the series' clearest example of the editorial statement.

"Harvest" dug into the problem of America's migrant workers, taking the strongest possible stand against the passive indifference which allowed these people to live so miserably. To strengthen the point, the program was shown during Thanksgiving week, when most Americans were enjoying the very harvest gathered by the migrants. Using the photographic record of environment and the direct interview, the *CBS Reports* unit (led by producer David Lowe and with Murrow as narrator) followed the path of the migrants as they traveled the harvesting route in ramshackle caravans from their Florida shacks. The cameras recorded their squalor and the deadly and hopeless monotony of their labors. In disturbing interviews we listened to mothers forced to leave children alone in rat-infested hovels because they could not afford the pennies to send them to a day-care center; or parents unable to provide milk for their infants more than once a week. As the film progressed, we were offered a devastating visual contrast between the shacks occupied by migrants and the comfortable, clean stables nearby. We saw scenes of cattle cars stopping at regular four-hour intervals in order to water and exercise the cattle, contiguous with scenes of the pitiful migrants riding buses and overloaded trucks for ten uninterrupted hours at a stretch.

"Harvest of Shame" was editorial documentary in its frankest manner. It was intended to shock, to make men aware of the deplorable conditions under which some Americans must exist, and dictated only one response — direct social action. Murrow summarized with specific points of legislation which he felt required immediate adoption. To be sure, there were interviews with various interested parties, including then Secretary of Labor Mitchell and an owner of a large farm where migrants were hired. But these did not seek to "balance" or make the presentation in any way impartial. The indictment of the system was too strong to allow a speculative conclusion. If there was any mistaking Murrow's statements, there was no misinterpreting what the film was deliberately intended to show us, and in this regard "Harvest" joined that long crusade against human suffering begun in the early 1900's by photographers Jacob Riis and Lewis Hine and pursued in the 1930's by the haunting photographic records of Walker Evans, Dorothea Lange, and others in Roy Stryker's FSA Unit.

CBS REPORTS — "Harvest of Shame"

. . . part of that long crusade.

But the editorial stand brought severe criticism. The charges of slant-ing or distorting a story, of magnifying problems out of all true proportion and of deliberately ignoring "the other side" of the question were answered by Richard Salant, then President of CBS News:

> . . . The price of avoiding angry letters is blandness; the price of blandness, in this field at least, is public indifference; and we cannot afford those prices either. Even the critical letters we've received on "Harvest of Shame" and "The Business of Health" . . . tend to show that we've accomplished precisely what we sought — to present facts and issues so as to stimulate people into doing their own thinking. . . . For the letters on the one hand have charged unfairness and slanting; on the other hand they've made quite clear that the letter writers were stimulated into examining the issues and making up their own minds — precisely in the opposite way from what they alleged that the program pointed them toward.[7]

The suspicion that Friendly and Murrow had abandoned journalistic precepts and "manipulated" the audience by clever techniques (notably the juxtaposition of scenes contrasting cattle and people, and emphasis upon visual details of sordidness) has, of course, been voiced throughout the history of documentary. In this instance NBC News producer Reuven Frank disputed such contentions:

> Pictures are like words — they are not facts — they are symbols. What-ever is selected will create a point of view. There was a wonderful story in the [New York] *Times* recently about a voter-registration meeting — in Georgia, I think. The reporter used a sentence describing a deputy sheriff

who was holding a five-cell flashlight in his left hand and smacking it heavily into his right palm. This symbol just popped out at you from the word-picture and you just felt the tension . . . that was generated.

Selection always creates a point of view. The question is not one of objectivity — but responsibility. Objectivity is a screen we hide behind. It's just a word. These programs cannot be done by computer. They have to be done by people. People must react. People who have no interests aren't worth anything at all to you. You are looking only for people who are sufficiently disciplined to approach a subject responsibly. "Fairness" is not an objective criterion. It is subjective. "Fairness" is not "equal by the stopwatch."

This brings up the matter, then, of decision-making. Every program has a large staff — platoons of people are needed to get anything on the air. But decision is restricted to only a few — a few people within the unit who are sympathetic with each other. Out of these people will come the myriad decisions. What film do you shoot? How do you edit it? How is it written? How is it spoken? And these become a unified whole. Successful programs are consistent in this way, and *CBS Reports* is about as good an example as you can get.

Consider Murrow's treatment of the migrant workers in "Harvest." If you were writing a book about migrant workers you'd make a big point about cattle being watered and exercised every four hours, while human beings travel for a full day without rest. It wouldn't be a fiction book, would it? Nor would it mean anything to take a picture of a bus going ten hours without a stop unless your program was ten hours long! That way you could get across the idea of boredom — like some of the new art-films.

But this was an important point to be made. So they compressed. The method they chose was to contrast that with cattle trains. Other equally skilled but different individuals might have used another way to illustrate it. . . . But they made their editorial point — an important point in the exposition — that way, and it worked.[8]

The parallels to be drawn between this defense of the News Documentary and Alistair Cooke's defense of *March of Time* are too similar to be overlooked.

But still deeper matters are raised in any attempt to make distinctions between editorial and other kinds of News Documentaries. The presentation of any kind of politically or socially controversial subject material has drawn fire from all sides. In 1963 Senator Barry Goldwater proclaimed that he "did not trust" CBS News after *CBS Reports'* review of conservatism in America, "Thunder on the Right." Outspoken liberals such as Howard K. Smith took public issue with the networks' failure to probe as "deeply as they should" into certain areas. And while political conservatives and liberals criticized TV's news documentarists, such film critics as Arthur Knight were characterizing TV documentaries as being "carefully neutralized."[9] It would seem, on the one hand, that for many of those who are politically committed, any report which does not reflect only their position is "unfair." On the other hand, the same kind of judgment often works itself out as a semi-aesthetic consideration of whether such a report is "good" documentary or not.

If the hope of avoiding criticism of its treatment of national controversy was faint, *CBS Reports* nevertheless continued occasionally to
explore this area of news. The lessons of "Harvest of Shame" had been
observed, however, and thereafter most of its programs did seek to present
impartial consideration of all issues within the limitations which Reuven
Frank has stressed. If the attempt to achieve balance and a reasoned presentation of all sides can casually be termed "neutralization," this is a
matter which must inevitably reflect upon the critic's understanding not
only of the journalistic function, but perhaps of television itself.

Impartial examination of the issues of our age are best demonstrated
in such *CBS Reports* programs as "The Population Explosion" and "Biography of a Bookie Joint," where the more or less typical methods and
approaches of the bulk of documentaries aired in the first five years of this
series can be observed. Aside from whatever editorializing is inherent within the process of subject-selection itself, each of these programs attempted
to provide as full and detailed an exploration of the subject as possible.
For its treatment of the population problem, the series chose to pose the
conflict as it has evolved to a near-crisis point in India, and selected
spokesmen for various points of view looking toward a solution.

"Biography of a Bookie Joint" was distinguished by the effort of the
experienced journalist to dig out his own story. Fully aware of the extent
to which illegal gambling is being conducted throughout the nation, *CBS
Reports* moved a unit to Boston and found the single story which reflected
this national condition. Producer-reporter Jay McMullen had moved into
the city with his staff, set up hidden cameras near a key-maker's shop, and
proceeded to record the remarkable business which the little store pro-
moted. Among the damning details were photographic records of the
regular daily burning of the policy slips on the street in front of the store
(a violation, no less than book-making, of a city ordinance). To make
sure of getting enough details to build his case, McMullen smuggled a
camera (in a lunch-box) into the store itself and recorded actual bet-taking.

The purpose of "Biography of a Bookie Joint" was evident. It sought
to bring before the American public the moral issue of gambling, and what
might be done about it. Although it relied heavily upon actual documents
to thread together the story, the program also made full use of the basic
technique of News Documentary which *See It Now* had pioneered — the
recording of people's faces as they contributed their opinions upon the
issue involved. "Biography" returned to each of five key figures several
times as the case developed, letting them pass comment in a direct face-to-
camera method.

Often reprehended for such reserve, Friendly made certain that the
shots were relatively static and the set for each interview carefully lighted.
Nor did it matter if the interviewer was occasionally seen. On one occasion
the program even used a straight hard-news, "on-the-street" interview to

CBS REPORTS — "Storm over the Supreme Court"

. . . a sense of grave importance.

CBS REPORTS — "Biography of a Bookie Joint"

. . . to bring a moral issue before the American public.

solicit the opinions of Bostonians. Friendly, producer McMullen, and editor John Shultz were concerned with getting facts across as forcefully as possible, relying upon the dramatic value of the story itself and the human-interest values derived from clear interview presentation. These sufficed, for as things turned out this single program created far greater impact than many more sensational treatments of similar topics. It said, editorially, only that the problem was *with us* and ought to be recognized.

As it entered its later years of production, *CBS Reports* had so refined its techniques of presentation that it could treat the major and minor tumults of the day with an authority and integrity which commanded re spect even from hypercritical print-journalists. It entered into less earth-shaking controversies in such studies as "The Silent Spring of Rachel Carson" and "The American Funeral" — both based upon disputatious books; but Friendly and his staff also explored such major controversies as smoking and lung cancer, civil rights for Negroes, and the historic Supreme Court decisions on prayers in the public schools.

The distinctive production style of *CBS Reports* was unmistakable in each of these programs. The technique of presenting strings of direct quotations in intercut narrative sequences was Friendly's basic contribution, it has been observed, to journalistic TV documentary. The dialogues conducted with an interviewer were normally trimmed to a smooth flowing exchange of pro and con monologues between the interviews — and the reporter was often edited out. When transferred to controversial treatments, the pace of intercutting between the interviews was altered to match the rhythm of argument.

Before long, there were diverse applications of this technique in other News Documentary series. Yet nowhere was it any better executed and more closely integrated with a story line than in *CBS Reports*. Friendly and his producers had come to grasp those exact points at which to depart from the comment of a narrator and cut into direct face-to-camera statements by the people involved. They never allowed an idea or a compelling expression to play itself out before cutting away to another face and another idea. We saw people only in those moments when they were intellectually and physically *committed* in important and vital expressions of opinion.

To date, the high point of this series of journalistic documentaries remains the three-part "Storm over the Supreme Court." In the first program the history and crucial role of the highest court in the nation was given a full description and analysis, and in the second the historic 1963 "school prayer decision" was reported. Eric Sevareid narrated the segments, tying each program together with commentary and questions. In no previous television documentary could one find more vivid writing, a more carefully gradated plot line, or a more compelling use of the faces and words of men. With all this, Friendly and producers Gene DePoris and William Peters succeeded in bringing a sense of grave importance to the subject.

The News Documentary production method of *CBS Reports* was given one final variation in treatment in the initial Supreme Court program when Mark Van Doren, Archibald MacLeish, Frederic March, and Carl Sandburg were engaged as "readers" to assist Sevareid in relating the evolution of the Supreme Court. They recited the observations of famous justices who had reflected upon the role of the Court in a free society, while the visual included impressive scenes of the court building and chambers and a dramatic series of shots of the statues of famous justices. Sandburg read for Lincoln in the Dred Scott decision and for Earl Warren; MacLeish read the comments and opinions of Charles Evans Hughes and Felix Frankfurter; Van Doren read for Thomas Jefferson, Oliver Wendell Holmes, and Hugo Black; and Frederic March for John Marshall and Louis Brandeis. Voice-over statements, borrowed from later sequences in the series, were used at the opening to suggest the sharp cleavage in opinion over the Court's function in interpreting the Constitution. Stills and paintings carried the burden of visualizing the history of the Court and its struggles, although on occasion we saw the readers themselves as well as portraits of those for whom they spoke.

As the historical account moved into the modern era, actuality films and voice recordings of Franklin Roosevelt, James Byrnes, Warren Austin, Arthur Vandenberg, and others were employed to recount Roosevelt's battle to "pack" the Supreme Court in the 1930's. As the story was finally brought to the present, Sevareid introduced Professor Paul Freund of the Harvard Law School, and conducted a direct interview with him on the Court and what prompts it to review cases. Statements by Justice Learned Hand ("In a society where the spirit of moderation is lost, no court can save it . . .") and Oliver Wendell Holmes ("When the ignorant are taught to doubt, they do not know what they safely may believe") concluded this remarkable presentation of one of our fundamental institutions.

Many would consider the second program in the series the most compelling, particularly in its intercutting of the arguments of attorneys representing both sides in the school-prayer case — a challenging summation of the issues involved. In all of these programs, however, journalism, history, and drama had been combined to provide public information at a level unsurpassed in television history, and perhaps in all of public communication. In a presentation which truly made drama from fact, dignity and authority were never weakened or subverted by theatrics. As journalism, these documentaries achieved a force and authority which removed them from any possible accusation of "slanting" or "propaganda," and dispelled once and for all the notion that the art of recording the great struggles of our society could destroy their journalistic validity.

By its fifth year *CBS Reports* had brought before the American public nearly 400 of the thinkers and doers of the world. Presidents, statesmen, scholars, and specialists from a dozen walks of life were sought out and recorded as they gave their opinions on matters relevant to the conduct and progress of our society. The entire CBS reporting staff was on call at one time or another in these years, and the programs benefited from the presence of the professional reporter, working at his task and bringing continuity and unity to each program. Friendly also developed a group of first-rate producers, including Gene DePoris, Bill Leonard, William Peters, Jack Beck, David Buksbaum, Jay McMullen, and others, who were assigned a limited number of programs in any given period and allowed sufficient time to bring their work to final readiness. With a working staff of no less than six photographers, six film editors, and the same number of sound technicians, Friendly, director of operations Palmer Williams, and the *CBS Reports* producers have been able to keep ten to twelve documentaries in concurrent progress.

After five full seasons of producing this remarkable series of News Documentaries, Fred Friendly might look back upon his own accomplishments in certain knowledge that he achieved what he set out to do — *involve* Americans in the urgent affairs of our nation and all mankind. "If these real struggles of men," he once said, "are not more dramatic, interesting and exciting than fiction, then it is my fault and the fault of others like me who are privileged to report, to impart to Americans some of the wonders (and crises) of the real world "[10]

NBC WHITE PAPER

The tradition established by *See It Now* and perpetuated by *CBS Reports* was matched by a comparable development at the National Broadcasting Company. Since 1956, when NBC brought an established west coast TV journalist, Chet Huntley, to New York to begin the *Outlook* series with producer Reuven Frank, NBC had been building a major news-gathering organization. But the "prestige" documentary still required a distinct unit of its own to be led by men of unquestioned story instinct, and NBC found this talent in Irving Gitlin, a radio and television documentarist of long experience and considerable reputation. Gitlin had been instrumental in the creation of successful CBS public affairs programs in both media. He moved to NBC News in 1960 to build there a special "Creative Projects" unit, and the first result of his efforts was the *White Paper* series.

The skill of creating the prestige documentary news program was not confined to Fred Friendly. Gitlin's instincts were equally sound, and he brought with him an able young producer, Albert Wasserman, who had been with him at CBS since 1953. Wasserman had been an important figure in the Gitlin CBS series, *The Search,* for which he had written, produced, and directed one of TV's finest programs on mental health, the unforgettable "Out of Darkness" in 1956. He had also worked with *The Twentieth Century* series and with *CBS Reports,* where he produced and directed "Biography of a Cancer." With Wasserman to assist him and with Chet

Huntley already cast in the traditional Murrow role of reporter-personality, Irving Gitlin initiated a series which won six major national awards with its first four programs.

White Paper began with a light schedule of only six hour-long programs in its first season, and avoided the natural pitfalls inherent in an attempt to rush too many such programs into its schedule. Gitlin promised that the series would "point its cameras squarely at some of the issues, trends and developments which many fear are sapping America's vitality or may suddenly explode into major threats to our way of life." He began auspiciously with a minute-by-minute chronology of Francis Gary Powers' ill-fated U-2 flight, the resultant collapse of summit talks, and the trial of Powers by a Soviet Court. Some 30 researchers worked on the task of tracing the story of the flight and its effect on America's political aims; their efforts resulted in a thorough and painstaking analysis which disclosed available facts in careful and measured terms.

In its general concept and approach, this first *White Paper* differed hardly at all from the kind of work the CBS unit was doing. But early in its history the creators of *White Paper* served notice of their willingness to seek out new means to illuminate the ongoing crises of our time. The Gitlin team then turned to one of the more urgent domestic controversies of the decade; and in "Sit-In" some subtle distinctions in approach became evident. "Sit-In" focused upon that incident in May 1960 when Negro customers approached lunch counters in six downtown stores in Nashville, Tennessee, and *sat*. Wasserman emphasized the interview technique as the program moved outward from this historic incident to an examination of the entire civil rights movement from gradualism to nonviolent action in the South. But he also introduced a different method to support the great amount of actuality footage. To lend added significance to outbreaks of violence, Wasserman meticulously reviewed all footage, identified key individuals involved in rioting, and returned to them later to record their reactions once the heat of the moment had passed. Against a replay of the actuality footage, these voice-over after-statements added a power to the records which far surpassed anything that a narrator or reporter could have described. Such variations represented a fundamental truth regarding the use of the documentary instrument, even within whatever rigidities are imposed by journalistic necessity: each story is shaped by an individual who will ultimately seek to tell it in his own way.

Another innovation was apparent in the third *White Paper*, "Panama: Danger Zone." In this study of anti-American demonstrations in Panama during 1959 and 1960, the program again used lesser incidents to introduce a comprehensive study of United States-Panama relations and of American policy in Latin America as a whole. Again, interview sequences played an important part in relating the story. Film was taken of the jungles, the plantations, and the cities; and historical background was presented through integration of film sequences showing original construction work on the

WHITE PAPER #1 — "The U-2 Affair"

. . . in careful and measured terms.

IRVING GITLIN

. . . the skill was not confined.

canal, Teddy Roosevelt's visit to the site, and Woodrow Wilson's official opening of the Canal. But a decidedly different method of seeking emotional involvement was added when the intensity of Panamanian resentment of the United States was heightened by counterpointing the improvised anti-American songs of Calypso singers against Huntley's narration. The method was described by NBC as a "new documentary technique," and in light of the preceding history of TV News Documentary it was. Friendly had been careful to avoid the use of music in his work, apparently because he felt it created agitated response unrelated to his journalistic purpose. Now, in this third *White Paper*, authentic music was not only recorded but purposely *scored*, and within the News Documentary this represented a distinct turn.

Such departures, however, were neither frequent nor dominant during *White Paper*'s early seasons. In most ways the program continued to reflect the general concern and approach of its predecessors. Its studies of the functioning of the state legislatures in American politics; of the economic struggle within the American railroads; of the evolution of the Polaris missile; of issues behind the establishment of the Common Market in Europe; of profiles of Japan, India, and Red China; and of a review of the National Health Service in Britain — these followed the course of the ongoing crises in national and international life in more or less conventional fashion. *White Paper* avoided, however, the almost patented interview documentary of *CBS Reports*.

White Paper also offered its own prime example, in the "Biography of a Bookie Joint" tradition, of the news story dug out by the reporter and cameraman under adverse, even dangerous, conditions. In "Angola: Journey to a War," the official Portuguese government version of native uprisings in Angola was contrasted with a disturbing filmed account of the revolt from the natives' point of view. The story was filmed and later narrated by director-reporter Robert Young, who made a perilous journey on foot through the rebel villages of Northern Angola and provided the American public with a full and impartial report of a story which would otherwise have been silenced. Young's account of his travels simply represented a reporter's version of what he saw and heard. The natives told their stories, describing the revolt as the camera recorded places and people. In one sense, here was a dispassionate news story, and yet it framed an undeniable picture of efficient Portuguese brutality in the subjugation of the revolt. Young's report of the sufferings the natives had endured — told sometimes in his own words and sometimes in translations of native accounts — was "balanced" by the Portuguese version, but there seemed a certain authenticity in the first account which could not be offset by any official statement. If the Portuguese government would not release this side of the story to the world, *White Paper* could, and did.

Nor could *White Paper* avoid the familiar charges of slanting and unfairness as it moved to more sensitive domestic issues. It created considerable furore with its investigation of the welfare dilemma in the city of Newburgh, New York. In this connection it was a tribute to both *White Paper* and *CBS Reports* that the Federal Communications Commission — while harassing networks on several fronts — defended them in behalf of "Biography of a Bookie Joint" and the NBC "Battle of Newburgh." Despite objections raised by various parties, the FCC ruled that both programs had met the Commission's "doctrine of fairness' in treating controversial issues.

Still, there is no doubt that "The Battle of Newburgh" approached the limits between impartial reportage and editorial statement, as had "Harvest of Shame." When Joseph Mitchell, City Manager of the little town on the Hudson River, decided to take upon himself the burden of ridding his community of "welfare chiselers," he attracted the attention of the New York City-based communications media, thereby unwittingly making his private solution to a local problem a national issue. The welfare problem, including such related matters as aid to dependent children, had been a subject of national dispute for years, and carried within it a smoldering political argument between liberals committed to the continuing support of the needy and underprivileged, and conservatives dedicated to a "help-yourself" point of view which decried the use of tax funds for "socialistic" purposes.

Joseph Mitchell's position in these matters was evidenced in his personal solution to Newburgh's tax problems: he simply proposed to ignore New York State welfare laws, and decide for himself who deserved aid and who did not. A sharp local battle developed, and it was into this situation that the producer and crew of *White Paper* plunged — in full possession of the knowledge that the very heat of argument would make even the most honest and impartial report of events at Newburgh subject to suspicion.

The program, narrated by Huntley, opened with a quick series of statements on both sides of the argument, including Mitchell's public remarks. Huntley then summarized the issues, and the balance of the program made a careful study of the City of Newburgh, its citizens, and its welfare cases. The evidence uncovered pointed to conclusions different from Mitchell's and thereby refuted his claim that the welfare ranks were filled with idlers and cheaters.

Wasserman later emphasized how *White Paper* sought to use the interview to illustrate its own reportorial points, and cited as an example the "Battle of Newburgh" interview with Tom Wiegand and his family.[11] The fact that some needy people in Newburgh had been denied welfare had been established by research, and the *White Paper* unit sought some dramatic illustration. The Catholic charities of the city arranged the Wiegand interview, which turned out to be as remorseless in its revelation of human despair as the vignettes Murrow and his staff had recorded for "Harvest of Shame." So devastating was the effect that Mitchell promptly charged that NBC had "paid off" those who testified before the cameras — an allegation categorically denied by *White Paper*.

WHITE PAPER — "The Battle of Newburgh"
Joseph Mitchell and the Wiegands

. . . No simple answers to big problems.

In this use of the interview, *White Paper* followed the established tradition of News Documentary at its best. In the astute words uttered by an elder statesman of the city of Newburgh, the program achieved a humane and philosophic declaration of purpose: "There are no simple answers to big problems — there aren't even simple answers to little problems." Those words brought "The Battle of Newburgh" away from editorializing and into the realm of impartial appraisal of great social needs, a kind of reportage before which all charges of "liberal meddling" became meaningless.

But while exercising its capacity to report events as they happened, *White Paper* also continued to find new ways to make such reports more vivid. Departure in form continued to mark the progress of Gitlin, Wasserman, and producers such as Fred Freed, Arthur Zegart and William Jersey, all of whom had earned recognition within the Creative Projects Division of NBC News. Their efforts were supported by operations manager Robert Rubin[12] and cameraman Joseph Vadala.

Another method was the "structuring" of scenes in which opposing points of view were recorded. Where Friendly preferred in most cases to retain the shotgun method of letting argument develop (and thus keep essential control of the story in the editing-room), the *White Paper* producers were seeking to make the camera a greater force in this development. In "The Battle of Newburgh" an early scene showed the progress of an argument in a local bar, which the camera recorded as a lengthy sequence in which various citizens vehemently stated their views. There was a trace of self-consciousness in their posture and attitude and in the general flow of argument itself, but the technique of *involving* the camera was excitingly new.

What had been happening to documentary journalism in the early 1960's, reflected in this shift at *White Paper* toward camera involvement, had its origins elsewhere, but the true changes were technologically inspired. While news and documentary producers depended largely upon the Auricon camera (designed in the 1930's) and the Arriflex, a German newsreel camera developed during World War II, the pace and spread of documentary communication in TV demanded a more fluid and imaginative set of tools. Robert Rubin and his associates at NBC News Creative Projects were experimenting with a variety of modifications of old equipment, seeking inventions which would permit documentarists to engage in more impromptu synchronized-sound recording of events. Their efforts made possible such a documentary as the 1963 *White Paper* on America's gambling problem — "The Business of Gambling."

Like "Biography of a Bookie Joint," "The Business of Gambling" was intended to set a moral issue squarely before Americans. Producer Arthur Zegart, cameraman Joseph Vadala, and a *White Paper* crew moved into four counties of southern Maryland that had legalized slot machines more than a decade ago. They proceeded to record scenes of gambling (often using a hidden camera) and the opinions of a variety of citizens with opposing viewpoints. These records were interwoven with a tight story by Zegart, who also scripted the program. Narration (by Huntley) over scenes of gambling establishments tied together the story; the comments of citizens were cut-in appropriately in a way that advanced the argument.

But there was also a greater emphasis upon capturing opinion in as near a natural situation as possible. The camera records may have been less crisp and the sound fuzzier than in Friendly's precise face-to-camera interviews, but there was a decidedly more dynamic quality here — derived not from the selection of more interesting people, but purely from the technique of recording them. As it had done to some extent in "The Battle of Newburgh," *White Paper* let people debate in front of the cameras, and then edited out those bits of action which were too stiff or self-conscious, thus preserving only the most natural and intense moments of argument. In a larger sense, Zegart was doing no more than Friendly's producers by selecting for his record moments of human interplay. But by shifting to natural environment, by allowing people to become involved with each other rather than with the formal camera, and by deliberately permitting both sound and picture to create a shaky and uneven flow, Zegart provided the viewer with a more intense feeling of immediacy.

The most effective illustration of this came near the end of "The Business of Gambling" when Zegart brought together two citizens in the aisle of a supermarket, where they expressed violently opposed opinions. What might have become a routine effort to introduce local color suddenly became an electric and utterly dramatic revelation of human conflict. In the restive shuffling of the men as they began to quarrel and in a number of quick, stabbing, facial and vocal expressions, these men suddenly displayed a complete unawareness of the camera. "Life itself" in all its unpredictability was there before our eyes.

There is little doubt that this technique was rare at *White Paper*. Too often the results of its application were flat and self-conscious or, if the sequences were edited to preserve only the naturalness, they became pointless. But in this instance and in others which were being recorded more and more frequently by 1963, the sheer drama of human perversity was being offered to us in journalistic reports in ways that had seldom been attempted before. The supermarket argument was no less honest than Jay McMullen's direct man-on-the-street interviews at the close of "Biography of a Bookie Joint," but it had eliminated the nonessential elements in the portrayal of dispute among men and brought to it the dynamism and restless energy of a free camera which added its own emotional power.

The question, and perhaps the final one, is whether such an approach could be legitimately employed in the service of journalism — in impartial reports of already emotion-fraught issues in 20th-century life. In less skilled hands it could reduce the portent of the serious issues of our times by resort-

THE GITLIN TEAM AT NBC NEWS CREATIVE PROJECTS
Fred Freed, Al Wasserman, Arthur Zegart, William Jersey

ing to arty, pretentious treatments which leave these issues pointless and further confused. In addition, as will be subsequently noted, changing techniques could produce equally undesirable results — the evocation of pure emotional response when human reason, above all, should be engaged. It is this question which dictates a breaking point within any discussion of these "prestige" efforts to document the ongoing crises of life, for these efforts of *White Paper* to depart from the more conventional approaches of the *See It Now* and *CBS Reports* series were comparatively minor. The purpose and concept behind all of these documentaries were uniform and similar.

Before moving on, however, to those major developments in News Documentary which had inspired the later changes in *White Paper*'s "The Business of Gambling," we must observe the fact that the major documentaries reviewed thus far were under the creative control of men whose experience and training were gained within the profession of broadcasting, particularly broadcast journalism and public affairs. Many had begun their training in radio, and carried with them a first allegiance to the spoken word. While film cameramen, editors, and audio technicians serving under them made significant contributions to the clarity and precision of the news narrative, the final control still belonged to the reporters. For them the spoken word still represented a chief means by which the essential framework of events was to be reconstructed. But respect was also paid to the visual power inherent in their accomplishments, and there were many who began to sense that even in News Documentary there were moments and sequences when the visual communications dominated.

If Friendly and his peers acknowledged that TV was a *visual* medium they did not always maintain that it was either a *pictorial* or a *cinematic* medium. The visual communication in which they engaged was still the communication of record. The possibility that the aesthetic tradition of the cinema — the emotionalizing power which only cinematic movement in its various forms can summon — might become a significant factor in the reconstruction of news events was not permitted to take hold.

It was not until the early 1960's that major national News Documentary programs were executed under the creative control and supervision of men whose entire training and commitment was to a pictorial and cinematic emphasis in the communication of experience. These men brought with them new insights — and new problems — to the processes of reconstructing the essential framework of reality.

6 / News Documentary: The Crisis Within

> I'm determined to be there when the news happens. . . . I'm deter-
> mined to be as unobtrusive as possible. . . . And I'm determined not to
> distort the situation. . . . I am a journalist.
>
> — ROBERT DREW[1]

> Who has influenced me? Paul White, of course. But I think Aris-
> totle, too.
>
> — JOHN SECONDARI[2]

IF THE HISTORY of documentary in all media reveals a thrust away
from fictional re-creation of human character, the processes of recording
life with a camera and editing the records into narrative sequence introduce
the problem of re-enactment at a different level. The men who take the pictures and then order them into narrative presentation can not only invest
reality with meanings other than exist in fact, but in a fine sense can trans-
form men into actors. The words and actions of men recorded in actual
circumstances may so be arranged, by either heightening or intensification,
that a viewer might assume motivations and characteristics at variance with
truth. It is this power of editing which enabled Frank Capra and Leni Riefenstahl to turn the same film sequences of Adolph Hitler toward entirely
contrary purposes in attempts to arouse different emotions. It is our understanding and fear of this power which has led some men to question documentary producers from de Rochemont to Friendly each time they entered
into treatments of affairs involving political and social commitment.

It is quite true that the use of a film technology must inevitably introduce some of the aesthetic characteristics of cinematic art. "The basis of
communication in the cinema is emotional," Walter Lassally has written,
"and once this has been recognized all sorts of enigmas can be solved."[3]
The procedure of joining one piece of film (a fact) to another piece of film
(another fact) will produce still a third phenomenon — an emotion — and
this is the final and unavoidable condition governing all forms of visual
communication-in-time, whether filmed, or of live studio origination, or

videotape-recorded. And such emotional sway may further be intensified by the "pre-editing" which takes place in the initial camera recording — wherein framing and lighting may unbalance content, and where the movement of the recording cameras themselves can create unexpected spatial displacements. The inward thrust of a movement toward the subject, the jarring sensation provided by an abrupt pan, the serenity of a slow withdrawal from a scene — these and many other camera movements in time and space create subtle alterations in the meaning of a recorded event. To all of this must be added the emotional assault of accompanying musical and sound symbols. The possibilities for emotionally structuring an event, then, are many and exist even before the spoken word (it, too, working with symbology) is introduced into the documentary process.

Given all of these possibilities for creation of artistic expression with a resultant distortion of objectivity; given the desire of men to objectively appraise events to promote intelligent reflection; and *then* given that intention to involve men in such intellectuality by emotional prods — given such complexities, it becomes difficult to formulate reliable methods and criteria which the News Documentary may employ.

We have seen that Fred Friendly and his peers sought to execute their intentions largely by placing the reporter in charge of not only *what* the cameras recorded, but of *how* such recordings were made. He was in command as well of the final edited reconstruction of the narrative. But in the history of News Documentary there are also numerous examples of the ways in which men might begin from entirely different premises and seek divergent goals. Upon the very nature of their departures rests the validity of their efforts as journalists.

THE LOGIC OF PICTURES

The ABC-TV network News Documentary series, *Bell & Howell Close-Up!*, achieved a remarkable impact which seriously altered the direction of News Documentary in American television. For some, its experiments merely enlarged upon the concept of TV journalism. For others, much of what it introduced was hardly new and did not constitute a legitimate approach to News Documentary. For still others, the experiments of *Close-Up!* marked the first genuine efforts to find a documentary form ideally suited to television — a form comparable in its depth and persuasion to Chayefsky's small crisis in video drama.

Close-Up! was initiated in September 1960 with "Cast the First Stone," produced by Walter Peters. This was a treatment of racial prejudice in the North. Two more programs in the prestige context, "Paradise in Chains" and "What's the Proposition?", were offered before ABC-TV announced that it would co-produce four one-hour documentary programs in conjunction with Time, Inc. and the latter's producing organization, Robert Drew

Associates. John Daly, then in charge of ABC News, objected to such a contractual arrangement because it would put the matter of production of news programs outside his own direct supervision, violating his conviction that news and public affairs presentation should be under the exclusive control of the department he directed. The network remained firm in its decision, and Daly resigned. The Time, Inc. contract remained in effect. Before John Secondari, who was executive producer of the series from the outset, could bring his own theories of News Documentary to fruition, he had to deal with those issues related to technique which Robert Drew posed for all of TV journalism.

Drew and such key members of his staff as Richard Leacock, Gregory Shuker, Hope Ryden, and James Lipscomb represented a new attitude toward TV news. While most were journalists (from the *Life* staff) they styled themselves as "film-makers," and seemingly represented the dedicated *cinéaste* who, on principle, resented the tiny image and the vaguely defined possibilities for cinematic art in television. Despite their lack of affinity for the medium, these new types of experimental film-makers — the exponents of *verité* — began, by 1960, to be attracted to television's salaries and audiences. It was *verité*, more generally called the "mobile camera" school of documentary-making, which forced television journalists to ponder, perhaps for the first time, the true implication of that difficult concept — documentary — which they once so casually adopted. Perhaps it was the *verité* method which led Fred Friendly to reconsider calling his own works "documentary."

Verité establishes its claim to television in the reality program. As a "school" it assumes at the outset that the camera is the only real reporter and must not be subservient to script, to preconceived thematic statement, to plotted narrative, to someone's idea of a story — to anything, in fact, but the chronological unfolding of events. The *verité* thesis and the difficulties which it posed for the video News Documentary was demonstrated in the early Drew productions for *Close-Up!*

"Yanqui, No!," the first of these productions, was aired in December 1960. Its subject was the threat of Communism in Latin America, and Drew's inclination was to approach anti-American developments in Venezuela and Cuba through the eyes of the natives of those countries. His announced intentions were to "do shows that employ dramatic logic — where the story tells itself through pictures, not through word logic, lecture logic, written logic or interviews."[4] The result was a raw and edgy technique which made extravagant use of extreme facial close-ups, deliberately blurred focus, and a camera that moved about restlessly. Jerky, partially focused pans and sweeps were common throughout. Wild sound recording, resulting in a fading, distorted voice quality, gave an additional dimension of immediacy. Drew also severely restricted narration, making it tense and terse. His narrator, Joseph Julian, employed a soft, underplayed style which reflected

FILM-MAKERS SHUKER, LIPSCOMB, RYDEN.

. . . the new breed.

ROBERT DREW

. . . no more "word-logic."

a total departure from the Van Voorhis "voice of doom" of the early *March of Time*. Narration barely introduced, and seldom explained, action. Finally, Drew attempted to eliminate, wherever possible, the sight and even the sound of the interviewer. These techniques were given a decided emphasis in all of his productions and were seen, after "Yanqui, No!," in "X-Pilot," "The Children Were Watching," "Adventures on the New Frontier," and later Drew programs in this series. A controversial 1963 production carried as an ABC news special, "Crisis: Behind a Presidential Commitment," also employed *verité*.

Drew's principal method was, of course, a TV adaptation of *Cinéma Verité*,[5] a school which has been emerging over the years in continental film-making. *Cinéma Verité* and its television counterpart were devoted, in one aspect, to preserving an essential reality by eliminating the subject's awareness of the camera and, in another, to eliciting emotional response from the viewer by making the camera an active participant in the events recorded. Considering the first of these in terms of dramatic art, *verité* represents no more than an attempt to break down aesthetic distance between the photographed subject and the viewer — the apotheosis in film of Zola's *Naturalisme*, which languished in the theatre simply because drama could not be both life and art at once. The logical argument of *Cinéma Verité* is that film, after all, *does* record reality, and the "aesthetic distance" of the theatre is of no corollary consideration.

The school has distinguished forebears. The force of the unobtrusive camera has been demonstrated in a thousand ways in every kind of reality film as well as in the entire history of live television — in those unexpected moments when, for any number of reasons (the heat of argument, a momentary lapse into total reflection, forgetfulness of the camera's presence) a human being loses all consciousness of being a subject and exposes himself to us with all socially conditioned behavior torn away. During that moment, or those sustained moments, he is absolutely "real."

This aspect of *verité* — the removal of the subject's self-consciousness — played a major role in such documentary films as *In The Street* (1952), in which Helen Levitt, Janice Loeb, and James Agee used hidden cameras to record life on the New York streets; Lionel Rogosin's *On The Bowery* (1954); and George Roquier's seminal 1947 film, *Farrebique*.[6] To capture the truth of life among the French peasants, Roquier lived on a farm for a full year, becoming almost a part of the family while recording everything he saw and heard. From his efforts came a faithful, and beautiful, record of humanity. The cogency of this film lies in its clarity of record and its visual poetry, not in its destruction of aesthetic distance. The hand of film-maker Roquier upon the performers is always, if gently, evident as he attempts to reconstruct important happenings in their lives. We see, in the twitch of a muscle, a gesture, a momentary pause of uncertainty in movement and, above all, the turn of a self-conscious smile on the handsome face of the eternally Gallic *grand-mère*, that these people are aware that they are performing. As a reconstruction of reality, *Farrebique* is beyond comparison in documentary film, but the evidence of reconstruction cannot be overlooked. *Verité*, however, seeks in its "picture logic" not so much to hide as to *obliterate* this evidence.

The candid-camera technique is everywhere. The improvement in equipment — light cameras, portable sound recorders, and new methods of achieving sight-and-sound synchronization — has made it possible for a small crew to work efficiently in gathering the records of reality. The key questions to be posed in relation to the use of *verité* are whether such a complete breakdown in aesthetic distance between camera and performer may be sustained for a total production, and whether regard for clarity in the recording process can contribute to a viewer's *Einfühling* with what he sees.

Television has demonstrated that at least the first of these can be answered affirmatively. In a 1953 *Omnibus* presentation, "The Young Fighter," film-makers traced the daily life of a young boxer as he trained, met his family responsibilities, and wrestled with the moral problem of attempting to combine the two. The technique was essentially *verité*, and along the way was created a fairly sustained impression of real life (in the sense that the subjects became so involved with their own lives that they were, for the most part, no longer performers). This was only one of many examples of *sustained* reality of this kind, as opposed to those brief moments of psychological revelation witnessed in innumerable contexts throughout the history of early TV. The film-maker can at least entertain the hope of becoming unobtrusive, and on occasion he can maintain this effect.

The more important matter of whether "picture logic" can avoid distorting a context by making the camera alone seek out a revelation of human character is best illustrated by one of television's most distinguished failures, the *Dialogues* of Archibald MacLeish and Mark Van Doren. This program, offered by CBS in the summer of 1962, was nobly conceived, displaying two of the finest minds of our time in quiet reflection at the peaceful MacLeish farm.

Warren V. Bush, the producer of *Dialogues,* proposed to bring these men together, let them talk for a weekend, and edit the results of their cerebrations into an hour-long program. He cannot be blamed for any error other than his decision to turn the recording of this meeting of minds over to a group of film-makers so dedicated to *verité* that they showed no reserve in the application of its techniques. The culpable parties were Hillary Harris and Albert and David Maysles (the Maysles brothers were disciples of Richard Leacock, a film-maker par excellence who served as Flaherty's photographer on *Louisiana Story* long before joining Drew Associates. They had contributed to an earlier *verité* success, the 1960 film on American politics, *Primary*). What the *verité* trio unintentionally demonstrated beyond doubt was that the visual alone can not sustain all human communication.

In their artistically self-conscious "picture-logic" recording of this event, little respect was paid to an intellectual content. With perhaps a traditional *cinéaste*'s disregard for the possibilities of television, they ignored the medium's potential of presenting an essentially unemotional content in a clear and thoughtful style. Worse, they made their record a contrapuntal force opposing the inherently rational content. As Van Doren was answering some pertinent question, the camera was disconnectedly rambling along in close-up pursuit of a coffee pot being passed over the table by a servant. Later, when Van Doren was discussing the "American dream," the camera rested on his hands — a mode of revelation not essentially bad in itself — but used at a moment when his hands were gently resting above the fly of his trousers, a shot which must have produced a general state of discomfort in most viewers.

With bursts of light, out-of-focus flashes, garbled sound, and that distraction provided by constantly wavering and restless hand-held cameras, Harris and the Maysles not only distorted but destroyed what they had set out to create. One can accept weak lighting. One can applaud a relaxed setting, even to the dubious extent of including scenes of MacLeish swimming. What defies comprehension is the resolute determination never to let us *see* and *hear* the protagonists wholly and steadily.

The tradition of *verité* and its desire to express reality in terms of the "picture logic" of an unobtrusive, moving camera, along with a disregard

FARREBIQUE — George Rouqier (1947)

. . . the evidence of reconstruction cannot be overlooked.

for conventional editing, contains its own potentials and its own pitfalls. It offers the possibility of seizing moments of fire and ice in human expression. It offers excitement — an overlay of blurred and breathless movement which can, of course, grip the emotions. By proposing to let us experience life (as well as merely see and hear about it), it stakes out a claim for continuing development in documentary television.

But *verité* has shown us also that it can nullify an essentially intellectual message — or impede, in annoying fashion, our appreciation and understanding of it. Because it can interfere with rationality (it is *designed* to do so), the question fundamentally is whether *verité* is legitimate in News Documentary; and the answer lies in two Drew productions: his "The Children Were Watching" (1960) and "Crisis: Behind a Presidential Commitment" (1963). Both of these programs involved presentation of an already emotion-laden issue in American life, civil rights for the Negro. If the *verité* approach is to be regarded as a true journalistic method, here, above all, is where it was obliged to prove that capacity.

One of the many tragic chapters in the Negro's endless struggles for human rights was written at New Orleans in 1960, when the attempt to integrate the public schools there brought out a mass of angry racists who hovered near the schools and proclaimed their brutality and ignorance in deed and word. The violent outbursts of mob action were fully disclosed in all the communication media. On assignment from Drew, Richard Leacock went to New Orleans to record this raw, boiling-over hatred.

He chose to tell his story primarily through the actions of a Negro and a white family, both of whom sought to answer the call for integration. First we heard the soft voice of a narrator saying, "Some will learn to hate and some to love." Opening scenes of the Negro home placed emphasis upon the faces of the children as they observed adults in hushed discussions of the events of the day. Following upon his instincts to react spontaneously to a fluctuating situation, Leacock resolved to remain as unobtrusive as possible and record the story to the finish. His hand-held camera gave us a sequence of unsteady pictures, as the loose pan, the zoom in and out (and the momentary adjustment of focus), and every other kind of externally imposed movement was introduced. Projected thus into the milling crowds outside the school, we began to experience the restless energy of the crowd in close-ups of elbows, backs of heads, and twisted faces.

Now we hear the word "nigger" spoken in contempt, and the frame drops to show a small child, listening. There is a momentary pause on a man's unshaven face as he speaks of "gittin' a shotgun" — and above and behind all of this the ugly shouts and screams of the racist women fill our ears. We move back to the semi-peaceful Negro home, where nerves are taut, and overhear the parents talk of their plans for their daughter's future. The camera pans to the family dog and to the father petting him.

RICHARD LEACOCK

gun-mike, grainy, hand-held — Télévérité *in New Orleans.*

Abruptly, with the briefest narrational transition, we are inside a car, riding along the trouble-ridden streets and listening to the words of the driver, a white segregationist leader. In a distorted blur his words crackle: ". . . Half of them are uninterested in bettering themselves. . . ." We cut away once more to the Negro home for more discussion, then back to the car and a hazy sequence of visual impressions as the white segregationist speaks of a "Communist plot — pushing the colored people to try and destroy our nation." The pattern shifts, and we are in a car driven by a Negro integration leader, introduced over a swirl of movement by the narrator's typical brief statement. We go intensely, abruptly, to Leander Perez, to the car of the white leader (and now the camera catches the blur of faces as they come rushing to the car, collecting money for the "white cause," and we are assaulted by the loud, tinny crash of a passing car radio). Next to a PTA meeting, then to the bus arriving outside the school where the shuffling, screaming crowd waits to take the white children home. More angry scenes, interspersed with curt statements by the school superintendent, then a cut to the school exterior and screaming "cheerleaders" hooting the white mother, Mrs. Gabriel, who attempted to take her daughter to school and finally retreated before the onslaught.

Now we go to the Gabriel home where the daughter, her face a study in terror, watches from the window as the shouting mob gathers outside. Inside the home there is confusion as the crowd hammers at the door and windows. The police appear outside. The tense action continues after a few words by the Police Chief and we are in the mob again, where a frightened mother gathers up her child and runs. Another face is suddenly seen, swearing, "We gave those niggers all what they got," followed by a quick pan to an infant sucking on a bottle as the words are still echoing in our ears. At one point the screen goes black as a tumultuous rush toward the cameraman makes us suspect that his camera has been destroyed.

We return to the Gabriel home and hear the agonized comment, "They are crucifying Him, just as surely as if He were right here." The tension grows more and more ominous. A missing son arrives, followed by the father who has quit his job under threat and pressure; his awkward admission of this with its intolerable despair, is recorded. The home is quiet. The narrator comes in again over the mob outside and asks, "What are the children learning?" Among continuing scenes of horror we hear that these "were some events of that week in New Orleans." And the credits fill the screen.

Is this a valid recourse for the journalistic documentary in a society groping to find answers to grave questions? Could it, by any honest measure of journalism, be called a report, or even a record, of an event? These questions must be answered, for what we see in "The Children Were Watching" is a drama affected not only by the mere choice of a climactic moment in a crucial social situation (which may, after all, be what journalism is all about), but largely by cinematic techniques.

Leacock went to New Orleans seeking to witness the same ugly miscarriage of justice which all thinking men knew was occurring there. But, while others were trying to explain the meaning of these events in order to invoke the sobriety of reason, he was predisposed to show only hate and fear at its most tumultuous level, leaving us no room, no avenue, for thoughtful action.

What *CBS Reports* had done in its "Mississippi and the 15th Amendment" was not far distant, in some ways, from what the Drew unit recorded. We saw the hate there, too; we experienced the same sense of disgust with the machinations of the racists; and we felt the same sympathy with those being denied their basic liberties. But we saw it all in the framework of journalism to which drama was merely an additive. In "The Children Were Watching" we witnessed not only the drama, but were made participants in it. Emotional involvement in this Drew production was no longer a method by which to lead people to intellectual involvement, but an end in itself. When used in this way, *verité* is a negation of that virtue which underlies the documentary idea.

Journalistic function aside, a part of a documentary's purpose is always social — somehow to let us discern more clearly, with greater compassion and vision, the issues we must resolve. *Verité* revokes such purpose when it leaves us no time for clarity, when it exploits instinct alone, and when it makes technique an enemy of reason. If we add the responsibilities of journalism to documentary, we realize that only by undistorted appraisal of the crises in American life can rational men report the facts as they see them. They may introduce the scenes of anger and hate, but they must also help us to maintain detachment. In one sense, television journalism can truthfully say, "This is the way it was" or even "This is the way it is," but it is not the function of journalism to say "This is *it*." Certainly the news documentarist fails, as Fred Friendly has observed, if he cannot involve people. But the crux of this involvement — the whole art of the documentary-journalist — is in the skill with which he shows and tells us about human beings in conflict, *not* in the skill with which he can make us forget that we are witnessing a reconstruction.

If the rough and tumble "picture logic" of "The Children Were Watching" resulted in a disjointed and emotional treatment, there were rare moments, particularly in the Gabriel home, when we saw, overpoweringly, people who had lost consciousness of the presence of a camera. Drew's producers had attempted to establish what has been called "a gray area," in which the camera can operate at a level equal to people in such moments of crisis. Their hopes of neutralizing the effects of the camera's presence had been realized often enough to give them hope that they could enter into the reporting process at entirely different levels within our society.

In Gregory Shuker's 1963 production for Drew, "Crisis: Behind a Presidential Commitment," the cameras were admitted into the offices of the President and the Attorney General of the United States throughout that period when Governor George Wallace of Alabama threatened to bar the entrance of Negro students to the University. The Drew production team pursued this legal combat between Wallace and the Kennedy administration in a program which purported to show us the decision-making process — the behind-the-scenes progress of a major national conflict.

Too much of this program followed the paths of formlessness of earlier Drew efforts, but the significant fact to emerge from the "Crisis" program may be offered as a simple law: the more responsibility men assume in democratic decision-making, the less they are willing, able, and liable to forget the presence of the camera. The promise that we would actually hear President Kennedy himself during this crisis never materialized, as he exercised his authority to delete his own comments throughout the conference. Obviously, no official would approve the recording of his full reactions at all times. What Wallace and the Kennedys allowed the nation to see were the official representations of their offices.[7]

This in itself might destroy the validity of the "gray area" as journalistic material, for what was seen was always, in one way or another, either staged or irrelevant. So great was this program's departure from accepted standards that New York's educational TV station, WNDT, followed the national televising of the Drew program with a discussion titled "Presidency by Crisis," and invited several spokesmen for varying points of view to comment upon what they had seen. Whatever consensus could be drawn from their discussion focused entirely upon these matters of the danger of misuse of the technique in such sensitive social circumstances. Political sympathies

ABC-TV's
CRISIS: BEHIND A PRESIDENTIAL COMMITMENT
(Produced by Gregory Shuker for Robert Drew Associates in 1963)

notwithstanding,[8] the participants were seemingly agreed on the point that the element of "play-acting" had entered the program on both sides of the controversy, and that the decision-making processes of our government had been brought too close to "show business."[9]

Valid comment upon how man lives can be enriched with *verité*, but its technique demands judicious handling and its range of subjects must, in the final analysis, be removed from the contemporary disputes which men must somehow resolve in the name of reason if they are to survive. The Drew approach would later find a significant niche in television documentary; but New Orleans, the places where the great national decisions are made, and all the other pressure points of a civilization cannot be the foci of application.

ABC Close-Up!

The primary production responsibilities for the *Close-Up!* series, however, were not assigned to Drew Associates (which offered only a half-dozen of its many programs between 1960 and 1963) but to John Secondari, whose contribution to the News Documentary has too often been underestimated.

Citing his debt to Paul White of CBS for a keener sense of the responsibility of valid News Documentary, Secondari also equated this form with Aristotle's fundamental definition of drama — men in action. For Secondari, documentary was a mirror of fact in which the dramatic values of people, places, and events determined the success of the story. To be sure, the idea of the "story" had been used again and again to define what the news documentarist offers, and yet our understanding of it in relation to both the formal theory of drama and to techniques of presentation becomes more complete as we trace the history of *Close-Up!* In both his theory and production, Secondari endeavored to establish the documentary link to drama. "Men in challenge," he has said, "is the thing the journalist must show, and to be effective, we must show men in *action* by focusing upon the proper thing — an identification with people."[10]

This belief was consistent with the tradition of story control by the reporter, but in matters of technique Secondari was eclectic. Despite a certain defensiveness about Drew, he was aware of the value of a restrained and intelligent use of both the intensely personal story as well as the possibilities of the free and unobtrusive camera. While Secondari directed or produced — and occasionally narrated — certain shows himself, he functioned as executive producer to bring together an expert group of producer-directors, including Helen Jean Rogers, Nicholas Webster, William Weston, and Sam Rosenberg, who were assisted by production manager John Lynch and a permanent staff.

During its three years on the air, this unit offered Americans such productions as "90 Miles to Communism," a filmed-in-Cuba report of Castro's conversion of the island into an armed camp; "C'est la Guerre," a report on the Algerian war filmed with the rebels during a night of battle; "The Flabby American"; "The Troubled Land"; and "Our Durable Diplomats." In these programs *Close-Up!* producers pursued a method which combined reliable reportage and the visible demonstration of men in action. In "The Troubled Land," for example, the "personalization" of social conflict in Brazil was achieved by examination of the ferment and political anxieties of Brazil's peasants through the eyes of one family. In "Our Durable Diplomats" a general condition was reduced to the personal by a treatment of the American Foreign Service in terms of the experiences of two young Foreign Service officers and their families. The skill and maturity which had been acquired in this personalizing technique were movingly demonstrated in September 1962, when *Close-Up!* aired Nicholas Webster's classic, "Walk in My Shoes," a study of the world of the American Negro told entirely in his own words and actions.

The opening of "Walk in My Shoes" is an impressive revelation of how *verité* had influenced *Close-Up!*. We begin to share the noise, the anger, and the dark corners of the Negro world. Then we are in a cab, where the driver is talking to us over his shoulder. He is an angry man of simple, blunt speech — committed to the belief that the "white man" has too long dominated him. We move next to a filthy apartment in a crowded tenement, where a woman answers questions about her future with the same sad resignation as in some of the "Harvest of Shame" interviews. But the free camera is always in focus and carefully deployed as it explores the darkness of tenement life.

Now there is a departure in technique. In the tenement a young man arises and makes ready for the routine labor of his day. Narration over this action describes his work and his hopes, but as he goes into the streets the narration becomes his — his own thoughts in first-person, voice-over narration. It seems that we are on the way to another exercise in unrestrained *verité* when Webster's direction suddenly catches hold. The young man is our point of involvement, but it will not be *his* drama. Instead, the balance of this program becomes a vehicle by which the Negroes of America *tell*, not *live*, their stories. In a series of semi-interview situations recorded in Los Angeles, Chicago, and other places, we see a number of intense discussions of Negroes' problems and dreams. We see the wealthy and the middle class, as well as the poor. We listen to Martin Luther King as he talks directly to us, and hear Percy Sutton — in what must remain the single most revealing interview ever recorded for TV — describing his feelings during his earlier "freedom ride." The shots are tighter than Friendly might sanction, but are not instruments of compulsion in themselves. The people are made important, and they are presented to us in *reflection* upon crisis rather than in the frenzy of it.

HELEN JEAN ROGERS, SIDNEY DOBISH, WILLIAM HARTIGAN
(On location for *The Saga of Western Man* Series)

JOHN SECONDARI

. . . we must show men in action.

One method of personalizing in "Walk in My Shoes" is to bring groups together in an informal living room, and record them as they try to reason with each other. The camera moves among them, catching their doubts, their frustrations, their private pains, but it never moves for its own sake, and diffusion and blur are gratefully absent. To be sure, Webster and his film-makers catch a touch of *verité* excitement during the meeting of the Black Muslims or during those scenes when the young man who asks us to walk in his shoes drifts among the sights and sounds of New York. But technique seldom creates added conflict.

A similar treatment was evident in the analytical "Meet Comrade Student," an intensive and rigorous examination of Russian education, first aired on *Close-Up!* in September 1962. Coming in the wake of increasing post-Sputnik speculation over the aims and functions of our own system of education (aggravated by such critics as Admiral Hyman Rickover) this detached yet dramatic summary of the strengths and weaknesses of Russian education showed Americans that all was neither good nor bad in the Russians' way.

The approach was subdued reportage, carefully controlled by Webster's exacting direction and Robert Lewis Shayon's spare but encompassing writing, and revealed how much *verité* had been softened and shaped in style. The quick-cut in sound and picture was often employed to force the flow of attention, but the faces and voices were always sharp and distinct. Webster had found the proper distance for the close-up, keeping the reserve strength of his tighter shots only for moments when subject-involvement demanded it. The Russian children, like all children, were compelling in themselves and free from that affectation of the adult before the camera. They performed, but only for their classmates and teachers; and this gave a certain added vigor to the observations of the unobtrusive camera. We saw no movement for the sake of movement, nor did we see the needless and distracting "pan-of-pursuit."

Out of classroom records of learning, interviews with students and teachers, and visual evidence of the day-to-day activities of Russia's rising generation, this program fashioned a tempered and logical evaluation of the socialistic task of building for the future. Yet, throughout the story, there was the thread of a greater logic made evident, not in a technique which dramatized at all costs, but in a journalistic respect which reservedly allowed the drama of the Russian spirit to speak for itself and permitted us to respond with all of our faculties intact. In its portrayal of the advantages and weaknesses of the Russian system, "Meet Comrade Student" issued a clear call to all Americans. Shayon's eloquent summary of that challenge forced itself upon us, particularly when he reminded us that ". . . it is not their weaknesses; it is their *strengths* that we are called upon to match."

These individual successes notwithstanding, *Close-Up!* left the air at the close of its third season (1962-63) as ABC was moving toward the

"MEET COMRADE STUDENT"

. . . a tempered and logical evaluation.

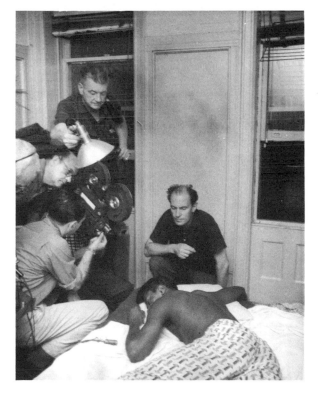

"WALK IN MY SHOES"

Nicholas Webster directs the actor in a New York tenement scene "special" context for its News Documentaries. The *Close-Up!* unit remained intact and entered into production of a series of historical documentaries — a shift from the News Documentary to the Theme Documentary which was presaged in the impressive color film, "The Vatican," offered during the closing season. "The Vatican" was in the still extant tradition of the travel or "interest" film, hence removed from the reporting of immediate issues of our time. Yet, one final offering of *Close-Up!* — in some ways an epilogue to this series — deserves attention: Sam Rosenberg's "A Vanishing Breed: Portrait of a Country Editor."

This study of Landon Wills, editor and publisher of the McLean County *News* in Calhoun, Kentucky, was neither the most exciting nor controversial of the *Close-Up!* productions, and yet it was a tribute to the emphasis upon great human drama which John Secondari had brought to journalistic documentary. Its face-to-camera monologues with Wills and his fellow citizens held a revelation of a poignant American problem — the rapidity of change in our society and resultant fading of precious institutions which are built upon a single man's conviction that there is a job to be done. In this sense, it was as vital and significant a look at modern life as any of the growing number of crisis-centered reports which the journalistic documentary had offered over the years. In this program was the suggestion that we are only too mortal: that by the slow attrition of time and change upon everything that is valuable and dear to us, we risk, in the long run, losing something vital and meaningful to American life.

Here was men-in-action carried to a sane conclusion. Reservedly edited, the program slowed the pace of this confrontation of men and social change by allowing the camera to linger — beyond the moment of conviction — upon the faces of these hard-bitten, yet gentle, Kentuckians. In doing this, television came close once more to Maeterlinck's dream of conflict and resolution within the single human being.

In Secondari's work, as in the later programs of *White Paper*, we find the sure signs of evolution in News Documentary. The influence of *verité* is plain in the new and jarring visual revelations of humans in deadlock. But the direction of the entire CBS tradition from Paul White through Edward R. Murrow and Fred Friendly is also seen in that impartial reporting style wherein people before the camera carry honest dramatic validity of their own. And Aristotle's aesthetic, translated by Secondari, is also here in the over-all form which is "story."

Perhaps, upon examination, the "crisis within" may be seen as a restrictive way to describe the work and influence of the experimental filmmakers who brought the *verité* tradition into the nationally seen News Documentaries of television. *Verité* itself has no firm limitations, and is often employed to describe any number of experiments and innovations in cinematic technique which are directed toward revealing new aspects of life. When Drew and his associates theorize upon it as a means of reconstructing reality, we share their enthusiasm for its great promise; but it is the same kind of promise held by any theory of how men will better recognize truth and reality. Theory is meaningless until it has been demonstrated in the fact of communication itself.

The notion, for example, that there is some inherent communicative power to be derived from simply letting the camera run through a full situation is subverted in fact by the editing processes we see in Drew's productions. There *is* cutting, and there is a reason for cutting. Once a cut has been made, the editor (or producer) has imposed himself upon the event. There is a point — a subject — at which the camera is aimed and there is a reason for the aiming, so the cameraman has imposed himself upon the event. There are words, however few, and they direct the viewer toward some meaning, and so the writer has imposed himself upon the event.

The whole concern of "the crisis within" comes down, then, to how much and what kinds of cutting, aiming, and writing are done, and for what purpose. It is surely as simple as that. Some have insisted that reconstruction is dominated by cerebral processes, and the more that cutting, aiming, and writing can assure clarity, the better. Others, in stressing that reconstruction is dominated by emotional processes, are willing to forego clarity to evoke emotional response. Yet none — not Friendly, not Drew, not Gitlin, not Secondari — can responsibly ignore Wilbur Schramm's fundamental description of the journalistic function as the reconstruction of the essential framework of an event. The substance of responsible reporting must lie in each man's independent determination of what he deems is *essential* for a civilization to know — and to understand.

Control of Theme: Art and Record

THE SECOND general approach to documentary expression in television shifts control of the interpretative process away from the journalist and to the artist. This method of presentation relies upon the active effort to create "worlds of imagination" — to design and execute some larger statement reflecting universal truths which are inherent within the documents of life. The creation of form, not the recording of it, becomes the central purpose of the documentarist, and the elements which contribute to his expression are selected, arranged, and intensified only as they serve that purpose. As a documentarist he cannot distort or subvert the records themselves, but he may extend controlling processes over them in such a way that the truth of these events *as he sees the truth* is emphasized. For he begins, like artists in all media and forms, by seeking that broader and deeper significance of the events of life which tells us something of man's condition in the great flow of time. This significance he expresses as a theme.

"The important thing," wrote George Pierce Baker in his discussion of theme as an element within the drama, "is that something seen or thought should so stir the emotions of the dramatist that the desire to convey his own emotions or the emotions of the characters who become connected with what he has seen or thought, forces him to write until he has worked out his purpose."[1] The expression which results from this working out of purpose we may regard as a "theme," and our understanding of the concept is further enlarged by Francis Fergusson, who relates it to the "men in action" represented in drama. Fergusson defines "action" as that which extends beyond the events of a story and becomes "the focus or aim of psychic life from

141

which the events in that situation result."[2] Jacques Maritain completes the concept for us by making a theoretical transition from this focus or aim of an event to the theme it carries. Action thus becomes, for Maritain, a "spiritual *élan* or motion which, emanating from a constellation of human agents, carries them along." The motion, he asserts, "commands a certain development of events in time, permeating it with a definite significance." And this significance which a witness must experience from sensing the motion or force of people-in-events is identified as the theme.

For Maritain this force or ultimate meaning does not exist independently from the action simply because it *is* the meaning of the action. A theme, whether in literature, poetry, drama — or documentary — is what the communication *proposes, intends*, or *wills*, not merely the communication itself.[3]

This argument is useful as we move to distinguish the ways in which the documentarist, by controlling theme, seeks to make his work reflect the world of imagination. For he surely works with the same documents of life that are the raw materials of the news documentarist. He is still bound to the essential condition of structuring life, and while it is convenient to say that in the journalistic documentary life controls art and in the Theme Documentary art controls life, the dilemma of documentary still remains. Control can be neither an exclusive nor dominant factor. It can be only a *discernible* intention.

When Baker speaks of the dramatist's impulse to convey emotions — his own or those of characters — we may sense this drive at work with equal force in both journalistic and poetic approaches to the documentary. No better illustration of this exists than the use of the phrase "point of view" in describing many of the great News Documentaries in television's history. In one sense, the determination of a point of view merely represents the traditional print reporter's search for an "angle" in the reporting of an event — a procedural approach to a specific production means. Is it to be a direct chronological account of the event? Should it seek additional involvement by personalizing — telling the story through the eyes of typical people involved in, or affected by, the happening? These are, at one level, purely technical considerations. Yet they are also decisions which may reflect aesthetic processes, for inherently the selection of a point of view suggests some natural desire to impose unity upon the formlessness of events in time — to *propose, intend,* or *will* a significance in these events. Obviously, the more dramatic and involved with the subject the point of view becomes, the closer it moves to the intention of creating a unity of experience and hence a thematic expression of life.

Still, a point of view must hold some distinction from a theme. There is a sharp variance on the circumstances in which they are to be applied, as well as the thinking which governs selections. The theme documentarist begins with an idea which has created an emotional response within *him*.

"THE TUNNEL"
Produced for NBC News by Reuven Frank. Correspondent Piers Anderton (left),
Cameraman Peter Dehmel (right).

. . . all theory breaks down.

It is a personal choice, a personal reaction, which leads him to find the proper subject by which to express his impressions of events. Conversely, the news documentarist considers the wider significance of the subject itself first. Yet he is also bound to seek ways to illuminate the meaning of the subject, to find the point of view which will make it unified and compelling. Thus he, too, approaches that larger meaning which is theme.

In theory the distinction may lie in the order in which the theme and subject are selected and determined in the documentary creative process. In fact, however, such a structure often breaks down. The journalist may have some particular awareness of a great human problem underlying a news event, and a desire to convey this awareness to others in the direct terms of reportage. Such a process describes precisely the way in which a 1962 NBC News special, "The Tunnel" (the first production of its kind to be cited as the program of the year by the National Academy of Television Arts and Sciences) came into existence. Reuven Frank, its producer, knew of that great surge of desire for freedom in the captive Iron Curtain countries of Europe, and felt impelled, as a reporter, to convey the significance of this to us. He found this in a story of escaping refugees from East Berlin. The particular subject was one of a million of its kind, no more newsworthy in itself than any of the others, but it was an available story[4] which gave Frank the opportunity to express his broader theme.

In "The Tunnel" all theory which distinguishes "control of theme" from "control of subject" breaks down — for in its technique of presentation it was pure and dispassionate reportage. Yet "The Tunnel" was as much art as record, because within the very selection of an event was implied the dramatization of the great theme of man's urge to be free, expression of whose universality is a true function of art. Thus, to the degree in which "The Tunnel" moved beyond the delineation of a social problem in a journalistic context, it entered into the realm of art — the world of imagination.

"The Tunnel" represents only one of many News Documentary programs which emphasize the slightness of that boundary between point of view and theme. We have indicated, however, that technique must play an important role in keeping distinct the kinds of control which are exerted in documentary. These elements, when combined with the expressed purpose of the documentarist, are key factors in establishing and maintaining all differentiation of control. Within the Theme Documentary class, the subjective purposes, enhanced and affected by artistic techniques, move to the fore. The use of symbolic structures is emphasized. The poetic power of words, pictures, and music is combined with the aesthetic of cinematic structure and the dramaturgical form itself to shape the documents of reality into thematic expressions of the human condition. The control shifts from the reporter to the artist.

The work of television's theme documentarists has evolved within three basic production methods. One is in the *compilation,* involving the creative application of techniques of cinematic organization, the poetry of the spoken narrative, and the suggestive power of the musical score. In the *biographical* method the same elements are present, with the addition of elements of dramaturgical structure as distinct from the broader narrative. There is also a greater use of dialogue within the spoken narration. In the *dramatic* method the use of historical material is minimized, as the functions of dramaturgy within the more immediate records of actuality become dominant.

7 / Compilation Documentary

. . . In all the programs, all the time, our plan of procedure from start
to finish is expressed in the following quotation from Walt Whitman:
"I seek less to display any theme or thought and more to *bring you into
the atmosphere of the theme or thought* — there to pursue your own
flight."

— RICHARD HANSER[1]

IF THE EARLY Pathé newsreels and the traditions of pictorial
journalism up through *March of Time* gave ideas and impetus to TV News
Documentary, such compilation series as Frank Capra's *Why We Fight* and
a number of other wartime films produced here and abroad showed men a
different method of presenting reality: a method in which the artists —
director, film editor, writer, narrator, and composer — could seek, each
within his own craft, common and purposeful thematic expression.

The crises of the contemporary moment as reported in the various TV
News Documentaries constituted, after all, only one aspect of history.
There were other events of the past, both the crucial and the seemingly
unimportant, which deserved to be given that kind of exposure which
television alone could offer. In the film vaults of the world were stored
incredible amounts of footage, shot by untold numbers of photographers.
Much of it had been seen by no more than a handful of people. In television documentary's first decade, this filmic record of yesterday's great
upheavals and minor clashes — the photographic memories of men and
civilizations in action — was brought to Americans in a continuing series
of compilation documentaries.

The earliest experiment in the creation of such compilations for the
medium was initiated by the *March of Time* organization, which offered
two series, *Crusade in Europe* and *Crusade in the Pacific,* in the period
before television had acquired a truly national audience. These were both
interesting and informative, but unfortunately did not command wide at-

145

HENRY "PETE" SALOMON

. . . out of war's brutality — compassion.

tention. It was not until 1952 that what was to become the great tradition of the historical compilation documentary scored its first true and enduring achievements in television.

VICTORY AT SEA

As Murrow and Friendly provided the inspiration and thrust for News Documentary in television, so the compilation form was given its greatest encouragement by the work of a single man, Henry (Pete) Salomon. Though unknown to most of the millions of Americans who witnessed, and were touched by, his work, Salomon was honored in England when, on the night of his death in 1957, BBC-TV interrupted its schedule to carry a special commemoratory program.

Some would call Henry Salomon the Robert Flaherty of TV, for although working with a distinct method of cinematic presentation, he brought to his art the gentleness of time remembered and an enlarged sense of humanity — a compassion for mankind and a capacity to create expressions of this compassion in terms of the pictorial records of war's brutality. It was Salomon who conceived *Victory at Sea,* television's early historical compilation series built around United States Naval Operations of World War II, and who later brought to TV the *Project XX* series.

As a Lieutenant Commander in World War II, Salomon had collaborated in the preparation of Rear Admiral Samuel Eliot Morison's 14-volume chronicle of the United States Navy at war, and when he took his first plans for a series to NBC-TV he was given unqualified support by his close personal friend, Robert Sarnoff, then executive vice president of the network. Utilizing the full resources of NBC, Salomon began to build a production staff of distinguished talents, many of whom would later make significant contributions of their own to TV Theme Documentary. From RKO-Pathé, a spawning ground for TV documentary craftsmanship, he brought Isaac Kleinerman, a film editor without peer in reality film, to serve as senior editor; Richard Hanser, a writer with a fine sense of the balance between words and pictures who worked closely with Salomon in story evolution; and M. Clay Adams, who directed the series. To these, Salomon added Donald B. Hyatt, a young Dartmouth graduate with training in sociology, as his assistant.

This nucleus was augmented by numerous younger men who executed a variety of functions in research under the direction of Daniel Jones. Then Salomon began the arduous task of finding films which could tell the massive story he had in mind. Combat film and related story footage were sought in the governmental bureaus and Army and Navy departments of many nations. Much of the film had to be declassified from "secret" status, an effort which in some cases required diplomatic negotiations. In the end, Salomon and his staff had viewed some 60 million feet of film which then had to be reduced to the 60,000 feet finally used in the 26 half-hour programs. When the project was in its beginning stages of production, Salomon engaged composer Richard Rodgers to create an original score, and Robert Russell Bennett to orchestrate it.

Victory at Sea was first telecast to American audiences in the 1952-53 season, and received unreserved critical and public acclaim. Within each of its 26 individual segments the distinction between the journalistic point of view and the artist's expression of theme was made clear. Each phase of the long battle history hinged upon a certain aspect of naval operations. In the segment devoted to the battle for Rabaul the importance of radar as a military instrument was emphasized. In "The Turkey Shoot," concerning the battle of the Marianas, amphibious warfare provided the key to story development. In "Magnetic North" the description of the operations from Alaska to Murmansk was a basis for presenting the role of weather in naval operations. Thus each major subject was given a specific point of view around which a thematic episode could be constructed. The selective processes of the entire unit sought the film, the words, and the music which could reflect the predetermined point of view throughout. This story approach directed the flow of the elements by providing an essential source of unification which extended beyond chronological development.

Yet the true theme of *Victory at Sea* was an expression of a dominant emotional statement about men and nations at war. This was evoked in different ways, as both aural and visual communication combined to transmit the artist's representation of life. Nowhere is the full significance of this statement more precisely defined than in these observations by critic Bernard De Voto:

> One first thinks of isolated moments and such special effects as climaxes. A falling plane skips on the surface of the water like a stone, or a burning plane sinks and the gas goes on burning. A Marine uses his helmet to shield the face of a wounded comrade from the rain. At Malta, nuns shepherd school children into a bomb shelter. A baby shakes with terror at Okinawa. At Peleliu, the surf rolls the body of a soldier in full combat pack up on the beach, Arabs dance to the pipers of a Scotch brigade on a dock. . . . Someone is reading a letter which had kisses printed on it in lipstick. Firecrackers snap as the first convoy of trucks reaches the end of the Ledo road. . . . An old man weeps as President Roosevelt's coffin comes down Pennsylvania Avenue. The face of a captured German is pure hate. . . . Some moments restore in full emotions we resolved never to forget: Hitler's turkey strut at Compiègne, the tinny bravado that makes every picture of Mussolini's corrupt, the anger and shame of Pearl Harbor. Or moments of excitement so intense that one could not stand much of them — the Anzio landing, a Kamikaze almost missing a ship, a convoy under torpedo attacks, the facing death of a carrier. "Roman Renaissance," the 14th episode, ends with the crowds hushed by the appearance of the Pope on his balcony. At the end of "Conquest of Micronesia," crippled planes land on a flight deck and burst into flame and the film closes with a solemnity intensified by the fact that not only the body of a pilot but his plane too is committed to the deep. . . .
>
> The documentary instrument is used here, and *Victory* must be the longest documentary film ever produced as Mr. Rodgers' score is said to be the longest symphony ever written. . . . The exhaustion, anguish, agony, sullenness, apathy, despair, or exaltation which the screen shows are not histrionic; they are actual. *But the faces blend and generalize and build up and create a realization of men in war, and this is not a function of fact but of art.*[2]

Perhaps what *Victory at Sea* offered to a wide new public was this expert function of "blending and generalizing" within the records of reality. The series had brought new and important uses to an older film style, for by the fact of its being carried on television it could and did reach more human beings than any other motion picture or TV series in history. After its network airing in 1952-53 the series was released for national and international syndication, and it continues to be run on TV stations throughout the world.

De Voto has touched upon the timeless art of the series — its emphasis upon human hope and despair, joy and sorrow. These were brought home to us in terms, not of cold imagery, but of the creative interpretation of what had gone before. It was this artistry which enabled the series to triumph over the memories of man, giving the victors a sense of oneness with their former enemies. Eight years after its first telecast the series was brought, in a special 90-minute form, to Japan, where it reached one of the largest audiences ever to view a television program. As a result of this reception the entire series was rerun on Japanese television in 1961. More than 20 years after Pearl Harbor, Henry Salomon's noble vision of humanity is as inspiring as ever.

PROJECT XX

Victory at Sea had brought together within a single unit some of TV Theme Documentary's ablest pioneers: Salomon, Kleinerman, Hanser, Hyatt, and Bennett as well as others who had contributed to the success of the series. They knew its needs, felt its demands, and had received their baptism of fire in its hectic, sometimes deadly schedules. These men were not journalists. They had some of the reporter's instinct — the documentarist's desire to record the changes in human existence — but they were artists concerned primarily with creative interpretation of the world around them and only secondarily with reportage.

At the conclusion of *Victory at Sea*, NBC gave Salomon approval to keep this unit intact and begin producing new programs in the tradition of *Victory*. *Project XX* was born, and in September 1954 it offered "Three, Two, One — Zero," and account of the development of atomic energy, which was produced and co-authored by Salomon and Hanser, edited by Kleinerman, and scored by Bennett. To narrate this production, Alexander Scourby was engaged. His style, phrasing, and tone were to become an integral part of the work on the project.

The future of *Project XX* was assured when it won the Robert J. Flaherty Award for outstanding creative achievement in the production of documentary film, and since then *Project XX* has represented television Theme Documentary's peak. Moving at its own pace, the unit continued to produce its theme compilations with expertness and precision, and from September 1954 to April 1962 it offered 18 special programs which earned world-wide respect. Many were given repeated airings for nationwide audiences (a total of 43 network airings in all), and by 1964 *Project XX*'s programs had won over 50 international awards in documentary film.

The artistry and achievement of *Project XX*'s compilation reconstructions of segments of 20th-century history were fully illustrated in three other early programs: "Nightmare in Red," "The Twisted Cross," and "The Great War." Here the techniques of bringing filmed records of life into a single, sweeping statement of a civilization's agonies were refined and perfected.

"Nightmare in Red" was brought to the American audience over a year after the unit's first telecast. Dealing with the birth of Communism in Russia and the growth of this system into a world threat, the film was not ready for airing until December 1955. Much of the footage discovered by

Salomon and his associates was virtually unknown. History was traced from the days of Imperial Russia to the present — through the old Czarist order, the Revolutions of 1905 and 1917, the Provisional Government, the Purge Trials, and World War II and its aftermath. Two research teams, one in Europe and one in America, found film of Czar Nicholas II, Tolstoy, Lenin, Kerensky, Trotsky, Stalin, Vishinsky, and Molotov. Some film dated back to 1893. Robert Russell Bennett's score gave an impressive flow to varied sequences such as those showing the gentle ease of life aboard Nicholas' yacht, the Czarina at a charity bazaar in Yalta (both rare film sequences), and the ominous executions (also rarely seen) during the Russian Civil War. Among the unusual finds were scenes of American troops in Vladivostok after World War I which also had not been turned up previously. Out of such footage Kleinerman put together a forceful visual account of Communism's growth — an editing masterpiece balanced against a sensitive narration delivered by Scourby. The film was re-telecast, by popular request, less than a month later and received subsequent showings in 1958 and 1960.

"Nightmare in Red" was followed by "The Twisted Cross," whose point of view focused upon the rise and fall of Hitler. In this program the unit turned to the vast supplies of historical film which described the growth of the Nazi movement through the eyes of the Germans themselves. Salomon had already observed, after *Victory at Sea,* that American audiences were even more absorbed by the segments of captured film than by our own combat footage, and in "The Twisted Cross" he kept the story entirely inside Germany.

Research for these earlier films uncovered sufficient material to indicate that still a third historical drama could be created, and in October 1956 *Project XX* offered its documentary study of World War I — "The Great War," combining once more the editorial work of Kleinerman, a score by Bennett, and a script by Salomon and Hanser. These first three programs were undoubtedly milestones in television's effort to document the past, and their portrayal of great conflicts within the living memory of man conveyed an urgency and significance unequaled by any history book.

It is difficult, when viewing any of these early *Project XX* triumphs, to single out individual accomplishments in the blending of music, poetic narration, and visual flow. The mastery of these films lies in the fusion of each element within a balanced and harmonious whole. With the conclusion of their work on this historic trilogy, Hanser and Robert Russell Bennett reviewed some of their discoveries. In a 1957 Seminar on Documentary at the University of Denver, Hanser reflected at length upon the factors involved in creating narration in this form:

> . . . The basic peculiarity is, of course, that the words have to be tailored to footage — a bastard form of composition that obtains in no other field, the stop-watch method imposed by the nature of the medium.

PART OF THE *PROJECT XX* TEAM: Kleinerman, Hanser, Scourby

... for each, within his craft, common and purposeful thematic expression.

Another basic factor is compression and placement. The right sentence with the right choice of words, planted at the right place, can, when combined with the right pictures, suggest whole areas of information and emotion in one quick stroke. (That is why reading one of these scripts is so often unsatisfactory; every sentence is designed to connect with, merge into, or enhance — or be enhanced by the pictures to which it applies. Conversely, as you know, to see the pictures alone is often confusing and even irritating, until the narration clarifies them and gives them meaning.) The bromide about one picture being worth a thousand words is true to a very limited degree. Over and over again, the pictures of themselves do not convey a clear impression and certainly not an accurate meaning. I think Maxwell Anderson (perhaps in his book *The First World War*) pointed out that a line of soldiers marching by themselves takes on entirely different meaning when it is known which direction they are marching in — to battle or away from it — an essential element in the feeling of the scene which the visual image does not of itself convey.

Another trick is finding a vivid sentence, or bit of information, or a quotation which, once it is delivered by the narrator, illuminates a whole following sequence — kicks it off, so to speak, in such a way that the sequence can then unfold, perhaps for a hundred feet or more, all by itself with no further explanation at all. The kick-off sentence has planted a suggestion, an emotion, a mood in the viewer's mind which then carries over throughout the ensuing footage. An example is the quotation from Goering which ends on script page 19 of "The Twisted Cross." Once this 66-word paragraph has been spoken, the entire Hitler adulation sequence then rolls for a good ten minutes with not another word. And the quotation is strong enough to suggest everything that needs to be said to launch and sustain this very long wordless passage.

The rule Pete Salomon and I work by all the time is: "The less narration the better." But this is a matter of judgment. Too little commentary can leave the pictures a confused jumble, with the viewer asking, "What the hell is going on here?" Too much narration can, of course, get in the way, be distracting and irritating. There is no known rule for gauging when precisely enough words have been written to clarify the pictures without cluttering up the sound track. It is a matter of feeling and instinct, as with practically everything else in writing when you get down to it. Sometimes we hit it just right, and sometimes we sin with too much, and again with too little.

Much, naturally, depends on the kind of sequence being dealt with. In "Nightmare in Red" there was a great deal of factual explanation necessary to convey some idea of how czarism fell in Russia after so many centuries, how the Bolsheviks came to take over, and so on. Naturally, where a mood, an emotion, is the aim, the pictures and the music together often perform this function more effectively with no spoken narration, or a minimum of it. In both pictures and narration our general idea, in all the programs all the time, our plan of procedure from start to finish is expressed in the following quotation from Walt Whitman: "I seek less to display any theme or thought and more *to bring you into the atmosphere of the theme or thought* — there to pursue your own flight."

Therefore, we do not get alarmed when somebody comes around later and says, "But you forgot to mention the Roehm purge," or "You didn't do justice to the Social Revolutionaries in the pre-Bolshevik period" or something of the sort.

In both words and film we want to suggest the essence of the event as accurately and forcefully as possible. And this, again, comes down largely to feeling and instinct — for which no infallible rules have yet been devised.[3]

During the seminar at the University of Denver, Hanser's observations on writing were supplemented by those of Robert Russell Bennett on music in an interview with James Nelson of the *Project XX* staff:

NELSON: How do you make music that fits the needs of the TV pictures?
BENNETT: Your problem is to find music that will not be consciously heard but will be felt; that will not take off on its own, but will push the emotions of the viewers in the same direction as the picture.
NELSON: When the program's footage has been cut down to size and before the narration is written, do you run the film for yourself privately?
BENNETT: Yes, several times — until I begin to hear some kind of musical accompaniment in my mind.

NELSON: Then do you wait for the words — the narration — to be written?

BENNETT: I would rather have words, if possible. Sometimes they are not ready, however, and we have to trust ourselves all to tell the same story.

NELSON: Do Pete Salomon and Dick Hanser change any words after they have heard the music?

BENNETT: Pete does. Pete and Dick work it out together. In every picture there are places where the music has suggested a change in the narration. Often, Pete wants to take out narration because the music explains it to him. Of course this has limits, because not all viewers are as sensitive to music as he is. Remember that what counts most is the fusion of all three elements — pictures, words and music. Or the *seeming* fusion because, sometimes, one or another will be dominant.

NELSON: After you know the program's mood and what it is trying to say, then what?

BENNETT: As soon as the show is cut near to size, I begin choosing musical fragments that will advance the story line. As I work, I have a shot list on my desk. This lists every scene (1,032 for "The Twisted Cross") and gives me scene lengths in terms of footage. I write the music to fit each piece of film. Of course, if I make a mistake in calculations, I have trouble — and so does the orchestra when I am conducting the score at the recording session.

NELSON: You are obliged to write every note to exact footage — is that so?

BENNETT: Yes. At the bottom of every bar of every page of my score I write down the footage which it will fill.

NELSON: When you are actually conducting the orchestra of 75 or 80 men at the recording session, how does that work differ from conducting the same musicians at Carnegie Hall?

BENNETT: I have three extra duties beyond conducting. I must watch the film that is being played for me on the screen that stands in back of the orchestra. I must watch the large footage meter that clicks away at my side. And I must watch the notations of footage on my score. Everything must synchronize. If I see that I am a little ahead or behind, I must reduce or step up the tempo to make us come out on the nose. Of course, certain film actions must be hit exactly by certain notes of music. This is precision not demanded in conducting a Broadway show.

NELSON: Is there much difference between composing and arranging a *Project XX* show and working on a Broadway musical?

BENNETT: There's a great difference. Our music is emotionally deeper than Broadway music. It's a much more responsible task than just bringing out the tunes of Broadway.

NELSON: Is it more exacting work?

BENNETT: Yes. For one thing we use a symphony orchestra. There are many more notes to be written. The scope of the music is much wider — requires not prettier music, but in many cases better music.

NELSON: You spoke of writing many musical notes. For a one-hour film program, how many pages of score might you write — including all instruments?

BENNETT: Depending on how fast or slow it is, the score of an hour of music can be anything between 400 and 1,000 pages.

NELSON: Do you do all that by hand yourself?

BENNETT: The full conductor's score I do. The parts for the musicians are
  copies from that.
NELSON: We spoke earlier of your adapting music. What are the problems
  of original composition? In "Three, Two, One — Zero" and "The
  Twisted Cross" and others you wrote practically the entire score.
BENNETT: An entirely original score fits the picture better, but arranging
  other men's themes is easier and often more fun for all concerned.[4]

Too few of Kleinerman's comments upon his own contribution are
available to us, yet it was his assembling and reworking of the visual records which also carried a dominant emotional thrust in these productions.
In "The Twisted Cross," for example, he was challenged by a task which
had baffled many editors — presenting some great visual summary, in a
limited time, of the human meaning of Hitler's early conquests in Europe.
So often, before and after this production, this kind of sequence had been
reduced to the whine of Stukas, bursting of bombs, scenes of ruined build-
ings, and scurrying refugees. Kleinerman, however, created a sequence
which has rarely been equaled in its cinematic power and remains an
example to be held before every student of the art of visual communication.

The force of this sequence rests upon Kleinerman's use of only a few
key elements. There is first a flash of pure light which stuns us, then a bit
of stock footage showing Hitler standing in the rear of an open automobile,
taken as the camera makes a 180° sweep around him (thus holding him in
the center of the shot as he gives the Nazi salute). Then there is a cut to
the faces of Europe's suffering humanity. The elements are simple enough,
but it is in their repetition, and the "effects" treatment Kleinerman gives to
them, that the dramatic surge is pushed forward. Over the Hitler shot, run
in negative to give it a weird and ghostly suggestion, flames are superim-
posed. The flames rise, and as they envelop him there is a cut to the faces of
those who endured his conquest. The same burst of light, the ghostly sweep
and the flames, are repeated as each country Hitler has ravaged is revealed.
Only the faces of the people change. Repeated again and again in a mounting crescendo, the sequence burns itself into the memory. It has rarely been
surpassed in television as a vivid and encompassing demonstration of the
art of cinematic montage.

The concepts and techniques which evolved in these early films continued to be seen throughout the *Project XX* history, as the unit went on
to create (in order of their production) such studies as "The Jazz Age,"
"The Innocent Years," "Life in the '30's," "Not So Long Ago," and "That
War in Korea." Each of these involved the basic construction of visual
narrative with film, employing no major changes in approach except for an
increasing reliance upon the "narrator-star," a departure which permitted
Fred Allen to provide narration for "The Jazz Age," Bob Hope to review
the post-World War II period of "Not So Long Ago," and Richard Boone
to add an eloquent and restrained narration for "That War in Korea."

Salomon lived to see the completion of his productions of "The Jazz
Age" and "The Innocent Years" (a portrait of the era between 1900 and

PROJECT XX: "THE TWISTED CROSS"

. . . a burst of light, a ghostly sweep — a masterpiece.

"CALL TO FREEDOM"

. . . for Salomon, a grand epilogue.

1917), both of which were aired prior to his death in late 1957. In many ways "The Innocent Years" carried the special mark of his authentic genius, making the past come to life in still another of those magnificent panoramas which always set before us that great concern for humanity which was Salomon's. It repeated the basic technique of historical compilation, unfolding the chronology of events, places, and faces of those early years of this century. Beginning with a carefully edited look at New York City at the turn of the century, the program's nostalgia was enhanced by Bennett's clever interweaving of the old songs — "Get Out and Get Under," "Come Josephine," "Yankee Doodle Dandy," and others out of the period. Salomon's compassion dictated the inclusion of the tragic: shots of children working long hours in factories, and some magnificently graphic film of the aftermath of the San Francisco earthquake and the Dayton flood of 1913. In the narration Salomon and Hanser sought the idiom of the era, using direct quotations from the newspapers, the sayings of the times, and the prose gems of Jack London, Theodore Dreiser, and "Mr. Dooley."

Yet, despite the fact that Salomon had directed the *Project XX* unit in these moving demonstrations of the compilation form, it was his next-to-final production, "Call To Freedom," which wrote a grand epilogue to his career. And curiously, it was the only one which did not give emphasis to the use of compilation footage.

In "Call To Freedom" (aired in January 1947) *Project XX* experimented again by moving a crew to Vienna, where they filmed the war-devastated *Wiener Staat Oper,* one of the world's great musical institutions, and recorded one of its performances. Salomon wished to combine this method of expressing the theme he had set for himself — the progress of civilization toward liberty and independence — by intercutting major scenes from a production of Beethoven's *Fidelio* with sequences of historical film treating Austria's long struggle for freedom in the 20th century.

In this venture Salomon and his staff created a startling innovation in television documentary. Bennett built his entire 90-minute score upon Beethoven's musical passages taken not only from *Fidelio* but from overtures, symphonies, concertos, and other works by the master composer. Hanser and Salomon were assisted by Philip Reisman, Jr. in preparation of a script which employed extensive quotations from Beethoven's letters and conversations, and which enabled the genius's words, as well as his music, to comment upon man's struggle toward freedom. In another remarkable single achievement Kleinerman worked together a sequence using the museum pieces of war — masks, helmets, suits of armor, and other weapons and artifacts — by which he brought to visual life a re-creation of the violent wars of 20th-century Austria. This "reality-animation" technique may have been used on occasion earlier in the history of film (and was imitated on several occasions thereafter by TV's editors), but it revealed again the inventiveness of Kleinerman's work.

By the time "The Innocent Years" was telecast, important personnel changes were being made within the unit. Donald B. Hyatt, Salomon's assistant, was listed as director for the program, and Silvio d'Alisera as senior film editor. The shift resulted from "Ike" Kleinerman's departure for CBS, where he was offered an associate producer's role with producer Burton Benjamin on *The Twentieth Century.* Kleinerman's last work for *Project XX,* the editing of "Life in the '30's," was already completed when he left.

NEW DIRECTIONS AT PROJECT XX

Donald B. Hyatt, Salomon's successor, could no more escape the influence of his predecessor than could Fred Friendly avoid the spirit and commitment of Edward R. Murrow. Further, the same creative forces which Salomon had drawn together were still active in the unit Hyatt now directed. Nevertheless, Hyatt still faced that personal conflict which every creative person must experience — the need to find his own unique means of expression.

In search of his own form, Hyatt turned back to the documentary film, where he found examples of the use of still pictures in a filmic context. In the work of Louis Clyde Stoumen and such individual films as Colin Low and Wolfe Koenig's famous NFB production, *City of Gold,* historical photographs had been combined with music, narration, and the moving image to create ingenious documents of life. These examples could well serve Hyatt's intentions, for he meant to broaden the purposes of *Project XX* by creating documentary treatments of the past where the religious, cultural, social, and political ideas of the 20th century were first formulated. Such events antedated the invention of the motion picture, to be sure; yet still photographs had been made since the mid-19th century, and beyond these lay a wide range of paintings and other works of art.

Utilizing these, Hyatt could construct Theme Documentaries in the Salomon tradition, and he began an impressive series of "still-in-motion" productions in 1958. With research director Daniel Jones and his staff, Hyatt examined over 25,000 prints, daguerreotypes, and photographs of mid-19th century life in America and selected those he would need to create his "Meet Mr. Lincoln," a program seen by over 30 million Americans when first broadcast in early 1959. In this production Silvio d'Alisera, working closely with Hyatt, earned distinction — and an "Emmy" — for his editing, and the film also reflected in every detail that care in scoring and narration which had distinguished earlier efforts by Bennett and Hanser. Just over a year later the unit recreated "Mark Twain's America" with 3,500 photographs and engravings carrying the visual narrative and a script founded within the great humorist's own account of American life in the last decades of the 19th century. The still-in-motion technique was continued in the early 1960's with two productions — "The Coming of Christ" and "He Is Risen" — employing the many religious paintings of

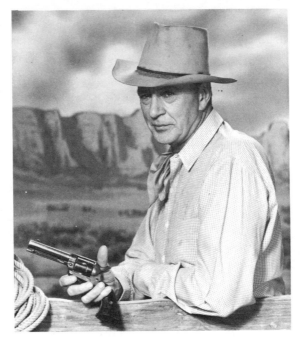

GARY COOPER IN "THE REAL WEST"

. . . romance, not sentimentality.

"THAT WAR IN KOREA"

. . . rarely do we ponder man's tragic spirit.

history. These programs were enhanced by the gentle narrational style of Alexander Scourby.

But the most effective of these productions remains *Project XX*'s "The Real West," which ranks among the finest Theme Documentaries created for American television. Before he started production of this epic, Hyatt had come to a full understanding of the creative principles which controlled the still-in-motion technique, and had developed a working philosophy which he expressed in this way:

> Whether it's a painting or photograph, there is a dimension to this moment beyond which the motion picture can't reach. When all these authentic flashes of history are treated with respect something uncanny happens — the dead come alive. "Respect" is the secret. The scene, the photograph, the painting you choose must be looked at as a director looks at an ordinary scene with live actors and movable scenery and props. The usual tendency with the still-in-motion technique is to continually move the camera in and out and all around Robin's barn, trying to excuse the fact you are dealing with immovable pictures. I move the camera only when there is a reason for it — to motivate action, not to cover up inaction.

While admitting that there were many limitations to the technique, Hyatt was convinced of its suitability in the medium.

> We continually strive for simplicity on television and often still photographs, particularly good portraits, are the simplest and most effective means of communicating, of expressing an emotion and for creating a mood. The creation of the right mood, or feeling, in television hangs on a very delicate thread. An expression on a man's face . . . is gone in an instant, and with it the emphasis, the emotion and the mood of that instant. Because this technique is less mobile it is often more effective.

Because he insisted upon original historical source material, and personally examined each item to be used in such production, Hyatt also grew to hold firm convictions about the necessity for precision in detail:

> You must climb inside each picture and meet the people and live with them. The people of 50, of 100, years ago were not the same as we are today. They lived differently, dressed differently, thought differently, and even walked and acted differently. We can never really recreate the past — no matter how authentically the actors are dressed or the scenery built. The mood, history, feeling of the past can only be captured by going to original source materials — the photographs, sketches, music, words of an era — and weaving them together in a dramatic form, attempting to capture the real flavor of bygone times.[5]

It was this understanding of how the faces and scenes of the past could be brought to life that built the great visual flow of "The Real West." Yet the insight of the script by Philip Reisman, Jr. also gave meaning to what we saw. With a sure sense of both ironic counterpoint and rhapsodic prose where each was needed, Reisman wove the reminiscences of "those who wested" into the visual narrative in such a way that we realized that these were real people, at once identifiable and to be identified with. At one point we saw a portrait of Belle Starr and were told that "those who said she was beautiful also said she was virtuous" (an irony, our eyes told us, of magnificent proportions). As we saw photographs of the long cattle drives north we heard a *vaquero's* wry observation that he was paid "damned few money and a hell of a lot of beans." As we witnessed an incredibly moving sequence of wind-etched faces of American Indians we heard their pleas for rest — for an end to war. And when Gary Cooper repeated the final words of an old-timer, "By damn, wouldn't it be fun to tear it all down and start over again?" we knew we had heard the poetry of common speech set within the lyricism of faces and places long forgotten. Unforgettable, too, was the final sequence depicting the tragic defeat of the American Indian, to which d'Alisera's contribution was a furious summation of all the battles, edited on the basis of paintings of the Indian wars. In its way, it was a duplication of Kleinerman's armor sequence at the close of "Call To Freedom." Again, a total fusion of word and picture, unified by Bennett's brilliant score, created a masterpiece.

"The Real West" also affords us some final appreciation of the differences in attitudes between Henry Salomon and Donald Hyatt as documentarists. Hyatt, to be sure, was working with a method which not only tolerated but encouraged a different *Weltanschauung*, but we may wonder whether the man sought the method or the method found the man. For Hyatt was more inclined to the romantic view, and the indications of it are found in his earlier treatment of "Mark Twain's America," where the bitterness of Samuel Clemens' views of life was sacrificed for his more sentimental rustic and homespun philosophy. Surely the selection of Gary Cooper as narrator for "The Real West" was, in itself, a concession to the great mythology of the west. Yet Hyatt never permitted romance to descend to sentimentality. And even had he been so inclined, the visual documents and the words of "those who wested" would not have permitted it.

Both Salomon and Hyatt sought the universal themes which could give man nobility and dignity. But Salomon worked with those records which closely reflected the foibles and brutalities of the eras he documented. Hyatt's records, so far removed in time and from the sense of actuality, would naturally force the more romantic view. Yet each could bring forth hope. Each could reflect the gentleness and sensibilities of humankind. The work of one was not less an expression of life's truths than the other. Had Donald Hyatt never led *Project XX* beyond "The Real West" and its still-in-motion predecessors, he would nevertheless be a worthy successor to Salomon.

In its later years *Project XX* came upon a number of new conditions which somewhat altered the nature of its thematic expression. The creators of the series had learned that a depiction of our nation's character need not always be made in terms of great and earth-shaking events. As the

"MEET MR. LINCOLN"

. . . for thirty million Americans, history in still-life.

DONALD B. HYATT

. . . "respect" is the secret.

portrayals of 20th-century life moved forward in time, the staff was confronted with new sources of film which, in abundance and at length, dealt with less significant events and personalities, at least insofar as history would regard them. New material on the performing stars of the popular arts was available, and comic as well as tragic, social, and cultural commentary on an era could readily be obtained. A shot of Fiorello LaGuardia reading comic strips to children could be intercut with shots of the latest divorce in Hollywood, a flooded Ohio Valley, or the latest social outing of the Ku Klux Klan. The processes of selection became more complicated, and the difficulties of establishing and unifying central themes more challenging. There had rapidly come to be so many records of people and events which were still within the living memory of audiences (and that were "musts" in a treatment of an era) that hope for the "sweeping" view became less certain.

Further, a treatment of the 1920's or 1930's might still show the dissenters — the unpopular figures of times gone by — without generating the controversy that such portrayal would set in motion if brought too close in time. But as the series drew nearer to the present, it naturally became involved with these questions. History had not yet always made its own selections of what was foolish and dangerous, or important and significant, and when men and events depicted were too fresh within living memory their treatment became the concern of the news documentarist. As a result, *Project XX* was pressed to narrow its focus upon contemporary life to those social and cultural developments which had only indirect political significance.

It turned first to a series of several productions which bordered upon a line between documentary and the "entertainment" special — programs which rounded out our view of 20th-century life by veering away from political crises and toward a more balanced expression of our society. The first of these programs was "Those Ragtime Years," which traced "the continuous sound-track of American life" from the late 1890's until America's entry into World War I.

In technique as well as in content, "Those Ragtime Years" represented a departure. It was, first of all, the initial "live-on-tape" presentation of the unit. Hoagy Carmichael, an accomplished composer and performer in his own right, appeared as both narrator and entertainer, and often these functions became confused. While the historical presentation of an important popular art was certainly a worthy endeavor, the art which *Project XX* had developed as its own seemed somehow lost here. Perhaps this accounts for the change in title given the *Project XX* unit in this period. As NBC's *Special Projects* the unit enlarged its scope and functions, and was soon engaged in a series of productions which no longer always carried the specific *Project XX* label. DuPont assumed sponsorship of several such specials in 1961 and 1962, and an assignment was given to Hyatt for the programs "Laughter, U.S.A.," "Merrily We Roll Along," "The Ziegfeld Touch," "Chicago and All That Jazz," "Circus," "Regards to George M. Cohan," "Cops and Robbers," and "The Beauty of Women." In addition to these lesser documents of our culture a separate unit within *Special Projects* was evolved to produce a series of biographical studies, *The World of* ——— which needs to be examined within a later context.

The *Project XX* imprint was retained, however, for certain Theme Documentaries in the Salomon tradition. Two of these, "Not So Long Ago," which treated the years between 1945 and 1950, and "That War in Korea" were more than worthy of *Project XX*. The study of the Korean War, in particular, reminded us that it was a war which has never really ended. When the program was finally offered to the American public in the fall of 1963, "That War in Korea" joined the small group of *Project XX* classics which moved beyond the reality of man's shattering conflicts to create once more the tragic and haunting theme of humanity, a theme which the artist alone can express when he extracts — from ugliness, brutality, and despair — the meaning of life. Rarely do we ponder man's tragic spirit, either in modern life itself or in television's reflection and transmission of it. Yet, in those scenes showing the long moments of waiting for a cease-fire at the 38th Parallel, we witnessed again that filmic portrayal of the inevitability of man's destiny upon this earth — to wait in hope. And when, accompanied by Bennett's splendid music, the flares signifying the signing of the cease-fire burst over the battle lines, the millions of Americans who watched "That War in Korea" knew and appreciated that sublime theme which the men of *Project XX* always sought to express.

8 / Compilation: The Successors

> If the compilation film is "just a collection of newsreel clips," then the history book is "just a collection of library clips" and no history makes any sense.
>
> — BURTON BENJAMIN[1]

FOLLOWING upon the esteem for *Victory at Sea,* American networks and independent producers began an outpouring of documentaries, cast in the compilation form, throughout the later 1950's. Concurrently with such later evolution in *Project XX,* these series indicated a variety of new styles and methods, each borrowing from and influencing the others; yet each also sought its own ways and means to alter technique and expand upon the basic form.

AIR POWER

The journalistic tradition initiated at CBS Radio in the 1940's was continued in that network's TV News Documentary by the work of *See It Now* and *CBS Reports.* Yet the strong emphasis upon news and public affairs was, to some extent, mitigated when the network brought its successful radio series, *CBS Is There,* into television in the early 1950's under the title *You Are There.* This amalgam of news and historical re-creation did not prove consistent with the visual medium. It was one thing to hear a CBS reporter suddenly thrust himself into the midst of Socrates' trial, but quite another to *see* it happen. The authority of the photographic record would not support the anachronism; and while the television *You Are There* provided interesting educational accounts of intense moments in history, the network probably experienced some difficulties in reconciling the appearance of its staff reporters on the bridge of a sinking *Titanic* and strolling among the barefoot in ancient Athens.

164

CBS had already begun to introduce actuality footage into *You Are There* in such later programs as "V-J Day," but this inclusion seemed only to accentuate the unreality of re-enacted sequences. Perhaps the network never really faced the issue squarely until 1961 when it eliminated Douglas Edwards from the narrator's role at *Armstrong Circle Theatre,* in which semidramatization was also the mode of production, but in which re-enacted events were taken directly from the daily newspapers. *Victory at Sea,* however, provided the example by which CBS could simply sidestep the issue by replacing *You Are There* with *Air Power,* a reality-based documentary series which was presented in 1956-57. The sponsor, Prudential Insurance Company, was quite content with *You Are There,* but when CBS concluded negotiations with the United States Air Force for some 77 million feet of film, Prudential accepted without reluctance sponsorship of the new series.

As early as 1954 CBS News and Public Affairs had engaged Perry Wolff, who had produced the earlier *Adventure* series for the network and who had earned two Peabody awards for radio documentaries while on the staff of WBBM in Chicago. *Air Power* was assigned to Wolff, and James Faichney was named associate producer. Norman della Joio was enlisted to compose a score which was conducted by Alfredo Antonini. Wolff later moved to further success in actuality television, notably his production of Jacqueline Kennedy's tour of the White House in 1962, but *Air Power* remains his foremost contribution to the documentary.

The principal task which occupied Wolff and his unit was the reduction of over 300 million feet of film to 26 stories which reflected the "grand theme" — victory in the sky. The elements of success, as in the case of *Victory at Sea,* were a balancing of the story mind (Wolff's), skilled film editing (by Peter Poor, E. Harlan Whitehead, Peter Curran, Leo Zochling, and others), the unifying quality of a fine musical score, and authoritative narration by Walter Cronkite.

The premise of *Air Power* was a simple one: that every advance in aviation reflected the changing times of our world. In the 26 programs the series carried us from Kitty Hawk and the Wright brothers through two world wars and into the Atomic Age, with its supersonic planes, missiles, and a prediction of space accomplishments to come. Its historic breadth gave the series additional opportunities for thematic variations which *Victory at Sea* could not attempt; and yet, in retrospect, its great appeal was much the same as *Victory*'s: the most exciting moments were those which gave us the drama of men and machines at war. Audiences were once more afforded a "this-is-the-way-it-was" survey of the conflict experienced less than a decade before — a struggle so tortuous that few men could, while living through it, see it whole and steadily.

In separate episodes *Air Power* treated the rise of the Luftwaffe, the Battle of Britain, Pearl Harbor, the United States 8th Air Force in Europe, the impressive daring of the bombing raids on Ploesti and Schweinfurt, the growth of long-range fighter escort in the skies over Europe, the new combat techniques evolved in the air war above Italy, the fall of France, and the final collapse of Germany. The programs then moved to the Far East and the Pacific, recounting the painful island-hopping war as American forces plodded their way from the Coral Sea to Iwo Jima and Okinawa, ending with the atomic blasts over Hiroshima and Nagasaki. The point of view followed the airplane and its uses in the arts of death, but the larger theme remained the men who fought and died in the massive enterprise of war.

In its efforts to give added dramatic power to various episodes, *Air Power* assigned certain narrational roles to individuals whose talents or experience best fitted them for the subject. Michael Redgrave narrated the "Battle of Britain" segment, and General Jimmy Doolittle helped to relate "The 1930's." The method begun with Fred Allen's narration of *Project XX*'s "The Jazz Age" was adopted, as Art Carney related *Air Power*'s version of the 1920's, "Fools, Daredevils and Geniuses." And for its story of the World War I era, Captain Eddie Rickenbacker supplied a firsthand commentary.

Beyond the addition of the special narrator to assist Walter Cronkite, this series followed the same purpose as *Victory at Sea*. Its visual substance was silent and sound film, shot by hundreds of unknown photographers, gathered together and welded into segments or stories — each with a different subject, but all reflecting the dominant theme. Not until late in its evolution did *Air Power* finally turn from historical records to originally shot film. For one of its two final episodes, "Starfighter," the crew visited the Lockheed plant in Burbank and the flight test center of the Air Research and Development Command at Edwards Air Force Base to record the problems encountered in tests on the then new F-104.

The *Air Power* series will probably always remain overshadowed by *Victory at Sea* simply because the latter came first. But Perry Wolff's documentary talents are of the first rank, and history must still assign to *Air Power* its rightful place among the best of American television's historical Theme Documentaries.

THE TWENTIETH CENTURY

The distinction earned by CBS's *The Twentieth Century* is as notable, although of a different kind, as that of its predecessors. Begun in 1957, this series has held to a rigorous and unvarying schedule ever since. Between 1957 and 1961, while *Project XX* presented less than 20 independent productions, *The Twentieth Century* produced 104 individual documentary programs, and by 1964, over 160. For a period of three years, between October 1957 and the onset of the 1960 season, it was the only regularly

WALTER CRONKITE IN *AIR POWER*

. . . CBS scores a victory in the sky.

BURTON BENJAMIN

. . . from films to television — the indispensable story instinct.

scheduled series of its kind on the air, meeting the demands of 26 original shows in each of these years. In its first four years it offered five hour-long programs and 99 half-hours, 90 of which were produced either by Burton Benjamin or Isaac Kleinerman, who joined *The Twentieth Century* after editing the entire *Victory at Sea* series and the first seven *Project XX*'s. *The Twentieth Century*, then, stands as a unique institution in American television documentary solely by virtue of such quantitative accomplishment — although the overwhelming reasons for its importance in television documentary's evolution go beyond the simple volume of productivity.

Executive producer Burton Benjamin brought to this series over ten years of experience as a writer-producer-director at RKO-Pathé, where he had worked on the *This Is America* screen-magazines. Equally creative in fictional and factual storytelling, he had written scripts for major dramatic series in television and executed various documentary writing assignments as well. Benjamin provided the essential story instinct; and when Kleinerman was engaged as an associate producer, a team which had worked together off and on since 1946 (when Kleinerman was a film editor at RKO-Pathé) was reunited. The latter's earlier work at *Project XX* assured *The Twentieth Century* of mastery in filmic construction, and he was given a producer's role in this series in 1961.

The activity of this unit throughout its long history can be divided into three major phases, only the first of which — the compilation history — is treated within this context. In addition to such efforts, however, Benjamin also developed a series of biographies, both compilation and specially shot, and several treatments of current events which brought him to the work of the news documentarist. This breadth of Benjamin's abilities gave the series fuller opportunity to record "the times we live in." It dealt with aspects of great ongoing crises, but with a different, more personal, concentration. It moved — when it chose to do so — more flexibly than *Project XX* into the small stories of recent history, seeking the incidents that reflected the mood and character of a place or an era with greater attention to theme and artistic interpretation.

The way in which *The Twentieth Century* adapted the compilation history approach is of interest, for when the series was initiated in 1957, American audiences had already seen many impressive demonstrations of this method. The urgent stories of conflict in this century had been told in the sweeping expressions of Salomon's early *Project XX* productions, as well as in the *Victory at Sea* and *Air Power* programs. The freshness of the approach had certainly worn off, and yet by 1957 the major film sources had hardly been tapped. There was still much of the past to be shown, and Benjamin's first important innovation was to move the compilation history to "the back of the book."

Early in its history *The Twentieth Century* offered a vivid account of those events at Peenemunde, Germany, in the 1930's and 1940's which changed the course of civilization. Here, in the two-part summation of German experiments in rocketry, "Guided Missile," was examined a lesser, yet important, story which the sweeping treatments could not emphasize. We saw the art of the "back-of-the-book" compilation — the smaller story which did not dominate history's headlines — evolve further in such *Twentieth* productions as "From Kaiser to Fuehrer," where Kleinerman borrowed from, and improved upon, Ruttman. Sequences from Ruttman's film classic of the 1920's, *Berlin*, were integrated within a broader study of the turmoil and terror of the German nation between the wars. The use of clips from the notable amusement park sequence to suggest the hollow, near-hysterical, national atmosphere during the boom-and-bust period in Germany provided a forceful illustration of how art and reportage could be blended.

The Twentieth Century continued to detail the history of major as well as minor stories of bygone eras in such programs as "War in Spain" (for which it was accused of pro-Franco and anti-Franco expressions by zealots at both ends of the political spectrum), "The Windsors," "New York in the Twenties," and "Paris in the Twenties." The latter, in particular, demonstrated how the series could, by narrowing its focus on time and place, maintain the power of thematic expression within a general view of a crowded half century and still create more detailed and intimate studies of people, events, and circumstances. In this way *The Twentieth Century*'s compilation productions complemented the virtues of *Project XX*.

Yet the history of these approaches in *The Twentieth Century* prompts a more specific review of the difficulties posed by the merger of certain journalistic techniques (including the presence of a narrator in a face-to-camera context and the heavy use of the interview) and of aesthetic processes executed by the film editor and compounded by the addition of a musical score.

There is little doubt, for example, that the very presence of Walter Cronkite was a concession to the requirements of the News Documentary. *Project XX* had, of course, used Alexander Scourby and others who were unmistakably performers, but it seldom introduced its narrators visually, other than in brief openings or closings. Benjamin, however, chose the dean of CBS reporters and gave him a more central role in all of its productions. Narrating, setting the problem and its attendant conditions, interviewing, making transitions, and summarizing, Cronkite was never out of sight for very long. His remarks introduced and "covered" the visual material (executing the same function carried out by Huntley in *White Paper* or by the many reporters on *CBS Reports*). This procedure was complicated by an important innovation of Benjamin's — the use of the "eye-witness." Benjamin himself would be the first to admit that the technique was not new to the visual media, and had long since evolved to a high art in radio. But the use of the eye-witness within the compilation history was a departure of significance; it was, in effect, *The Twentieth Century*'s unique contribution to TV documentary.

For its story of the Allied Armies' good fortune at the Remagen Bridge, *The Twentieth Century* found the German captain who had been charged with its defense. For "The Movies Learn to Talk," it enlisted the assistance of Jack Warner, whose company initiated the sound film. In the study of the fall of China, Generals Wedemeyer and Barr recounted the military failures there, and Pearl Buck told of the suffering of the Chinese people. For "The Battle of the Bulge," it found American General McAuliffe and German General von Luttwitz. All in all, *The Twentieth* employed 75 authentic eye-witnesses to the great and small events of the century which it treated in its first 105 productions.

It was the use of this particular technique in Theme Documentary which aroused once more that difference of opinion about documentary method which characterizes a cinematic, as opposed to a television, documentary form. The introduction of the visible reporter and eye-witness in *The Twentieth Century* has raised again the charge that television is merely an "impure" form of the cinema. Speaking of the evolution of TV documentary in Britain, Norman Swallow reminds us that the visible reporter is "decidedly a television device and one that is very much and very rightly despised in the cinema."[2] Swallow's attitude is enlarged upon by the American TV documentarist, Gordon Hyatt:

> Why must a continual flow of talk, or narrative, of the senator behind the desk, the interview, and the statement form the basis of nearly all our documentaries? Why haven't we learned from the film-makers to try to make a film or two — not a spoken newspaper piece or a radio program with visible people?[3]

The controversy echoes the same debate seen in the emergence of aesthetic processes in the News Documentary, where such criticism might be countered by arguing the necessity for control of subject. But we saw in these compilations at *The Twentieth Century* a sharper emphasis upon the control of the theme. Music, as well as Kleinerman's capacity for creating cinematic construction, certainly played an important role in these films. Indeed, an additional innovation of this series was to engage a variety of composers — including such gifted musical talents as Darius Milhaud, Morton Gould, George Antheil, Paul Creston, George Kleinsinger, and Georges Auric. Why, with these talents and in this form, did the visible narrator and the eye-witness figure so importantly in Benjamin's design?

The answers are found in those conditions by which television attains maximum effectiveness as a documentary medium, as well as in the demands imposed upon any series which attempts to meet the most fundamental pressure of American commercial television: a rigid, week-in and week-out schedule. Despite the rapid methods by which film can be shot, collected, and processed for use, the careful and time-consuming work of editing which is at the heart of Theme Documentary must curtail the rate of production. Even a biweekly schedule would be nearly impossible to maintain without the aid of those natural breaks when the reporter or eye-witness can face the audience directly and, with words, carry the story forward. What must be recognized here is the speed and frequency with which *The Twentieth Century* programs are brought before the public.

The use of the interviewer and narrator on camera permitted *The Twentieth* to preserve a high level of quality in its shooting and editing while meeting its demanding schedule. Rather than relax its standards, the series quite naturally adopted the best of alternate documentary methods available. *The Twentieth Century* has preserved quality and quantity; in terms of social effectiveness documentary depends upon both.

The presence of Walter Cronkite, however, is not a mere matter of convenience. It was no accident, for example, that when the *Huntley-Brinkley Report* on NBC threatened to dominate the evening news audience, CBS moved Cronkite into its news program to stem the rating tide. Cronkite is beyond doubt an important national figure. An experienced and astute reporter, he is also a television "star" — a personality whose authority and restraint perpetuate the CBS News tradition. Above all, he commands an audience in his own right. Such use of a star is an added advantage when he is employed in narration of Theme Documentaries.

But another reason underlies the evolution of the narrator and eye-witness. The question was opened by Rudolph Arnheim, who once observed that no really complex series of ideas could be conveyed by visual means alone, an opinion further advanced by Stuart Hood, Director of Television Programs for the BBC. In a discussion of whether some topics involving logical argument at an intellectual plane can be given the simplifying process necessary to mass communication, Hood observed:

> Television is in some ways an imperfect medium for communication. This is partly because the viewer's visual memory can play strange tricks. From a sequence of newsfilm, or from a documentary, it may retain some striking but irrelevant detail — a child's face in a crowd, a gesture, some distracting element. . . . Again, information in itself is useless if it conveys nothing more than a jumble of discrete facts, *disjecta membra*, incoherent and unrelated.[4]

Such comment supports, so it seems, the need for some additional and necessary information which only the spoken word can convey.

The truth, perhaps, is that the arguments of neither the unreconstructed *cinéaste* nor the unrepentant "radio mind" turn upon the crux of the matter — the intimacy of the communication of human character which is television's unique and ultimate achievement. There is nothing more visually compelling than the face of a living being, animated and alive, as he *talks* to us. To understand this we have only to look again at *The Twentieth Century*'s small triumph — "Paris in the Twenties."

To tell its nostalgic story of the American emigration to the City of Light, a great deal of film and a few stills were used against a light and

"PARIS IN THE TWENTIES" — Janet Flanner, "Ike" Kleinerman

. . . television's power — the talking face.

sentimental score. Cronkite introduced the program face-on, then moved to voice-over narration, and soon introduced Janet Flanner. It was she who provided, from her intimate knowledge of those rare days, a genuine feeling of their warmth and gaiety. Her wit, her tone of faint-but-fond reminiscence, and her wistful recollections of the great and near-great created a counterpoint to Cronkite's descriptive narration and an excellent contrast in mood and pace.

Cronkite gave a "sweep" narration: the verbal thread linking together, over the omnipresent *le jazz* background, the rapidly moving bursts of film clips showing the artists' flight to Paris, the invasion of the tourists, the triumph of Lindbergh. But it was Miss Flanner who contributed the slower, more sensitive moments of insight into the life and art of Paris. She reviewed, in gentle and sometimes solemn recollection, the influence and activities of Gertrude Stein, of Scott Fitzgerald, of Picasso. She was the echo of *temps perdus.* Sometimes in face-to-camera close-ups, sometimes voice-over, her verve and grace helped us to share with her the sentiment that "there was a gilt on the cage of life" in the Paris of those days.

On one occasion another eye-witness, Man Ray, described the Dadaist rebellion, leading into a clip from a *cine-poème* he had assembled, and continuing his remembrance of the audience's reaction to it as the collage of light and black raced by. But the dominant and unifying element was Janet Flanner and the total style of her delivery. Paris in the 1920's shone out from her face and echoed hauntingly in her voice, lending to the filmic representation a sweeter meaning — a new sense of that wild and carefree flow of existence on the boulevards and in the cafés.

These "functional" interviews, then, extend beyond reasons of mere procedural convenience. They are also a dramatic contribution; they add an important "you-are-there" aspect to documentary. It is not always sufficient that the viewer witness compilation film on a Murmansk convoy, for instance, or see German planes sinking merchant ships in the Arctic. Another and more immediate phase of such drama is offered when he sees and hears, close up, someone who actually participated in the event and managed to survive. The eye-witness or participant account has long been a vivid contribution to printed journalism, and on film it becomes even more forceful. As further illustration, in *The Twentieth Century*'s two programs on the bomb plots against Hitler there was the effective use of Axel von dem Bussche, an anti-Hitler plotter who is now middle-aged, speaks excellent English, and is unusually intelligent. Having him tell about his participation in the plots was to present a startling form of history. The use of the Countess von Stauffenberg, whose husband planted the bomb in Hitler's headquarters (and who was executed for it), was another such instance. No history book, no matter how deliberately written, can reproduce such an effect, and neither can an over-all compilation film by itself.

Benjamin's instinct for authenticity in a story often led him beyond the eye-witness and to emphasize a new role for the writer. Few television-trained writers were engaged for the series. Instead, Benjamin sought out experienced reporters and worked their special skills and knowledge into the format, coaching them on the limitations of time and the conditions of production, but allowing them to develop their own style and expertise. Hanson Baldwin, military editor of the New York *Times*, wrote "Guided Missile"; an old White House hand, Merriman Smith, wrote "F.D.R.: Third Term to Pearl Harbor"; and similar knowledgeable authors, correspondents, editors, and critics contributed scripts. Nineteen such experts were first brought into television by Benjamin, and their work added further prestige and authority to *The Twentieth Century*.

Although this series successfully attempted other documentary approaches, the discussion here has dealt with only the historical compilation and upon the inherent problems faced by any series which must maintain a *continuing* documentary output. In the widest view of documentary purpose and function, it must be acknowledged that frequency of communication is an important asset. The troubles of our time do not always wait for a new program idea, a new season, or that ultimate perfection which time alone may help the artist to find. *The Twentieth Century* created its documentary immediately, and did it well.

THE VALIANT YEARS

When ABC-TV came to offer a compilation series in the historical-theme documentary, it found the ground thoroughly turned. *Victory at Sea* and *Air Power* had already covered the expenditure of American military power in their programs, and the *Project XX* specials had detailed the decades of this century in terms of its great social and political upheavals. Further, by 1957 *The Twentieth Century* was concentrating upon the events, people, and conditions of those upheavals, ranging among a variety of techniques and combining both Theme and News Documentary approaches.

While the amount of fresh historical footage began to dwindle, there was still film which had not been seen, and even if seen, could be used again within different contexts. (It is difficult to estimate, for example, how many times TV's documentarists have used segments from Leni Riefenstahl's *Triumph of the Will*.) ABC's decision was to review once more World War II, but this time in terms of the life of one man, Winston Churchill. In the fall of 1960 *Winston Churchill: The Valiant Years* was offered to American television audiences. Based upon Churchill's six-volume epic, *The Valiant Years*, it was a series of 26 half-hours in which story and narration were structured upon Churchill's own prose.

The production team for *The Valiant Years* was led by executive producer Jack Le Vien. The working producer was Robert D. Graff, who earned his television experience as producer of NBC's earlier *Wisdom* and of such documentary specials as *Assignment Southeast Asia* and *Assignment India* in the early 1950's. Graff brought his knowledge of both films and theatre to television, and among his first decisions was to enlist Louis Clyde Stoumen as his associate. (Stoumen's admirable record in film documentaries includes Academy Awards for his features, *The True Story of the Civil War* and *The Black Fox*.) Churchill's words were delivered by actor Richard Burton, who simulated the ringing Churchillian style. Gary Merrill served as the narrator and, in keeping with the intention of matching the prestige of similar efforts, Richard Rodgers composed the score.

Visualization for this series followed an established compilation procedure: its stories were primarily traced with collected film footage. Additional emphasis, however, was given by use of animated maps, drawings, and stills — a technique in which Stoumen excelled — in relating the events of that period which began with Churchill's return to office as First Lord of the Admiralty. Specially shot sequences featured re-enactment of a sort by picturing historic locales as narration described what occurred there. Also included were the reflections of many individuals who were involved in events of those troubled years. Approximately a third of *The Valiant Years* involved new footage of this type. Finally, following a pattern established by *The Twentieth Century, Valiant Years* used an impressive number of reporter-writers to fashion individual scripts. Quentin Reynolds, William L. Shirer, and Richard Tregaskis were only a few of the writers who contributed episodes.

The Valiant Years profited from what had preceded it. Graff and Stoumen had had full opportunity to observe eight years of work, and could add to this their own judgments. TV documentary had made use of sub-narrators and eye-witnesses long before 1960, and Churchill's prose had been quoted again and again in earlier programs. Yet there was some distinctiveness to the idea of creating a biographical theme for an entire series. World War II was seen in terms of what Churchill said and did, what concerned him, and how it affected him. The grand theme became the personal theme, and this lent added richness.

The approach of the series is best revealed by analysis of techniques employed in one of its episodes. "The Ravens Return" concerned Churchill's account of the Battle of Britain during those months in 1940 when the *Luftwaffe* first began its incessant bombings. The opening sequences used compilation footage of life in London just after the fall of France, and were followed by specially shot footage of peaceful country towns. The visual then shifted again to already existing film showing the evacuation of the children from London and the critical shortage of British aircraft. This was followed by the first of four eye-witness recollections.[5] In one case an Englishman, in a humorous description of Lord Beaverbrook's hard-driving management, told of the "Beaver's" make-over of the wartime aircraft industry. The account was followed by compilation footage of the first air battles as Nazi bombers came over, and this in turn gave way to the testimony of another eye-witness — an RAF veteran who recalled those battles of over 20 years before.

Some additional specially shot inserts were next employed, leading into compilation scenes of air-ministry planning and dogfights in the air as the RAF grew stronger. This material shifted in content, along with narration, as the Nazis continued their heavy attacks upon London, tracing bombing strikes, the clean-up operations, the people in their shelters, and the anti-aircraft units in action around the city. From this sequence we moved to still a third eye-witness account, by the former commander of London's Anti-Aircraft Defenses, who told how he and Churchill could never agree upon whether too much or too little ammunition had been expended. The pattern continued, making extensive use of historical footage for the balance of the program, relieved by one final eye-witness; Churchill's housekeeper at Number 10 Downing Street, who told of activities there during the heaviest raids. The Quentin Reynolds script featured its own natural climax (the last raids on London) and provided a moment of triumphant resolution

after "Britain's darkest hour" when we again looked upon calm and peaceful skies. But the words of Churchill himself provided the unforgettable
denouement: "Never in the field of human conflict was so much owed by
so many to so few."

The Valiant Years all but completed the innovations within those
major compilation series which dominated the network Theme Documentary. By 1961 the field was occasionally represented by programs of NBC's
Project XX, NBC's *Special Projects,* and CBS's *The Twentieth Century.* It
was as though all the television classics that could be woven out of the photographic and filmic records of this century had been achieved. Henceforth
compilation at the networks focused primarily upon the "back-of-the-book"
feature and the occasional up-dating of a great era gone by.

THE ENTERTAINMENT COMPILATION

We have reviewed to this point only those efforts which were created
under the control and supervision of American television networks. Few
nationally seen documentaries were produced outside the networks, and for
the most part the planning and execution of these were confined to New
York. The influence of the Hollywood film industry, which by the mid-
1950's had become a strong factor in television entertainment programming
(both network and syndication), had never caught hold in the documentary
field. Yet before 1959 this system had not really been tested, largely because
few who were engaged in production of Hollywood's staple — entertainment
— paid much attention to documentary or that strange and foreboding
invention of broadcasting called "news and public affairs."

The single figure who broke this pattern was David Lloyd Wolper, who
was not a creative producer so much as an entrepreneur who grew from a
film salesman's role to become an important force in American TV documentary. His initial work came within the compilation tradition, and the
bulk of his output has remained there. Within three years after his first venture into the movement, David Wolper became America's third largest
producer of documentaries for television.

The conditions which favored Wolper's entry into national television
originated in 1961, when Newton Minow, then Chairman of the Federal
Communications Commission, charged that American television was a "vast
wasteland." The phrase generated more than controversy. To be sure, there
was little that any governmental agency could do to influence existing network programs in news and public affairs — other than to stimulate an increasing number of such efforts. But America's television station owners,
even when they demonstrated a public consciousness and a desire to present
more informational programming, were hard-pressed to find the range of
talent required to produce convincing documentaries. Many began to develop such creative specialists within their own staffs, and others intensified

the work of units already in existence. All stations, however, now were seeking significant informational material to add to their schedules — programs which might not only attract sizable audiences, but earn the plaudits of the FCC.

Wolper's first documentary program, "The Race for Space," was carried by 105 local TV stations in April 1960, and for the first time a non-network documentary received near-national audience coverage.

After a second compilation offering, "Project — Man in Space," Wolper's unit was enlarged. With Jack Haley, Jr. as his working producer and Elmer Bernstein scoring productions, Wolper began to hire additional talent from networks. From *The Twentieth Century* he brought Mel Stuart, who was formerly associated with the early *Project XX* at NBC and was a film researcher for *Victory at Sea*. From *CBS Reports* he hired Arthur Swerdlow, and for some narrational assignments added Mike Wallace. Later he employed Marshall Flaum, who had done research, and written two of Benjamin's scripts, at *The Twentieth Century*. Alan Landsburg was brought from NBC Radio. Retaining most of his original "Race for Space" unit, by 1962 Wolper Productions had a staff of over 200 employees.

Wolper found that there were some documentaries which networks, too, would carry — so long as they could be classed as "entertainment" documentaries and thus not conflict with the networks' direct supervision of their public-affairs programming. While such documentaries as Wolper's "D-Day" and "The Making of a President" were eventually given network approval and aired, Wolper had his own second thoughts about the matter of public affairs as opposed to entertainment documentaries. He turned to the Hollywood studios for a series of historical compilations on the motion picture, told in terms of those perennial stars and lavish productions which had been a part of American life for nearly a half century. In November 1961 his "Hollywood: The Golden Years" was telecast on NBC-TV, and was followed by two more such special programs, "Hollywood: The Fabulous Era" and "Hollywood: The Great Stars." These were simply organized documentaries, relying upon the drawing power of clips from old feature films and a narration by established players.

By 1963 Wolper's unit had also developed (for NBC) a series of half-hour "miniature specials" on Hollywood, using star-types and Hollywood eras as a basis for thematic structure. Along with these, his unit had created an additional series of compilation-biographies and many specially shot biographical treatments, both for syndication, as well as six historical compilations released in late 1963: "The Yanks Are Coming," "December 7 — The Day of Infamy," "American Women in the 20th Century," "Ten Seconds That Shook the World," "Berlin: Kaiser to Khrushchev," and "Rise and Fall of American Communism." By early 1964 these were being shown on over 70 local stations.

In reviewing Wolper's work it may be said that not until his 1964

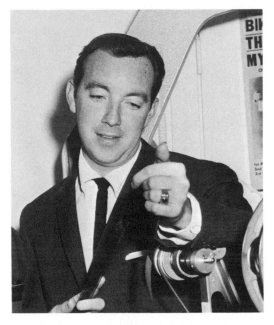

JACK HALEY, JR.

. . . a new force in American TV documentary.

MEL STUART, DAVID WOLPER, THEODORE H. WHITE

. . . in 1964, a poignant story, a great writer, an Emmy.

Emmy-winning special based upon Theodore H. White's "The Making of a President" did any of it carry the mark of first-rate writing — and in this case success was due in large measure to White's own script and the poignancy of the death of John F. Kennedy. Throughout all of the "Hollywood Specials" much of the creative originality belonged to those who first made the films which Wolper's editors clipped together. Many of the "miniature specials" descended to the level of the teen-ager's fan magazine, their narration often slipping from honest nostalgia to banal sentimentality. To be sure, there were brilliantly edited sequences within some of these, among the most notable being a "summation" of James Cagney's career — shooting, dying, falling, fighting, manhandling the ladies, and then shooting again. Within the entire compilation form, however, the achievements of David Wolper should not be casually dismissed. His unit has attracted considerable attention, and the entertainment documentary itself is a part of the story of our society which deserves to be told. The additional work of his unit has also had importance, and will be reviewed later.[6]

From *Air Power* to Wolper's entertainment documentaries, the work described above represents television's continuing effort to bring the past to life for massive audiences. If he owned a television station, Carl Sandburg once said, he would fill the screen "with history — TV out of the past." This has been the commitment of the men whose productions have been reviewed here. Instructed by the classic documentary compilations and inspired by Henry Salomon, each theme documentarist, pursuing his own judgments, has brought experiment, innovation, and creative spirit to the task of telling millions that "this is the way it was."

9 / Human Drama: Biographers to Plot-Finders

IT HAS BEEN IMPLIED here that there is a difference between those documentaries which seek to make the lives of men in action *dramatic* and those which attempt to create a *drama* from the raw material of life. Both aims employ certain techniques of storytelling to assure that change and conflict in the documents are intensified, emphasized, and structured so as to create for the viewer a steadily rising line of involvement leading toward a resolution. The methods in fiction are distinguished largely as they follow Aristotle's dictum that the creator may imitate by narration — in which case he can take another personality, as Homer does — or he may present all his characters as "living and moving before us."

If the story of human life is to carry a theme of purpose, it must reveal, whether in a narrative or dramatic form, elements within the human character which do not display him as merely passing through the external conditions of life. He must actively respond to life's circumstances, reacting as they arise and making decisions which reveal the operation of his private will. Biography must let us sense this exertion of will. If it cannot, as drama does, put such effort before our eyes, it must then constantly suggest it by careful attention to what is narrated and what is pictorially presented.

In documentary, where all people shown are, in the truest sense, "living and moving before us," the difference between the narrative and the dramatic is not so clear. The documentary which sets out to treat a single life — drawing therefrom a human theme of crisis-met-and-mastered — can never be completely free of some narrative device whereby the documen-

180

tarist *tells* us something about this crisis as well as *shows* us the contributing causes. Yet once the documentary in television began to concentrate upon stories of a biographical nature, focusing upon the individual life or the lives of a small, interacting group, there was also created the possibility of shaping such stories by principles of dramaturgy. In the biography movement within television Theme Documentary we may discern the stages through which these accounts of individual experience moved from a pure narrative to a nearly pure dramatic form.

NARRATIVE BIOGRAPHY

It is in the recording of lives out of the past, notably in the historical biographies of *Project XX, The Twentieth Century*, and David Wolper Productions, that we witness the strongest emphasis upon a narrative form — a form in which the storyteller sets out to relate the conflict and crisis of a life, and then finds the visual and aural records which will support that conflict which he *says* existed.

This search for and use of such records poses special problems for the documentarist working in historical biography. He must first recognize that his efforts can never truly capture the essence of lesser lives of the past within independent contexts. As De Voto observed and Salomon and Hyatt demonstrated, he can only find the isolated single pictures of forgotten faces, couple these with brief transitional phrases, and "blend and generalize" them into an emotional context with other faces and phrases in order to establish a story about a *kind* of life, a general statement about human experience — the life, for example, of American pioneers in "The Real West." And even when there are sufficient written records of a lesser individual life upon which to build a biographical study, the chances of discovering visual records to reconstruct that life are slight. It is history's edict that the unobtrusive life goes unnoticed.

The point would need little elaboration were it not that it leads directly to an understanding of the difficulties inherent within the alternate possibility — the documentation of the great and important lives in history. Here the visual records are often numerous; yet the very fact that they *do* exist limits their value toward the revelation of a human will in action. Such records were made almost exclusively under conditions in which the individual displayed his public, not private, self. Hence, they rarely reveal the personal *Angst* and joy which frame the larger humanity. The gray area, in which today both a camera and a microphone can be brought to bear upon a public figure as he undergoes crisis, is impossible to reconstruct from materials in the historical past. The records of the great lives of history were normally made for journalistic rather than artistic purposes.

So it is that the historical biographies of television have dealt not only exclusively with the famous, but generally only with those of whom visual records are in sufficient abundance to provide biographers with that range of choice and selection which will aid them in revealing the personal crisis.

Project XX seldom created independent biographical treatments of individuals, and when it did, either within the still-picture or compilation-film method, the burden of exposition was shifted to the words of a narrator. Oddly enough, this narrative emphasis enjoyed greater success in such total still-photo studies of Lincoln and Mark Twain than in the compilation-film treatments of Will Rogers and Gary Cooper.

It is as though filmed records are less capable of supporting those emotional overtones which can be drawn from a series of carefully selected stills. Film may be more revealing, of course, of physical attributes — of the *wholeness* of a man in action — but for that very reason it is often less useful to the narrative storyteller. Because the film is more likely to have been made in a broader public situation, the possibility of witnessing expressions which are private and inward are reduced. More important, however, is the limitation which the very authority of the record places upon itself, making film more difficult to structure in an unrelated context. There is, for example, very little film of Will Rogers which shows him in any other way than we have come to remember him. Even while "relaxing," Will could not resist perpetuating his public role by clowning before the camera. The suggestion that he experienced the same concerns as ordinary men was better provided in those moments when a still picture, supported by music and explained by words, gave us an *impression,* rather than a record, of the American humorist. The implication thereby of the meaning of life was perhaps just as strong as it might have been had we seen him during moments of privacy.

At *Project XX* the few productions dealing with individual historical biographies were given the form of crisis-met-and-mastered by the art of writing — by a story structure determining the point of view — which, in turn, dictated the selection of supportive visual and aural records. The same principle was applied at *The Twentieth Century,* which initiated the biographical approach in its first 1957 program, "Winston Churchill, Man of the Century," and continued it throughout a series of compilation-biographies of such figures as Woodrow Wilson, Gandhi, Mussolini, Theodore Roosevelt, Goering, Al Smith, and Wendell L. Willkie. Because the element of "public performance" was evident in most of the footage employed in these productions, the more intimate moments of these lives had to be structured first in words. Here Benjamin's use of the eye-witness — providing verbal reflections upon the subject — added immensely to each treatment.

More important, perhaps, to the technique of presenting biography from the past is the simple recognition by *The Twentieth Century* of Emerson's declaration that "there is properly no history; only biography." By framing its studies of individuals within the larger events of the age in which they lived, *The Twentieth* stressed the conflicts of man against society. Here the lack of records which emphasized the private conflict of man against himself, or man against man, was of less importance. The portrait of Teddy Roosevelt became a history of his times, the rise of Goering was made a part of the whole evolution of Naziism, and Woodrow Wilson's conflict was told in terms of his fight for peace. The story — point of view — shifted to a broader base, and the subject of a human life became less vital than what that life represented in an era.

Early in 1962 David Wolper Productions also began a series of historical biographies told with the compilation-film method. Produced by Jack Haley, Jr., the *Biography* series was released in syndication through Official Films and has received a heavy showing over local stations. Although generally uneven in quality, the individual production was commendable when its characters were set against the greater social changes of their time — and when the sources of footage were rich enough to permit a still greater range of selection in showing the triumphs and failures of that life in the most personal of terms. The two-part study of Harry Truman was outstanding, as was the story of Babe Ruth. Yet other studies were often flat and uninteresting, and the narration of Mike Wallace or the musical score of Elmer Bernstein could not bring to life such figures as Richard Byrd or Nazi hero Erwin Rommel. In both of these biographies the weakness of visual illustration was compounded by a written narrative which also failed to intensify the exertion of will. The narration merely followed a chronology, and too often there was no relationship at all between the verbal and visual accounts of one man's decision to change the course of history. We were left, in such biographical accounts, with a simple recounting of events that carried none of the interplay between the character and the situation.

It is this interplay which, in the deepest sense, constitutes the plot of any story; and when all elements of production are not brought to bear upon its revelation we have no "story" — merely a chronology incapable of sustaining a theme.

But there remains another possibility for creating a biographical documentary: making drama from life. Biography in any form, we have noted, seeks out the facts of life to elicit therefrom a meaningful statement. Documentary seeks to make drama from the facts of human existence. Because it involves the record of the actual it may pull the biographical account closer to the structure of formal drama and away from the narrative form. It can present the view of a protagonist "living and moving before us," and this carries it closer to the structure of drama — of rising action, crisis, and resolution — all played out before us in time as a protagonist seeks to exert his will in the overcoming of obstacles. The historical biography approach, even at its best, minimizes the possibility of showing such action, moving as it does away from drama and toward the biographical novel. The storyteller, concerned primarily with narration, has supremacy.

THE WORLDS OF BILLY GRAHAM, JACQUELINE KENNEDY, BOB HOPE

. . . not what life is, *but what it* means.

One method is not aesthetically superior to the other. Each is a distinct genre: and we must recognize that the art of making drama, rather than dramatic narrative, from the raw material of life can be done most effectively when the story of individual life is moved into the present, and can be achieved only when the totality of a dramatic crisis, unfolding in life itself, is captured and set in motion before us.

LIVING BIOGRAPHY

Advances toward this hope of making drama from life came when TV documentarists proceeded to record a life in the present, where the "struggles within" still burned, could be captured by the camera and the microphone, and then woven into a story. Once this step was taken, the question of recording the "small" life lost importance, and Burton Benjamin's plea for a kind of documentary which looks at "man from the inside out"[2] became the *leitmotif* for a great number of TV documentarists.

Benjamin had asked for the "little" film about man, implying by "little" not the size of the life portrayed so much as the scope of the portrayal. Even with conventional equipment, and discounting the added possibilities afforded by new technology for recording intimate human expression, the documentarist working with the living subject could examine not only the personal moods of ordinary men in a style which Mosel, Chayefsky, *et al*, had first brought to television over a decade ago, but could also reveal the inner states of those who were far from ordinary. After 1961 several TV units brought about a new evolution in Theme Documentary, and the great changes they wrought suggest unlimited possibilities.

A transitional phase must be noted in which historical narrative was combined with the direct recording of the "inward crisis" — several biographical programs which NBC's *Special Projects* created for Purex in 1961 and 1962, *The World of* ———. For this series, production responsibility was in the hands of Eugene S. Jones, who engaged Joseph Liss as his writer and Alexander Scourby as narrator. A group of cameramen led by Cy Avnet recorded the lives of the important subjects chosen for inclusion. The visual sources, edited by John Christophel, included stills, existing footage, and a great deal of freshly shot material.

For its first program the unit chose Bob Hope as its subject, following with portraits of individuals who were not only colorful, but newsworthy — Jimmy Doolittle, Jacqueline Kennedy, Sophia Loren, Billy Graham, Darryl F. Zanuck, Benny Goodman, and Maurice Chevalier. A few of these productions were exceptional in their intricate and reflective assessments of the deeper meaning of these interesting lives. The series demonstrated that it could effect "showmanship" by selecting figures who were great audience-pullers in their own right, yet moved beyond mere biographical details to reveal the personal *raison d'être*. The success of *The World of* ——— lay in its thematic concepts, involving in execution a carefully controlled relationship of all elements which contributed to this larger statement.

In *The World of* ———— we became aware how two parallel influences in the TV documentary of the 1960's were moving together. The narrative tradition of *Project XX* was present, and was best illustrated in the stylistic unity and flow of such sequences as those devoted to the girlhood of Jacqueline Kennedy, wherein Robert Emmett Dolan's score, a script treatment by Liss which included bits of Mrs. Kennedy's own girlish poetry, and a mixture of stills in motion were all complemented by Scourby's precise phrasing. It was a sequence which was never allowed to become sentimental. The same kind of narrative approach gave to similar sequences in the portraits of Bob Hope and Billy Graham a finely drawn insight and power.

But these were sequences employing visual and aural records of the past, and lent themselves naturally to full narrative treatment. Even when the specially shot footage of the current lives of the subjects was used, the narrative overlay was predominant. The story-mind was still in control of the entire process.

These series also included scenes in which the mobile-camera technique was utilized to allow the figures to reveal themselves. Here formal narration dropped off, and emphasis shifted to the essentially dramaturgical method of setting characters "living and moving before us." In "The World of Bob Hope" we saw a nervous, natural recording of events and characters in the entertainer's milieu — an exciting succession in which the unobtrusive camera revealed the frenetic rush of Hope's life. The camera patiently "studied" Hope, as it did Billy Graham, Benny Goodman, and Jimmy Doolittle in other programs, in moments when the subject paused to reflect and consider. Gone was the interviewer and his "structuring" questions; we saw these people alone, out of the public context, as protagonists in the eternal conflict of man against himself.

Some additional methods of this kind seen throughout the series included the loosely structured discussion, portions of direct intercut comments about a subject by the people close to him (best executed in the Bob Hope and Billy Graham programs), such extraneous movement-adding techniques as the "interview-in-the-moving-automobile," and a skillful interweaving into the story of considerable stock news footage (best done in the story of Mrs. Kennedy).

Particularly startling was a devastating scene in a Manchester pub in the Billy Graham story. This stark *verité* record of the tragedy of small lives in a fierce world showed how powerfully the unobtrusive camera can operate in that situation where noise, smoke, and liquor have dulled human sensibilities to that point at which, if a subject is aware of the camera at all, he regards it as a roistering companion. In the white-masked face of the pub songstress there was little human characteristic whatever. No other depiction of despair could have set the contrast for Billy Graham's exhortations to Manchesterians nearly so well.

EUGENE S. JONES

... biography in transition.

Yet throughout this series the moments of intensity of inward expression were too fragmented to hold the fullness of the crisis and resolution. They were not structured for us in themselves. Narration was necessary to move us from witnessing the inward conflict to a clear understanding of its meaning. The sequences of people in concentration still only said to us "here is an interesting life." The imposed structure from without told us "this is what this life means." In *The World of* ————, however, we observed the transition which had come over the biographical method in documentary as it sought to focus upon contemporary individual lives.

DRAMATIC BIOGRAPHY

The Twentieth Century also offered several "living biographies" — specially shot stories based on major and minor figures of the times, ranging from a professional football player to a dedicated American doctor working abroad. These programs still further evolved toward dramatic biography as the unit showed us more and more of the inward and outward conflicts of men as they were actually experienced. The idea of crisis-met-and-mastered began to dominate these documentaries. Formal narration was reduced, the camera and the viewer became more involved — more a part of the action — and the words which were spoken bore a closer resemblance to dramatic dialogue itself.

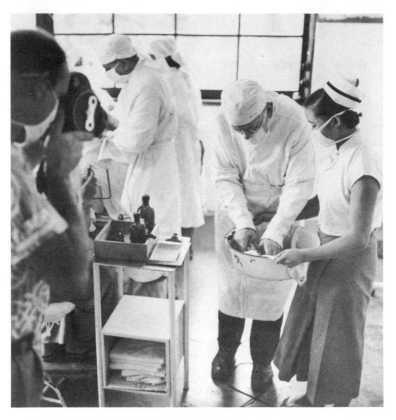

"THE BURMA SURGEON" (CBS-TV's *The Twentieth Century*)

. . . the conditions superb, the timing flawless.

In "The Violent World of Sam Huff" there was still much narration "from the outside" as we were told of things which were happening to the football star during his training period, but the influence of the mobile-camera (and natural-sound) methods led to such an innovation as putting a microphone in Huff's padding during a scrimmage game. We heard the thuds, the grunts, and shouts of men in physical contact. (The technique was repeated in a later study of a professional hockey player with equally forceful results.) Throughout, there was the excitement of felt experience, but these moments were still interwoven into the narrative form decreed by the storyteller.

One of these biographies offered by *The Twentieth Century* stands out, not only as a record of a magnificent life, but also in terms of a technique which brought the biographical documentary even further away from the narrative form. This was "The Burma Surgeon," the story of Dr. Gordon Seagrave and his life of service to the Burmese people. The program held a form and structure in which a human life was *shown* within a moment of crisis, as well as told about and illustrated by the visual record.

Although "The Burma Surgeon" contained some continuing narration, this was built entirely upon the reflections of Seagrave himself. The details of his daily existence were provided by his own thoughts, by the use of the contrapuntal voice-over. We saw Doctor Seagrave in his office, examining patients as he talked about the massive health problems of the Burmese and how he tried to help overcome them. We heard exposition about his life, but in the patterns and figures of his own speech. Some scenes were obviously reconstructed as the unit attempted to catch him in typical moments (chiding his devoted nursing staff for tying "granny-knots" in bandages, cheering on his team as he loped awkwardly about a softball field near the hospital). In these scenes Seagrave's image and speech carried the slightly self-conscious behavior of all who feel the presence of cameras and microphones. But when he looked at us directly and talked of his crushing disappointments and hard-won successes, and when he told us about his fears for the future, we saw a life in which all the elements of drama were movingly present.

But this biographical study of the Burma surgeon also went beyond the subtlety of inward crisis to the depiction of outward events which constitute a climax of *dramatic proportions* — a climax in which Seagrave was a living character, moving and speaking, acting and reacting. By a careful reconstruction in time of real events recorded, the program was brought to a climactic moment where Seagrave delivered a baby:

> The delivery is complicated, and there is some concern over whether the child will survive. "How's that baby doin'!" demands Seagrave urgently as he continues to attend the weakened mother. We cut directly to a full close-up of a nurse's face — her dark, anxious eyes above the white surgical mask — as she administers oxygen to the child. The tension mounts, then is broken by the wail of the baby and more cuts to the smiling faces of the nurses. The crisis has passed, but our emotions are not fully released until we hear Seagrave's moving statement: "When you've got a live mother and a live baby you've got a mother that's *more* than alive, Granny used to say."

The dramatic conditions were superb, the timing flawless. A true moment of dramatic crisis had been made by the documentarist. From this climax we moved to the sense of resolution — an inward and outward balancing of life's forces which sets the viewer at ease. In the closing scene there was a wide shot of the hospital at Nahmkahm, and we followed Seagrave as he got into his battered old sedan and drove up the winding path. A lazy pan trailed the car as it moved off, and we heard the voice-over reflections of a man nearing the end of a long and useful life as he confessed his fear of going back to America because he "may die there"; for unless he dies "right here in Nahmkahm" the people he has served will lose their faith in him.

Perhaps in no other program of the early 1960's was there a better example of how the documentary might move toward a change in form than in "The Burma Surgeon." Here we were confronted with the possibility that the camera and microphone could be taken into areas of life where the potential interplay of character and situation might not only reveal the meaning of a life but might also lead to some inevitable crisis of major proportions for a central character — a protagonist who carries audience sympathy with him — which must be resolved in *life*.

This program, and others which followed a similar pattern, calls attention to the question of "legitimate reconstruction" of living records. The argument is better reviewed after an examination of other developments in dramatic biography, but we may note at once that there was often no relationship in time to what was heard and seen in "The Burma Surgeon." The entire climactic scene may have been recorded on the first day of shooting, while the opening scenes may have been saved for the last day. Voice-over lines may have been recorded later or earlier than the visual documents over which they were spoken. In such reconstruction freedom of time is most essential. So long as the documents themselves are actual, both the news documentarist and theme documentarist must possess this freedom if they are to construct a story. This has always been the license of both fact and fiction narrative.

We must not lose sight, however, of the fact that "The Burma Surgeon," while it is a dramatic biography, remained essentially narrative in structure and form. It was not drama. Narration of other times, places, and conditions was still a part of Seagrave's function. He still carried the role of the *Sprecher* who informed us what had happened, what was happening, and what might happen. To be sure, within the story there were elements of true drama, and these were combined into the story-in-time to give us the sense of suspense, of rising action, and of a final crisis of deep intensity. The *structure* was dramatic, but the action was not a drama. Borrowing only those techniques of *verité* which seek to reduce subject self-consciousness before the camera and microphone, all other techniques in "The Burma Surgeon" were carry-overs from the narrative form, particularly the compression and rearrangement of editing and the emphasis upon spoken narration. Editing — in words and pictures — must always take place in any story, but the *verité* approach holds the possibility of reducing editing to a minimum.

The break with the story narrative itself came when documentarists moved to combine *plot-finding* with the "picture logic" of *verité* at a new level of synthesis. This evolution was seen, in its initial stages, in some of the work of David Wolper Productions, which moved to "living biography" when it made two specially shot films, "The Biography of a Rookie" and "The Rafer Johnson Story." "We call these dramatic documentaries," said Wolper, "and we try to make them like any other drama with a hero, a villain, a conflict and a climax."[3]

In these documentaries Wolper's unit was seeking the natural man and the natural story, and the free camera was employed to add a sense of excitement. The idea of personal conflict dominated these early sports-centered films, as the crew pursued the struggle to its own conclusion with the *verité* method of finding the loosely structured situation and relentlessly following it to its end, all the while using wild-sound recording and the unobtrusive camera.

These two programs were successful enough to lead Ziv-United Artists to engage Wolper to make a series of similar stories for syndication release; and Wolper soon developed *The Story of* ———— series, 38 programs of which were released to local stations beginning in 1962. Subjects were chosen from among the more interesting types in our society — a boxer, a singer, an artist, a prisoner, a patroness of the arts — none of whom were well known, but all of whom were out of the ordinary. Yet producer Mel Stuart, under the influence of a technique which is difficult to control, occasionally let the dramatic concept evade him. In the earlier "The Biography of a Rookie" there was that sharply focused man-against-man conflict as a young baseball player competed against others for the right to play. In this context the *verité* method let us share the conflict-within aspects of the life portrayed. These same outward-and-inward elements were dwelt upon in "The Rafer Johnson Story," a recounting of a young American Negro's victory over social obstacles.

But such later productions as "The Story of a Patroness" — a study of a wealthy San Francisco woman devoted to encouraging the arts — leads us to question the validity of the loosely structured situation wherein the elements which shape a thematic statement about a life are lacking. This program, as Robert Lewis Shayon has pointed out,[1] presented no more than a study of eccentricity — of a life in which no real crisis, inward or outward, existed at all. Surely there should have been some sense of dedication in this life, some reason for her interest, and yet the records did not even suggest it. The patroness was obviously doing something worthwhile, but we were not led, as we were in *The World of* ———— treatment of Jacqueline Kennedy, to understand why.

There are, of course, generic differences between *The Story of* ———— and *The World of* ————, and these extend beyond the selection of "important" and "unimportant" names (although the very significance of the lives portrayed is related to some greater expression of the theme of one human being's existence). The difference is the *verité* technique of the loosely structured situation, and herein lies, again, the separation between art and record. By setting out to record an "interesting" life as it is lived, the documentarist can give us no assurance that what will happen must have a meaning. In one sense the *verité* biographer and the "theme" biographer can be distinguished by whether the determination of what is said rests solely with the camera-recorder, or whether his work (*verité* or not in the techniques of recording) is subject to the larger point of view overlaid upon a production by writers and/or producers. Great drama can exist in records alone — a possibility noted in earlier considerations of the still photographer's work — but it can also be an expression of conflict which does not build toward a larger theme-producing totality. Without careful preselection and the purposeful recording of a life there exists the constant danger of statement without meaning.

The question remains: Can the combination of the loose structure and the excitement of the free camera be applied in those life situations where the full form and structure of drama already exists — where, however loosely a situation is recorded, some dynamic and dramatic form holds an *a priori* existence and a protagonist, rising action, climax, and resolution? This is the challenge which some documentarists have sought to meet. Their solutions have had considerable impact, for in the course of their work we witnessed the documentary producer becoming, in effect, a dramatist — a playwright with a camera whose function is not to *make* plots, but to *find* them in life itself.

Circle Theatre: The Plot-Makers

We cannot overlook the aims and functions of a very popular and — by television's standards — venerable dramatic program series, *Armstrong Circle Theatre*. Because it made use of actors, scenery, and theatrical conventions, *Circle Theatre* remains outside the documentary form, and yet, in its attempts to create drama based upon "indisputable fact," the series requires our attention. There is, indeed, some justification for believing that the reason for its demise in 1963 is the simple truth that the television documentary was doing better and more truthfully the job which *Circle Theatre* had set for itself.

Circle Theatre came into network television as a half-hour fictional drama series in 1950. As TV's live drama began to wane by 1955 — as the hour-long drama series left the air — *Circle Theatre* took a different route. It chose to stay in New York studios and continue to originate live production. Instead of giving up, as others had done, in the difficult search for original material, it chose to observe Philip Dunne's dictum that "truth is not only stranger, but *stronger* than fiction," and went to the factually based story.

This "documentary-drama" series was initiated in February 1955 with a program based on the account of a hard-bitten prospector who made a 60-million-dollar uranium strike. This was fairly routine drama, with all the elements of despair, crisis, and eventual triumph as the miner persisted in his search even after so formidable an agency as the Atomic Energy Commission had declared barren the land he was exploring. It was a rags-to-riches story of the Sunday supplement variety, but the difference was that it was "true" in every last dramatic detail.

Among the general principles which *Circle Theatre* established in its search for stories was the demand for "the theme of success over obstacles, long-awaited and long-deserved, hope fulfilled, or a crisis met and mastered." Its selection criteria called for "understandable problems," which would include "basic situations that anyone can grasp, and situations in which anyone can find himself." Next it was suggested that "basic human characteristics must be behind each triumph — courage, honor, love, righteousness, honesty."[5]

Executive producer David Susskind engaged Robert Costello as producer for *Circle Theatre.* Costello set further guidelines for an approach to the unique format, observing:

> We aim to combine fact and drama — to arouse interest, even controversy, on important and topical subjects. . . . We support them with authoritative statements by recognized leaders in specified fields. . . . We can't use an idea only or a news story only, we must also be able to present some potential solution, some hope for our citizens to consider, to think about.[6]

With a team of specialists brought mainly from dramatic series, Costello worked toward a format which offered two basic methods of dramatization. In certain cases it was found advantageous to deal directly with a real person, and in others it was found best to create a purely fictional character which represented several real people or a shared attitude. Costello's writers were sometimes pushed to create real or composite characters which were founded upon accurate factual observation, and yet also had range and depth as characters in their own right. The link to documentary now was broken.

The history of *Circle Theatre,* when set alongside documentary developments in American TV after 1959, significantly reveals an increasing duplication of subjects treated. Not only did the series present parallel treatments of many controversial and newsworthy social problems attempted by the News Documentary, but its smaller "back-of-the-book" theme dramas were also given identical attention in terms of actual documentation. The series revealed, in its inclusion of such documentary programs as *Project XX*'s "Nightmare in Red" and an expanded version of *The Twentieth Century*'s "The Burma Surgeon," its own incapacities. It was forced to acknowledge the limitations of its own mutant form. However authentic *Circle Theatre* might have been, as a form it was really neither fish nor fowl. On the one hand, its commitment to the faithful duplication of events and people limited its freedom as drama; on the other, the use of actors and theatrical conventions deprived it of any validity as documentary.

Circle Theatre failed to recognize that documentary and fictional drama not only cannot exist side by side in television, but can better strengthen and inform each other only when they do exist independently. The two are, in principle easily kept apart. One gives the statement of a human event to a plot-maker, and the other to a plot-finder, a recorder of life whose ability to fashion the elements of plot is limited by the nature of the event. One consciously and deliberately represents fictional people in fictional situations, and the other, by custom, may *represent* in extremely limited terms only when it cannot *present* reality. Drama can use the interplay of fictional situation and fictional character to the end of creating a crisis and a resolution which *satisfy* an audience, not in the sense of an "up-beat" ending, but as an outcome which closes the system of events and leaves the audience psychologically at rest. It is this "closed-system" resolution which completes that ordering of life we call dramatic art. Documentary can offer such a closed system only when an event inherently possesses this possibility, and when the documentarist can capture it in life as it unfolds. This was the whole thrust of the work of Robert Drew and Irving Gitlin.

THE LIVING CAMERA

When Robert Drew turned away from the often unstructured, raw conflicts of great and immediate social import, as well as from attempts to present public figures in private crises, his work displayed immense power. Drew found a significant place in television's documentation of life when he moved from treatments of ongoing public crises to the study of the individual moments of stress, a statement which could be made in the terms of the artist. When he engaged in the theme-controlled documentary, he found a true home for that restless experimental technique which he had been instrumental in bringing to television.

In 1963 Drew Associates completed a series of ten programs devoted to people in crises, productions which traced — with "picture logic" — a crucial day, week, or month in the lives of their subjects. Released in syndication, the series was titled *Living Camera* and described as unique entertainment. "It's unscripted, it's unrehearsed . . . for the first time the camera is a man. It sees, it hears, it moves like a man. . . ." If Drew changed his métier from "journalism" to "entertainment," the technique remained the same. He had simply entered a phase of documentary work in which human insight and revelation were set into an almost pure dramaturgical structure, and the combination of approach and technique was remarkably effective. "Like the best of the novelists," stated a descriptive brochure for this series, "the *Living Camera* truly enters into the life of its subjects and lays bare, layer by layer, their character under stress."[7] Despite Drew's eagerness to dissociate these documentaries from "theatre drama or the kind of television drama that has hitherto existed," his efforts nevertheless revealed that essential characteristic of drama which, William Archer insisted, is the "art of crisis."

The eventual evolution toward the "living camera" was implied in Drew's first nationally shown Theme Documentary, his 1962 "On the Road to Button Bay." This colorful and sentimental *tour de force*, made to commemorate the 50th anniversary of the Girl Scouts of America, disclosed for the first time how forceful and intriguing a device is the free-swinging pursuit of the loosely structured situation, especially when the latter holds the possibility for meaningful revelation of the smaller life.

The very success of Drew's method in "Button Bay" stressed the reason for its failure in almost all of the News Documentaries which Drew's unit produced. The recording method — tracking a series of interplays between characters and ever-changing situations — occurred within a broader study of the travels of a troop of Kansas Girl Scouts to a jamboree in Vermont. In "Button Bay" there was a natural rising action, a crisis for a central human being, and a sentimental and poignant denouement. The protagonist with whom all could readily identify was the troop leader, who in the course of the trip passed through an important stage in her inward growth from a girl to a young woman. This inevitable crisis, outwardly expressed in a tearful scene with the adult leader when the girl finally came to grips with her responsibilities, represented Drew's finest achievement in the documentary —a true dramatic form built out of living experience captured informally, and for the most part when the subject was totally preoccupied with her problem.

"Button Bay" was a tribute to the entire concept of the "gray area" which Drew and his associates could never hope to create in their studies of the terrible ongoing crises of men and societies. Men do not become "gray" before the camera when the fate of societies rests upon their actions, and the great public controversies of a society do not lend themselves to dramatic form simply because they are never really in a state of either-or resolution. But in "Button Bay" the unity of climax and resolution was inherent in the story.

In the *Living Camera* series Drew's purpose became surer, the focus narrower, and the crises depicted more direct and specific in terms of a sharp either-or moment of resolution. This series treated human beings who, in terms of outward action, were heading for a crisis of greater magnitude. We saw a driver getting ready for a critical race, Jane Fonda preparing for an opening night, two football coaches just before a crucial game, and similar examinations of human beings who were undergoing inward stress because they faced an outward crisis which, in one way or another, would close the system. Of these, none carried a greater significance — a more definite finality — than "The Chair."

In "The Chair" Drew's film-makers found all the eternal elements of the great courtroom drama clearly set in motion, with an inevitable crisis impending. The film detailed the case of Paul Crump, a Negro convicted of murder over a decade ago and sentenced to die. Through a series of legal

"ON THE ROAD TO BUTTON BAY" (Robert Drew Associates for CBS-TV)

. . . a true dramatic form out of living experience.

"THE CHAIR" (Robert Drew Associates, in *The Living Camera* Series)

. . . a definite finality.

moves his execution was delayed; and Drew's unit moved to Chicago to follow a young attorney who was fighting a major battle to have the sentence commuted. As the actual hearing neared, New York attorney Louis Nizer agreed to present the brief, which was, in effect, a strong argument for the possibility of rehabilitation.

The facts of this case happened also to be the precise conditions of drama. The hearing obviously would be held, and from this great crisis in Crump's life there had to come some resolution. This was, however, the only loose end, and in these terms it made little difference whether he won or lost. "The Chair," then, was laid out in the form of the trial drama, and Drew's unit had to do no more than capture, with as much impact as possible, the total situation: the efforts of the protagonist (the young attorney), of the antagonist (the state's attorney), the crisis in the courtroom (where Nizer became assistant protagonist), and the final decision of the hearing board (a resolution to commute the sentence). The denouement was a traditional happy ending (if one chooses to regard a man's return to prison for life as an improvement upon electrocution), showing the buoyant young attorney off to the race-track on a bus.

The difference between "The Chair" and a typical *Perry Mason* segment is dramaturgically small — and yet the severe distinction between them is that nothing seen in "The Chair" was not made from the raw material of life. In that difference lies still another testimony to *verité*. On two occasions, for example, the attorney totally forgot the camera and sound equipment. At one point he learned, in a telephone conversation, that a highly placed community leader planned to make a public statement in behalf of Crump's commutation — a stroke of good fortune beyond his wildest hopes. The conversation ended and suddenly he was in tears, a reaction so intense and natural that it was a full minute before he recalled the camera's presence. And again, when he was informed that people in Steubenville, Ohio, were collecting pennies for his cause, there was an overpowering moment of choking back his emotions. Not since the early *Philco Playhouse* production of Mosel's character study of Howie in *The Haven* did one see a more naturally motivated analysis of a man so deeply moved that he wept before us — and only with great concentration can we remember that one was a drama and the other the revelation of a real man intensely involved in a real situation.

LIVING DRAMA

But the climactic moments in men's lives do not happen at the convenience of cameramen and sound men, however unobtrusively they may wait. A dramatic situation must not only exist, but it must be approaching some definite climax when the producers arrive to record it. And if these elements are not present they must be manufactured. If they are manufactured, the documentarist runs the risk of destroying his very purpose. This was the challenge which Irving Gitlin and his producers at NBC News *Creative Projects* faced in a series of DuPont-sponsored productions in 1963 and 1964 which were called "living dramas." Several of their works over a two-year span are especially worth noting — William Jersey's "Prisoner-at-Large," "Incident on Wilson Street" and "Manhattan Battleground," Albert Wasserman's "High Wire: The Wallendas," and Fred Freed's incomparable "Fire Rescue."

One of Grierson's requirements for documentary was that a part of a society should see and comprehend the meaning of the lives of other parts of that society; if Grierson had seen "Fire Rescue" it is probable that he would have approved, at least in principle, its motive and achievement. The NBC camera crews followed the men of New York City Rescue Company One for a period of three months, recording them at work and in their moments of relaxation. Edited into a one-hour film, the story of these men held overwhelming power, carrying the Flaherty theme of man's indomitable spirit — expressed in ultimate terms of his capacity to exercise normality of function in the face of suffering, omnipresent danger, and death itself.

In "Fire Rescue" a classic unity of time was overlaid upon the story by the editing — reducing it to a single 36-hour "routine watch" for Rescue One. The dramatist's plot-making function was exercised as clearly as if the entire story were fashioned independently of reality. Working within a three-months' collection of records, Gitlin and Freed condensed and rearranged, building a rising line of action toward crisis and resolution.

The structure of the program was built upon the fact that at one point during those three months a member of Rescue One died while fire-fighting. The cameras were there to record not the death itself, but the reactions of men of the unit when they first learned their comrade was missing, to follow them in their search, and to film them as they discovered his body. Walter Mathau, in a reserved narration, spoke only those few words which told us that one of the men of Rescue One was missing, and for an almost unendurable length of time we shared the search in awesome silence: the diggers slowly picking their way among the debris, the chaplain standing by, the anxious faces of the men of Rescue One.

The men begin to burrow deeper. And, without warning, we know the missing man has been found. Not because we are thrust into the scene (the camera shot is still long) but by observing the silent movements, and the deliberate,

"FIRE RESCUE" (NBC-TV *DuPont Living Drama* Series)

. . . Flaherty's theme and Grierson's function.

almost formal, stances of the searchers. We *know*, even though we have not yet seen the discovery. Then we hear Mathau telling us that "by tradition the removal of the body is a task for the man's company." The tension is broken. Because of the very absence of theatrics the deeper knowledge of the death comes to us with dignity and simplicity.

This scene in "Fire Rescue" remains one of television's few respectful deaths, and its achievement repeats that same quality of those extraordinary still photos which tell us the meaning of death in terms of the living. The immense theme of "Fire Rescue" emerged from that climactic moment of a man's death, but its force as a drama lay in our having been prepared for the tragedy. Freed gave us a full study of men-in-action fighting fires, enjoying quiet moments at the firehouse as they baited the unit's cook (". . . The peas is given out!" he scolded when they attempted to usurp his lordly function in the mess room), and attending a funeral at St. Patrick's for another city fireman who lost his life in the line of duty. Yet all of these only presaged the climax we sensed would come, and when Mathau finally stated the cold fact that a man of Rescue One was missing, we were prepared for it almost in the same manner that Shakespeare prepared us for the death of Macbeth or Hamlet.

There are two differences in the dramaturgical approaches of "Fire Rescue" and "The Chair." In "Fire Rescue" the single hero was replaced by the small interacting group in which all members were protagonists, and the antagonistic elements were the inward fears and anxieties of each as well as the external dangers. Also, the chronology of events in real time was of less significance. The death of a fireman may have been one of the earliest scenes recorded, but as a plot-finder Freed recognized its dramatic value. This may have influenced not only the final structure of the work, but may have dictated additional shooting to fill a line of rising action — scenes which would support and unify an already recorded climax. The order of recording is sometimes unimportant in relation to the *truth* of the records.

In Jersey's "Manhattan Battleground" (1964) the drama of Paddy Chayefsky's "small crisis" and Benjamin's "man from the inside out" were once again reflected in the story of a young social worker's final weeks in a neighborhood where, with love and dedication, he had given new meaning to the lives of young people. We saw him as he walked the streets, counseling the weak, inspiring the indifferent, cheering the despairing. His indefatigable powers for good were chronicled for us by the camera which drifted with him, lingered as he lingered, and seemed almost a companion at his side. The boys prepared a little skit for his going-away party, and we shared their awkward expression of gratitude. Slowly, tenderly, we moved toward that moment when the van was finally loaded and there was no longer any reason for delay. And then we felt the reality of human experience: voices were breaking; out of the blur came faces, tearfully committed

**"PRISONER AT LARGE," "MANHATTAN BATTLEGROUND,"
"HIGH WIRE — THE WALLENDAS"**
(NBC-TV *DuPont Living Drama* Series)

. . . crisis enough to sustain a moving human drama.

faces, to say a last farewell. A life of force and vigor and hope was being withdrawn from that small social situation. Something of a corner was turned; and this, in the final accounting, was crisis enough to sustain a moving human drama.

The high tragedy of "Fire Rescue" was lacking in "Prisoner-at-Large," but the study of a Massachusetts parole officer who struggled to prevent a young man from destroying his life was made memorable by a treatment which involved intense examination of human beings in moments of emotional torment. Producer William Jersey also worked in that pre-selected structure which held its own inevitable climax, just as surely as had Drew in "The Chair." Made with the cooperation of the Massachusetts Parole Board, this film was designed to acquaint the public with the work of a parole officer whose efforts were directed toward the rehabilitation of a young criminal. This natural line of action ended at a meeting of the Parole Board, at which time the young man's future was settled.

In this case the relationship with these two characters was established in a series of fine *verité* scenes, and we became involved as we began to share the officer's conviction that the young man might reform. But the boy did not wait for the prestructured climax, and instead committed a criminal act while still on parole — an act which sealed his fate before the Parole Board even came to consider his case. The crisis spilled over, and finally was properly focused not in the Parole Board meeting, but in two scenes of intense emotional conflict between the officer and the criminal — the first when the officer confronted him after he had been arrested for house-breaking, and the second when the officer told him the Board had decided he must serve out his new sentence before being reviewed again for parole. In these scenes of raw hurt and anger the tensions were too high for the presence of any camera to hold them in check. We saw first the despair of the parole officer, whose faith and convictions had been ripped away by the boy's stupid and willful act, and later the desperation of the boy when he was told that he would have to serve out his new sentence.

Again, so intense was the feeling that playwright and actors would have been hard-pressed to so effectively reconstruct it. Perhaps the only comparable scene in all of contemporary drama was that moment of confrontation in the taxi between Marlon Brando and Rod Steiger in the film *On The Waterfront*, a reference which leads us once more to appreciate the inevitable power of living drama in a situation that is carefully preselected to incorporate natural dramatic crisis. In "Prisoner-at-Large" we saw that power at work, and also learned that the unpredictable can add even greater impact to a preselected crisis. The events of reality shaped a different climax and theme, emphasizing not a battle won or lost for the boy, but a battle lost for the officer.

In the same Gitlin series, "Comedian Backstage" and "San Francisco Detective" raised some questions with relation to the techniques of justifiable reconstruction. In both of these programs the treatment moved to the very edge of a manufactured crisis. Thus we sensed more than chronological rearranging of sequences; instead, the producers staged climaxes which not only seemed inconsequential, but betrayed the obvious tinkering. The loosely structured situation did not produce results in terms of genuine character revelation, and in their efforts to give the work a climax which did not naturally arise from what had gone before, the producers of these documentaries became not plot-finders but plot-makers.

In "Comedian Backstage" the climax consisted of Shelley Berman's tantrum after a backstage phone rang during the finale of his act, allegedly "breaking his mood." The richest and only true moment of the sequence came when Berman, attempting to find someone upon whom to vent his rage, took a long, smoldering stare at the camera (which probably revealed more than he intended). Ostensibly, the program was designed to present those 24 hours between Berman's arrival at the supper club and the climax — when, after all the arrangements had been completed and he had attended to all the preliminary details, he would give his first performance. Actually, his "performance" began upon his arrival. He was conscious of the camera from the outset, and we seldom saw him otherwise. Perhaps the phone-ringing incident did not actually occur on the opening night at all. This kind of reconstruction is not invalid of itself — indeed, without it, "Fire Rescue" would have lost its meaning. The point is that, in "Comedian Backstage," it was not consequential. The program was conceived in the hope that something *would happen*, and when it did not, a crisis was fabricated. It was a highly unflattering character study, and fell short of living drama precisely for this reason. Berman was not a protagonist at all, and because he elicited no sympathetic response, his "crisis" meant nothing.

In "San Francisco Detective" there was no climax; not even an inconsequential one. There was a scene near the closing in which a very sincere detective tried to discuss with a colleague his reasons for being in police work. It was a forced discussion, and the ideas expressed were stilted. An earlier scene, in which he interviewed a San Francisco "kook," was more exciting, but accomplished no dramatic purpose.

In both of these programs a legitimate documentary approach was in force. They did not arrive at living drama, for when the climaxes were either forced or inconsequential they became something else. The documentary instrument came under suspicion. Unlike *The World of* ———— biographies, where the scenes were controlled by the external force of story line, music, and narration, these weaker examples of living drama *went inside the record of a natural situation and imposed direction upon it*. If it were done in a play, we would say it was a bad job. But when perpetrated in a documentary, form itself is destroyed.

Such judgments are hard to make. Surely, on any number of occasions, even a *verité* photographer has asked a subject to move in a certain direction, discuss a certain point, or follow some specific instructions.[8] Where this occurs, it becomes difficult to discern the difference between a subject and an actor — between a person and a character. In this regard, it might be valid to consider *Circle Theatre* as a documentary form, but to do so would be to jeopardize all distinction between drama and documentary. The issue, at bottom, is that if we are told we are seeing actuality, then any tampering with human action and emotion within a scene will, to the degree that it is committed, weaken the entire idea of documentary.

From these experiments and departures in the documentary method of television some immediate conclusions may be offered. We are justified in saying that a true television aesthetic may exist, and that principles discovered in the golden age of the live television drama in the early 1950's strongly influenced the golden age of television Theme Documentary in the 1960's. For whatever method or style that documentarists have employed, as documentary began to record the life and the living which surround us in time, the form moved toward the *dramaturgical* — following Aristotle's division of ways in which we are told of men in action by pursuing the task of showing men living and moving before us. All that is missing is the full significance of Aristotle's *imitation*. Whether television's documentarists have served that method which emphasized plot building (as Benjamin and Eugene Jones have), or whether they have minimized narrative and become plot-finders (as Stuart, Drew, and Gitlin have), none of them is a plot-maker. None is free of the necessity to remain with the actual, and to structure it as his own conscience and honesty demand.

Part Four / DOCUMENTARY DEPARTURES

10 / The Networks: Variations

> The documentary idea, after all, demands no more than that the affairs of our time shall be brought to the screen in any fashion which strikes the imagination and makes observation a little richer than it was. At one level the vision may be journalistic; at another it may rise to poetry and drama. At another level, again, its artistic quality may lie in the mere lucidity of its exposition.
>
> — JOHN GRIERSON[1]

MUCH DISCUSSION HERE has been devoted to those national programs which best typify the alternatives of documentary method. Yet there remain numerous efforts which also merit attention, for, whatever their special content and procedure, they still answer Grierson's challenge that the affairs of our time be brought before us in a manner that "strikes the imagination and makes observation a little richer than it was." These series and individual programs in the first 15 years of television's history must be brought under the documentary rubric.

INFORMATIONAL DOCUMENTARY

In the early and mid-1950's a number of generative program series were broadcast. One of these, in 1952, was *Omnibus*, begun by the Ford Foundation, and later supported by commercial sponsors. Irving Gitlin created *The Search* for CBS in 1954, and in 1956 NBC originated *Wide Wide World*. These were prime examples of the documentary's direction in areas of informational, educational, and cultural content.

The Search investigated developments and breakthroughs in research and scholarship at American universities. A well-known documentary filmmaker, Henwar Rodakiewiscz, worked in close association with Gitlin in producing many programs in the series, and it was here that such writers and producers as Arthur Zegart and Al Wasserman increased their own abilities. *The Search* represented, at a different level, the kind of documentary inquiry to be seen in such later programs as the Frank Capra science series for Bell Telephone, and the television offerings of the indefatigable Walt Disney, who has long tried to make the worlds of science appealing to youthful audiences.

Both *Wide Wide World* and *Omnibus* began that spirit and method of the general cultural-informational documentary which are sustained in such series of the 1960's as CBS's *Chronicle* and *Accent*, the individual works produced by Lou Hazam at NBC and John Secondari at ABC, and a growing number of similar presentations at all networks. *Omnibus* did more, perhaps, to popularize the established film documentaries than offer new works, but it also experimented in semidocumentary forms.[2] It was on *Omnibus* that Robert Flaherty's *Louisiana Story* was first shown to a wider American audience, and this function of perpetuating interest in the documentary film tradition is continued in programs presently being circulated by National Educational Television.

Wide Wide World was conceived by Sylvester ("Pat") Weaver during that remarkably imaginative period when he served as program head at NBC. Under the production supervision of Barry Wood, the series explored the possibilities of live documentary. Until the practicality of videotape, demonstrated in late 1957, made such attempts seem less dramatic and exciting, *Wide Wide World* was an important contribution to the classic documentary function of "bringing the empire alive." Such people as Herb Sussan, John Goetz, Ted Rogers, and Alan Neuman produced 90-minute panoramic surveys of the nation at work and at play, typified by "American Theatre '58," which studied the national theatre movement in several live pick-ups from Broadway to California, and "Flag Stop at Malta Bend," a look at the American railroads. These programs revealed the potentialities of live pick-up within a documentary context, demonstrating that even the cumbersome electronic cameras (and the limited editing which live television permitted) could serve as a useful tool in the creative interpretation of actuality.

The high technical, as well as artistic, superiority of *Wide Wide World* was apparent in a sequence carried during the 1956-57 season wherein an attempt was made to re-create a "City Symphony." A number of TV cameras were set at various points around New York, and near each was placed a musician. As he played in concert with his widely scattered fellows, both sound and picture were fed into a control center, and these were mixed into a vivid portrait of the city — a poetic creation built out of actuality-of-the-moment.

A further example of how the very lack of camera mobility and the slower editing pace of live pick-up could be turned to fresh advantage was seen in a gripping segment of the 1962 CBS *Accent* series, "Pearl Harbor — Unforgotten." In this production, narrator John Ciardi took us to the scene of the Japanese attack. The program opened with Ciardi standing aboard a sight-seeing boat which was cruising the hallowed battle area; and his narration was counterplayed against the standard tour-lecture delivered by a young sailor to solemn tourists. Live cameras recorded the entire area from selected vantage points around the harbor. As Ciardi related how each ship had been sunk or destroyed, we saw only the dark water below him. And as the toll of death and terror slowly mounted in the narrator's restrained account, we were gripped by the scene itself and shared the awe of those who had come to visit this shrine.

Without benefit of a single film clip of billowing smoke or exploding bombs, we were led to an emotional grasp of the enormity of what had occurred at Pearl Harbor. As Ciardi told us about the first moments of the attack, the cameras scanned the gray skies above Oahu and we heard the faint, nearly imperceptible sounds of approaching aircraft. Although we knew these sounds did not exist in fact, we felt that we heard them because of our involvement in a tragic story. Thus, a documentary thrust carried this program beyond technical problems, and limitation was turned to advantage.

As a production method, live pick-up retains great usefulness in the broad documentary work of recording the life around us. Short features are often seen on such programs as NBC's *Today*, where remote originations from points here and abroad are recorded and played back. Such features hold the possibilities of documentary treatment, as do a variety of studio re-enactments of various real life problems. The latter technique probably also originated in such early *Omnibus* vignettes as "A Village Incident" — a staging of the problems encountered when a small community in India must attempt to meet modern social and technological change. Derivatives are still evident in such series as *Look Up and Live* and *Camera 3*.

If the coming of videotape made such live accomplishments seem unsophisticated, the value of the electronic camera was greatly enhanced by the new freedom in editing which videotape introduced. Still, live pick-up, even with the advantages of videotape, is seldom used any longer in an independent Theme Documentary context. Here, film — with its infinitely greater potentials for creative construction of narrative — is now the dominant tool. But in the News Documentary the use of videotape sequences continues to be extensive.

Our concern here remains with a number of network efforts which have, with some artistry, brought us awareness of the world around us. A major creator in this work has been Lou Hazam, a free-lance documentarist working on special assignment for NBC. Hazam's superb contributions to the TV documentary were his two 1962 biographical productions, "Vincent Van Gogh: A Self-Portrait" and "Shakespeare: Soul of an Age"

Like the background of many of his fellow TV documentarists, Hazam's lies in radio and in his earlier TV work within the actuality news and News Documentary field. One of his first TV series, *The March of*

LOU HAZAM, GEORGE VICAS

. . . the mere lucidity of exposition.

Medicine, received the Albert Lasker Medical Journalism Award. Hazam also developed reports on new research in medicine for the *Breakthrough* series, as well as "The Encyclopedia of Communism" for *White Paper.* Among his later achievements was a series of programs in which the travel film was brought to a more popular level: "Japan: East Is West," "U. S. #1: American Profile," "The River Nile," and "The Orient Express." Yet none of these have won for Hazam such wide respect and praise as were given his Van Gogh and Shakespeare productions.

"Vincent Van Gogh: A Self-Portrait" is memorable for its development of a subjective treatment of the artist's life, enriched by Guy Blanchard's cinematography, the dual narration of Martin Gabel and Lee J. Cobb, and Jacques Belasco's score. The idea of "camera-personification," in which the camera's perspective represents that of a character's, was first introduced to TV in this program. The technique is, of course, almost as old as film itself. In Robert Montgomery's 1947 production, *The Lady in the Lake,* the subjective camera was sustained throughout the entire film; and it is difficult to forget its use in Orson Welles's *Othello,* where, in the final scene, we "experienced" the sensation of weaving, spinning, and falling with Othello in his death throes.

In combination with Van Gogh's paintings and sketches (captured by Blanchard at a rare Paris exhibition which included many of the artist's less famous works), as well as his own words (read by Lee J. Cobb from Van Gogh's letters to friends and relatives), Hazam's documentation included specially shot footage of the places where Van Gogh lived. We walked the fields of Holland as he walked them as a boy, looked, as he had looked, upon his house and upon the church where his stern father preached. Through the sensitive camera eye we experienced his world, ending in that climactic moment when we stumbled and fell with Van Gogh as he took his own life. In "Vincent Van Gogh," Blanchard, director Ray Garner, and Hazam created a program which set high standards for the television use of camera-personification.

Derivations were soon in evidence. In 1963 NBC offered "American Landmark: Lexington and Concord," in which camera-personification took us to the site of the first battle of the Revolutionary War. Narrated by Fredric March, this program also had moments when the subjective camera pulled us into the action, notably when the British retreated from the fight. We stumbled, again, with the wounded and dying. Animation techniques were also employed, as lead soldiers and statues were worked into a symbolic representation of the battle.

By the mid-1960's television's theme documentarists were employing variations on the technique of camera-personification and the bringing-to-life of the inanimate, both of which proved particularly effective in dealing with historical content. By using dramatic lighting and deliberate camera movements, NBC producer George Vicas brought "life" to a scene in his starkly beautiful "The Kremlin" (1962) which re-created the murder of Peter the Great's family. Flags in motion were used to represent Napoleon's capture of the Kremlin in 1812. Such partial realism in "The Kremlin" was combined with film, taken within the edifice, of places which had never been shown before. This record of the architecture and past and modern furnishings of the grim old citadel stands, along with John Secondari's "The Vatican," among television's triumphs within this semihistorical travelogue genre.

It was Secondari, too, who brought still further innovation to the camera-personification and animation methods. In the 1963-64 *Saga of Western Man* series, the former *Close-Up!* unit — now designated ABC News *Special Projects* — treated decisive years in the history of our civilization: 1492, 1776, 1898, and 1964. In the first two programs Secondari and producer Helen Jean Rogers combined the subjective camera with actors' voices and a strong reliance upon visual re-enactment. The latter marked a departure of some note in the TV documentary, and yet it was the logical step beyond the "interpreter" reading the letters and speeches of historical figures. In "1492" the actor portraying Columbus was seen only in long shots or in silhouette. Secondari let us see close-ups of Columbus only in terms of paintings and lithographs. This visual method kept the documentary concept intact, and yet added new qualities of life which animation devices and the suggestions of the subjective camera cannot always sustain.[3]

There are possibilities and possibilities, limited only by personal vision and skills of execution. A program such as Hazam's "Greece: The Golden Age" (1963) reminds us there is no exhaustion of the documentarist's imagination. In Hazam's production there was an unusual sequence in which accelerated movements of ripe wheat and red poppies in a field "re-enacted" the battle of Greeks and Persians — while the statuary served as rigid onlookers. Even the technology of color television can become a creative tool for the inventive theme documentarist.

All of these network series and individual productions represent that profusion of documentaries seen by national audiences in the past dozen or so years. Whether "true" documentary, semidocumentary, or simply programs which make use of the documentary idea and method, they are indicative of the spirit of that kind of public communication which brings us, through the mere lucidity of exposition, explanations of our world and our human history.

NOTEBOOK DOCUMENTARY

Since the mid-1950's there has also been remarkable growth in that kind of journalistic documentary which reflects news happenings seldom commanding the headlines. In such series as *Chet Huntley Reporting, David Brinkley's Journal*, Frank McGee's *Here and Now*, NBC's irregularly scheduled *Our Man in ——* programs, and many of the works of *The Twentieth Century*, there has evolved a reportage of the lesser news event in what might be called "Notebook Documentary." In most cases emphasis is placed upon the reporter himself, and occasionally the approach involves no more than a lengthy "lecture with visuals."

In content, these programs extend from a two- or three-story "magazine" to the single report devoted to social problems or conditions, or to a personality. Frequently these series go abroad to delineate social and cultural changes in other nations. The lighter tone often prevails, as in *Our Man in ——* programs such as Brinkley's treatment of Vienna (which was a wry commentary upon the political and dietary habits of Austrians) or in one installment of his *Journal* when he examined art, letting his wit play upon scenes of apes dabbling in "modern art" and an American expatriate in Paris "creating" by shooting at balloons filled with paint. Chet Huntley's series has covered such subjects as drug addiction in Britain and the attitudes of American college students toward their alma mater. *The Twentieth Century* continues to present full analyses of foreign countries — as it did in "The Berliners: Life in a Gilded Cage," or such two-

"NOTEBOOK" DOCUMENTARY — BRINKLEY ON THE MISSISSIPPI

. . . the lighter tone often prevails.

part studies as "Ireland: The Tear and the Smile" and "Sweden: Trouble in Paradise?" — as well as reports of domestic significance, ranging from the new problems of air traffic to the work of the famed Menninger brothers in mental health.

When the necessary film was available, however, and a proper story executed, such efforts came near to News Documentary. Often individual programs in these series were moving and significant expressions of life as found in the long tradition of the "social-analysis" school of documentary film-making. Frequently these programs carried the quality of "prestige" News Documentaries which have higher budgets and less rigid schedules. At these levels it is difficult to see much difference in design, execution, and social importance. At all events, the Notebook Documentaries fill an important role, and when the documentary method is applied to them in fullness and honesty, as in *The Twentieth Century*'s "So That Men Are Free," they become vital social instruments.

"So That Men Are Free" represented the venerable documentary film tradition brought into television and shaped in the context of the News Documentary. This story of the Vicos experiment in Peru was directed by Willard Van Dyke,[4] who began his film career in 1937 as cameraman on Pare Lorentz's *The River* and made such respected documentary films as

The City and *San Francisco 1945*, the official film of the first United Nations Conference. His capacities for visually revealing the human condition gave a Flaherty tone and style to this description of how Peruvian descendants of the Incas — men who have never known freedom — became the first Indians in the history of Peru to buy their own land. Earl Luby's script traced the narrative history of this experiment conducted by a Cornell University anthropologist, but it was Van Dyke's emphasis on the faces of men, and sensitive illustration of how they lived, which brought this program away from a "notebook" report and into the realm of serious documentary statement.

It is not implied that "notebook" approaches elsewhere accomplished something less than effective documentary journalism should attempt. Yet their intention was simply to "backpage" informally the circumstances which surround us in life. It is in such works as "So That Men Are Free" and "The Tunnel" that the heights to which the Notebook Documentary may aspire are fully suggested. The first was made with that care and precision which only a great visual craftsman — a man who writes with a camera — could apply, and the second was a technically imperfect recording made by amateur "filmos" under incredible conditions; yet both told of events which, in Roy Stryker's way of putting it, were "an affirmation, not a negation" of the human spirit.

HARD NEWS AND HUMAN DRAMA

Among those in television whose basic function is to gather and transmit news, increasing respect for television's distinct capacities has created the same restiveness which led de Rochemont and Edward R. Murrow to follow the path to documentary. Since the earliest *March of Time* the intertwining courses of news reporting and documentary have been given impulse and direction by the man who, following events, is compelled to set them in a broader context of meaning. His compulsion is to illuminate news reports by structuring them in ways which will involve others in the reasons for their occurrence, explaining their social dimensions and activating responses concerning their outcome. In each case, existing technology has modified his intentions. When videotape was perfected, it served only further to spur his aims. Videotape gave to the reporter a facile instrument which could serve alongside film as a means for bringing new dimensions to his ambitions. By the 1960's the growth of experience and increased size in news units, together with more advanced technical developments, made it possible for networks to move into a distinct kind of hard-news reporting comparable to the newspaper "extra." Major news stories of the week began to be treated in a series of "specials" in which the documentary method was undeniable. These forms may be categorized somewhere between the full documentary instrument and the hard-news story.

NBC PHOTO

McGEE, HAGAN AND "INSTANT HISTORY"

The 1960 Eisenhower travels abroad, for example, were only one segment of *Eyewitness*, an unprecedented television series in which CBS News displayed speed and ingenuity in offering a regularly scheduled weekly news special. *Eyewitness* attempted to overcome one of the basic distinctions between print and electronic journalism — a totality, as well as immediacy, in transmission of news. The series continued this schedule for three full seasons, executing the mission of presenting the top story of the week in depth, despite hectic pressures and last-minute shifts when unexpected stories broke.

Often the attempt to establish a point of view within a story as it unfolded gave some of these *Eyewitness* specials a quality far closer to the News Documentary than to hard-news presentation. A full half-hour devoted to the single subject enabled the team led by producer Les Midgely — who was a member of the original *See It Now* unit — to create a more structured document.

At NBC the "Instant Special" became the product of a research and reporting team led by producer Chet Hagan, director Robert Prioulx, and correspondent Frank McGee. This unit, operating since the early 1960's, was not committed to regularly scheduled programs. Instead, it regarded the function of such specials as similar to a newspaper extra — planned on

short notice to cover happenings which were, at the time, headlines. The
NBC specials, like *Eyewitness*, varied, however, between the presentation
of the completely unexpected and those events which threatened to occur
but were still no more than predictable.

The NBC unit operated in a less continuous pressure situation than
Eyewitness, which was forced to present a "big" story each week and yet
had to allow for the unforeseeable major event which, despite deadlines,
remained its first responsibility. With the development of the daily half-
hour news program in 1963, CBS abandoned the *Eyewitness* concept and
also adopted a plan of irregularly scheduled extras, under the production
helm of veteran news-producer Don Hewitt. Both NBC and CBS units continued to draw upon the full resources of their far-flung news operations.
Available to them were the reports and materials compiled for either daily
hard-news shows or the major prestige News Documentaries. And, of
course, each unit remained free to employ reporters on network assignment at home and abroad.

The way in which "instant" documentaries are pulled together under
the restriction of limited time is disclosed in a choronology of activities at
NBC News following the announcement that the atomic submarine *Thresher*
"appeared to be lost" in the Atlantic at a point some 200 miles off Boston.
The announcement was made on the night of April 10, 1963, and NBC
News quickly assigned a group of newsmen throughout the northeast to
cover the catastrophe. These were the preliminary moves that resulted in
an hour-long special program the following night — a program that, with
films and live interviews, told of the *Thresher*'s disappearance:

> 1 p.m. — The decision is made firm to televise "The Loss of the *Thresher*"
> at 7:30 p.m. The sponsor, Gulf Oil Corporation, has decided to omit any
> commercial messages because of the nature of the program. Producer Chet
> Hagan, researcher Mona McCormick and Frank McGee, who will "anchor"
> the program, have already been gathering material.
> 2 p.m. — Associate producer Jerry Jacobs and news editor Gene Farinet
> screen films taken by an NBC News cameraman from a plane flying over
> the ocean where the sub went down. The NBC plane was the first on the
> scene Thursday morning.
> 2:30 p.m. — Production assistant Marian Biskamp finishes typing the "rou-
> tine" of the show. This is an outline showing where various film segments
> and live pick-ups are spaced in the program.
> 2:35 p.m. — Jacobs and Farinet screen a portion of an NBC News special
> broadcast that dealt with the atomic submarine *George Washington*. A seg-
> ment showing the diving sequence aboard the *George Washington* is edited
> out for use on the night's program. The film clip will last 27 seconds.
> 2:44 p.m. — Farinet spreads large maps of the northeast coast on the floor
> of Hagan's office. They select a map for reproduction by visual technicians
> for use on the program. It will be seen by viewers for about 20 seconds.
> 3:20 p.m. — Everyone is typing except Badami. He is talking long distance
> with a mobile TV unit being set up at San Diego, Calif., where correspond-
> ent Roy Neal will interview an officer of the bathyscaphe *Trieste*.

3:40 p.m. — McGee is typing at his desk with long sheets of copy paper spread out before him. Hagan enters his office and the two discuss the outline of the show. The pieces begin to fall into place.

4:30 p.m. — Stopwatch in hand, McGee reads to himself the script he has written. He yells, "How long is the dive sequence?" Farinet yells back, "50 seconds." McGee clicks his watch and reads on.

4:35 p.m. — Farinet has located some film of the *Trieste*. A messenger has been dispatched to Jersey City to get the film. He has not returned. Farinet checks and learns the film is enroute.

5:10 p.m. — The film of the *Trieste* arrives. Portions of it are germane to the program. It is edited and prepared.

5:37 p.m. — Badami is on the phone talking with Washington for a remote pick-up on correspondent Martin Agronsky who will interview Captain James F. Calvert, former skipper of the nuclear sub *Skate*.

5:45 p.m. — The mobile TV unit arrives at New London, Conn., and establishes communications with Badami in New York. Joseph Michaels will broadcast live from the unit with late word on a Navy board of investigation that has been convened.

7:12 p.m. — In the control room, Hagan scans late wire copy, searching for any late news breaks that will alter the factual content of his program.

7:13 p.m. — Director Robert Prioulx has alerted directors at the remote pick-up sites.

7:24 p.m. — There is difficulty clearing up the video line to the New London pick-up. Within a minute, the line is clear.

7:30 p.m. — An announcer says: "*Wide Country*, usually seen at this time . . ."[5]

A similar ordeal was endured by Don Hewitt's CBS "extra" staff which presented a half-hour treatment of the same story.

Beyond the identification given to these reports of a prominent news story as it unfolds — the "flash" or "instant" documentary — there is some further difference in method between them and the planned in-depth analysis which characterizes News Documentary. If the variations in documentary approach (in terms of whether the individual effort is governed in execution by a control of subject or theme) is to hold some further validity, we may note that the flash documentary — once it moves to the "extra" concept — is not merely controlled, but *dominated* by events. The values of urgency added to the flash documentary (by aural and visual records which are summoned under pressure of time) lie generally in the area of *illustration,* not interpretation. Events are totally in charge of the reporting process. But for News Documentary to exist, the reporter must be in charge. The shift in emphasis, however slight it may sometimes be in fact, marks the boundaries between the merely illustrated report of a happening and the story about events and their significance which is preplanned by the journalist.

We must finally accept the dilemma of all reportage in television — voiced in the challenge first raised by de Rochement and echoed at every turn in the evolution of the technology of public communication. The addition of sight, sound, and motion to the reporting process must introduce the possibility of that communication experience which intervenes at all levels of reportage and which extends beyond illustration. This dilemma has no relationship to the extra or flash concept of reportage because here the immediate event itself is dominant. Nor is it related to Notebook Documentary, where the necessity to go beyond illustration is already embraced. Rather, the dilemma rests within the emerging hard-news report, where the entire nature of journalism itself is undergoing change — where, for the first time, some men are admitting the real possibility that *all* news presentation on television is, in fact, documentary in nature.

For many years there has been a continuing demand for the longer and more comprehensive daily news program at a national level. Criticism of the television medium, linked to a mounting concern over the speed of change and confrontation in a time of social upheaval, generated a movement in the 1960's toward the half-hour news program at the American networks. This direction had been actively sought within television's emerging journalistic profession.

The TV journalist is not dissatisfied because there is *more news* than there used to be; his dissatisfaction is with the amount of time in which he may report the news. The searching reportorial mind in non-print media needs time, because time, not space, is at the heart of his craft. The human being *moving through time* is the *raison d'être* of his work, and the TV journalist alone possesses the capacity to transmit the actuality of the moment in sight and sound. With the instruments of recording now at his disposal, only time can help him to make that shift from news reporting to interpretation which, essentially, is what he earnestly seeks. Nowhere is this expression of need made more convincing than in these observations of Reuven Frank:

> . . . I keep coming back to the real possibility of transmitting experience — of giving that new dimension of information that is *not contained in words alone* and is applicable in every situation where human beings are in contact. In conflict, if you prefer . . .
>
> What could the extra time mean? It could mean a seven-to-ten minute "take-out" every night. What is it like to starve to death in Algeria because they can't make up their minds about the kind of government they want? Now we could find the symbolic thing that opens this up, that illuminates it. Television does that. It illuminates the news. It *pictures* much better than it explains. You can pick on little things, and by examining them you can light over a larger area. This is the function of pictures. It is as true on the tube as it is in the theatre. It is as true in fact as it is in fiction. . . . This is what the the half-hour news show will let us realize and explore.[6]

When asked to cite an example of the "dimension of information not contained in words" Frank described that sequence of news film shot during the Alger Hiss trials which followed Hiss as he left the courthouse walked to a subway station, and sat reading a book as he rode home

REUVEN FRANK

. . . the transmission of experience.

Everyone knew about Hiss and the trial by then, and yet here was the central figure in a national crisis, sitting alone and reading. "People were swaying," Frank said, "This was a dimension. . . . There are some who would say this isn't journalism. I think it is. I believe it is."[7]

The comments are revealing in themselves, but their greater value lies in the fact that Paddy Chayefsky, the dramatist of live television's "golden age" who did more to frame an aesthetic for the medium than any other playwright, created a similar study in "The Mother" — one of his early *Philco Playhouse* scripts which he described as his play best suited to television. In a short scene coming immediately after an aging woman is fired from the job which held the promise of her independence, Chayefsky wrote a vignette in which she returned home, defeated and despairing, on the subway. The camera merely observed her. Chayefsky asked for the feel of the crowded subway car — the passengers swaying — and for an intense focus upon her tired face. This was the entire action in the scene, and yet it carried the full thrust and power of all unforgettable drama.

If these descriptions of what a veteran TV news-producer and a renowned playwright sought to create are not sufficient matter on which to generalize, they are at least too closely related to be ignored. A simple revelation of how humans undergoing a "conflict within" can reflect the natural and most fundamental capacity of televised communication had been discovered by both a maker of fiction and a reporter of fact. The hard-news TV journalist constantly seeks to make this same discovery an intrinsic element of his work. And as he does so he moves closer to structuring the news.

The *story*, then, following upon structure, is the promise of the half-hour news program — the "take-out" which affords the added time for a longer analysis of a major event in the day's news and becomes a "small" documentary, revealing the small crisis of conflict and change within the individual. Here are the possibilities of beginnings and endings that make the news meaningful. When such possibilities are realized, *documentary*, in the broadest and truest sense of that elusive term, will find a new existence.

11 / Local Documentary: An Overview

> The broadcaster, then, is asked to search, to confront, to agitate and to understand; to make a commitment, to do his homework, to look ahead, and to remain detached. And when will he know whether he has done his job and discharged his obligations? Like the rest of us dedicated to the public interest, *never*.
>
> — PAUL YLVISAKER[1]

WHILE the efforts of network documentarists have spurred the local station documentary movement, the extension of documentary across the nation in this decade reveals an additional growth in talent and ideas. It may be proper, of course, to attribute to former FCC head Newton Minow this burgeoning in local public-affairs programming, yet a good number of stations were offering efforts in the semidocumentary and documentary forms since the early 1950's.

THE RISE OF LOCAL DOCUMENTARY

Without doubt there are still too many American TV stations where some concept of the public weal is manifested only in a heavily sponsored half-hour or hour of news, sports and weather each evening, and two or three overpublicized, artistically weak, and socially insignificant "documentaries" each year. Such stations were, after Minow, the first to protest against their freedoms being taken away by regulation, and by and large they have made little creative contribution since. Those stations, however, which exercised conscience from the outset kept right on doing so, and have continued to make important public-affairs documentaries since 1961, when the "wasteland" bomb was exploded over American commercial broadcasting.

In this connection it is worth noting that the 1960 Television Information Office inventory of public-affairs programming, based upon a survey of 562 stations then on the air, disclosed that only 264 felt it necessary (or were perhaps able) to respond. Of 1,038 programs included in the final report, 83 were eliminated because they were either straight news broadcasts or syndicated programs in which stations were not directly involved. This left a total of 955 programs or series (produced by 264 stations over a period of 18 months) which the stations themselves considered outstanding examples of public-affairs efforts. Of these, a great number were talk, interview, or panel-discussion programs, but many were clearly identified as documentaries, in which both film and videotape methods of recording were combined. The sample held, of course, only representative choices of their "best" by individual stations, setting an example for approximately one-half of America's TV stations which offered no response at all.

In the 1960's, however, the trend toward local documentary productions saw a sharp increase, as regulatory pressure and the standard of excellence set by more aggressive stations stirred the entire industry.[2] The possibility of viewing even a fraction of the thousands of regional and local documentary programs produced in the first years of this decade is faint, and one is reluctant to accept at face value the glowing descriptions of programs carried in trade-press advertising. Yet the documentary in local television has gotten under way.

In outstanding local documentaries, the vision and purpose of early British film documentarists is given still further application. It is on the community level that the people of various regions and locales are brought to grips with their indigenous problems, and it is here that some concerted action which moves toward the immediate solution of everyday problems can be sought. The networks and other national documentary agencies best accomplish effective communication on issues of national urgency and concern, and the local documentary can offer essential complements. In terms of social purpose and effectiveness the two run parallel paths.

There are, however, some recognizable limitations in the matter of applying critical standards to the reportorial and creative achievement of local efforts. One need only compare the typical $100,000 budget for a *CBS Reports* program to a total expenditure of $150 listed for "Urbandale, U.S.A.," a production by educational station WMSB-TV in East Lansing, Michigan. Certainly the level and quality of each aspect of production here must be inferior to the full network report, and yet a representative of the Lansing Welfare Department called "Urbandale" the "finest study on a local community problem" he had ever seen. A single standard in analysis of creative achievement, then, cannot apply in all cases, and social effectiveness must remain an equally important consideration in evaluation. The community itself is less inclined to be critical when a documentary depicts local people and local problems. The station documentarist enjoys, in some ways, the advantages of the local newspaper, whose reporter at

City Hall, although not a Walter Lippmann, still covers the ground with which people are familiar and which is of vital importance to them.

This may seem defensive in advance, but should not be so construed. Many local television stations have produced series which compare favorably with network offerings. In every case where this has occurred, however, the individual station has accepted the role of documentary seriously, provided the wherewithal to develop production talent, and then given its producers proper equipment and freedom to do the job. Within the competitive framework of American television, those who have undertaken this task conscientiously have recognized that the local documentary must battle for audiences, and the creative level of the best local work is attested to not only by a slowly but steadily growing audience, but by constant improvement in the capacities of staff producers.

The local station which assiduously practices documentary programming recognizes that it cannot maintain the rigorous schedules of networks and syndicates because the problems are not only financial but human. The superiority of talent in network entertainment programs and syndicated series applies also in the case of documentaries. Only a truly national medium can support the first-rate talent of a generation, in entertainment or documentary, and the best talent will constantly seek the top. One may perhaps ask whether many individual stations might not spend more of their profits to develop and retain such talent, but the laws of supply and demand are immutable in matters of artistry. For the first time in television larger stations now "raid" the staffs of smaller, just as networks have hired away the best of the local station personnel. The situation, uncomfortable as it may make the lives of station managers, is a hopeful one for community and nation.

A single public-service-minded station such as WBNS-TV in Columbus, Ohio, provides an example of this turnover in public-affairs staffs. By the mid-1950's WBNS-TV was producing regular series of specials (called "telementaries") in the documentary style, discussing subjects of local and regional concern. Its first public-affairs director, Charles Cady, went to the National Association of Broadcasters as a consultant in the Television Code; John F. Cox, who replaced him, later joined the National Education Association as a creator of educational programs. Gene McPherson produced several fine documentaries for WBNS-TV, and was promptly called to head a newly formed Documentary Unit at the Crosley Broadcasting Corporation, where his 1963 "The Last Prom" was given a regional Emmy. Jack Hunter, who created award-winning News Documentaries at that same station, was selected to fill an opening at a Westinghouse station — following the route of Jerome Reeves who, after initiating the entire WBNS-TV public-service thrust while program manager there, went on to manage *Group W*'s Pittsburgh outlet, KDKA-TV. This pattern was repeated again and again throughout the nation as far-sighted stations sought experienced talent with a demonstrated record of achievement, just as NBC hired William Monroe away from WDSU-TV in New Orleans, where, with Louis Read, he had helped to write one of local television's most courageous stories — the battle for reason in the 1960 New Orleans integration crisis.

Whatever the problems and challenges, and whether the broadcaster is motivated by conscience or by regulatory demands, there is sufficient evidence to support the belief that American local television has begun to assume a more professional and responsible attitude toward its communal responsibilities, and has sought to make the documentary program a chief instrument in executing its charge to serve the public interest, convenience, and necessity. For a few, Robert Shulman's admonition that those engaged in documentary at the local level must either "dare and lead — or forget it!"[3] has offered too easy an alternative — they have forgotten it. But most have responded in positive ways, and these responses are our concern here.

THE ACHIEVEMENT OF LOCAL DOCUMENTARY

The local station output in the 1960's has differed in purpose and effectiveness. Nearly all stations which have engaged in documentary have turned, at one time or another, to regional or civic issues and problems; and here the Westinghouse stations (including WBZ-TV, Boston; WJZ-TV, Baltimore; KDKA-TV, Pittsburgh; KYW-TV, Cleveland; and KPIX-TV, San Francisco) have been among the most prolific and active. With encouragement from a parent corporation which advances a dynamic philosophy of the role of television in the American community, member stations have developed extensive documentary units within their public-affairs divisions, and these stations have gone about the job of creating intelligent studies of community problems. Typical of this dedication was WBZ's *Complex Community* series.

Complex Community offered continuing analyses of such pressing social questions as the suburban explosion, highway and transportation problems, urban renewal, tourism as a New England industry, state government, Massachusetts blue laws, tax structure, and education. "The Next Move" was an examination of the problems of urban renewal and redevelopment. The photography of WBZ's Bob Cirace was startling, crisp, and honest — carefully framed records of slums, tenements, housing projects, and new construction. Yet, too often, the visual material seemed unintegrated with a narration that rolled on at an alarming rate, pouring out facts and figures. Even occasional interviews within the total context did not pose the problem as urgently and precisely as one would wish. Missing was the sustaining point of contact between what was said and what was shown.

In another documentary of the *Complex Community* series, "The Three-Way Street," the same WBZ unit brought to public awareness the traffic problems of Greater Boston. Here there was the establishment of a clear and immediate point of view. This program used film and the "documentary why" in exceptional co-ordination. At the opening we saw a Boston driver and were told what he paid for auto insurance. Then there was a contrasting cut to a Detroit driver, and we learned that *his* insurance rates were only one-half those of the Bostonian's. For the remainder of the program this comparative visual and aural examination continued in similarly direct terms, explaining why and how Detroit had managed to solve so many of the automobile control problems which were besetting Boston. In production skill this program matched many more expensive network efforts, as the story line brought film and narration into intelligent juncture.

This same kind of expert documentary reportage was being executed at other *Group W* stations. KPIX, for example, added to the breadth of its own work in this "problem-solving" area with such series as *San Francisco Pageant,* an imaginative survey of that city's history. The *Group W* activity in public-affairs programming represents the most advanced state of the art from the viewpoint of group ownership of TV stations in America, an art also reflected in the efforts of the Crown, Triangle, and Corinthian stations, as well as the NBC and CBS chains of owned-and-operated stations. These have provided significant documentaries for local audiences and, along with *Group W,* represent leadership in this field.

An important measure of the growing importance and impact of the local station public-affairs program is evidenced by the introduction, in 1962, of special category awards for such programming into the annual recognitions of the National Academy of Television Arts and Sciences. In 1963 eight such regional programs were named by committees at the National Academy; and WCBS-TV's "Superfluous People" was judged the best.[4]

It should be noted that no less than four entries originated in these CBS owned-and-operated stations: New York City's WCBS-TV, Chicago's WBBM-TV, Philadelphia's WCAU-TV, and Los Angeles' KNXT-TV. Indeed, "Superfluous People" was only one of over 60 filmed documentary programs produced at WCBS-TV in 1962, where producers such as Gordon Hyatt and Warren Wallace have consistently sought to equal the level of their network peers. Hyatt's abilities have emerged in such reminiscence pieces as "La Vie Élégante," a film re-creation of the gilded era in Manhattan mansions, and the slightly tongue-in-cheek assessments of manners and mores seen in "Automobiles and Attitudes" and "The House That Jack Built," wry commentaries on the art of planned obsolescence in America's cars and homes.

But it was Warren Wallace's look at the social welfare issue, "Superfluous People," which was selected to represent WCBS-TV, and which deserved the national honor it was accorded. This documentary was an hour-long essay built out of that single statement by an elder of Newburgh, New

"LA VIE ÉLÉGANTE"
(Produced by Gordon Hyatt for WCBS-TV, New York)

York, which summarized the theme of the earlier *White Paper*: "There are no simple answers to big problems — there aren't even simple answers to simple problems." Wallace brought a warm heart and cool head to his study of the plight of New York's welfare cases. At times, his scenes of elderly derelicts, high school drop-outs, and the chronically unemployed reflected the reserved social "analysis" of Rogosin's *On The Bowery;* and at other times we were drawn into pity and sympathy for the human lives set before us — the universality of spirit which touches all mankind when we see babies awaiting adoption, children at a city shelter, and displaced elderly citizens to whom the "progress" represented by new housing projects meant only the bitterness of not belonging.

KNXT's entry, "Burden of Shame," narrated by actor James Whitmore, was a straightforward treatment of the sexual psychopath in our society — relating the history of a child molester in abrupt and often shocking terms. This documentation of a typical patient admitted to Cali-

"SUPERFLUOUS PEOPLE"
Produced by Warren Wallace for WCBS-TV, New York

fornia's Atascedero State Hospital employed the stream-of-consciousness narration in early scenes where the associative thought processes which led to the criminal act were revealed. Music and soft focus were blended with voice-over reflections of the sick man as he recalled the circumstances of his crimes and his eventual capture. Once he entered the hospital, however, we saw actual scenes of his treatment and the camera became subjective. The most vivid moments were those in which the inmates were gathered together for therapy. The camera eavesdropped on the actuality of men in inward torment as they tried to identify themselves and the reasons for their acts. Far from being sensationalistic, "Burden of Shame" was a rational plea for increased attention to, and understanding of, this serious social problem — an issue which television has seldom touched upon.

From WCAU-TV in Philadelphia came a first-rate documentation of a broader problem of modern civilization, "Conformity." Reported by Harry Reasoner, whose wit complemented this often humorous analysis of a technology-bent society, the program brought into telling illustration the theories of the "mass society" advanced by so many social scientists. Several individual scenes of the way in which men become slaves to machines and processes harked back to Ruttman's *Berlin* and such later documentary films as *The City*. During some of the re-enacted scenes — as when a school-teacher questioned students who have become mere puppets reciting by rote — the argument was forced and unreal, yet on the whole "Conformity" was a considerable achievement in making us aware of that world in which "everybody is taking refuge in being nobody so that they will not have to be somebody." In accordance with a CBS practice of exchanging programs among its various stations, "Conformity" was later shown on the west coast.

Station WBBM-TV in Chicago was represented by "The Wasted Years," a half-hour study of prison routine at the grim Statesville Prison. Producer Hugh Hill, director Bill Robbins, and a WBBM-TV crew went inside the prison to make their record — a revelation of the spiritual and intellectual impoverishment of prison life. Added power was given "The Wasted Years" by a segment at the closing in which the student drop-out problem in Chicago's schools was related to preceding content. This was an interview of two brothers whose thoughtless crimes of their youth had led to their incarceration. When WBBM-TV manager Clark B. George ended the program with a sharp, face-to-camera statement, the force of the documentary itself came immediately home to local audiences. The technique deserves greater consideration in all TV documentaries aimed at the younger audience.

From the southwest came "Time's Man," the regional winner from WKY-TV in Oklahoma City and the only compilation documentary included. This nostalgic treatment of the life of an early western photographer, James B. Camp, was really a study of Oklahoma's history as well.

"BURDEN OF SHAME"
(Produced by Mike Kizziah for KNXT, Los Angeles)

"THE WASTED YEARS"
(Produced by Hugh Hill for WBBM-TV, Chicago)

Camp had been engaged as newsreel photographer by Pathé in the earliest years of this century. His work for Pathé, beginning in 1912, is still preserved, as are scenes from western movies for which he was also a cameraman, and a great amount of footage which he enthusiastically recorded throughout a quarter of a century. From this wealth of footage was derived an insightful and sympathetic portrait of Camp himself, but chiefly in terms of Oklahoma and its people.

The work of WKY-TV is of larger interest, for its program manager, Joe Jerkins, has set forth a unique and forceful philosophy of the role of documentary at his station in preserving the heritage of the southwest. He has encouraged his creative personnel and exhorted his fellow managers to follow along, and his attitude and commitment have resulted in such works as the above-mentioned "Time's Man," "The Pioneer Painter" (a beautiful biography of Augusta Metcalfe), and "The Run" (director Gene Allen's nostalgic account of the land rush in Oklahoma). These were all included in the WKY-TV *Oklahoma Heritage* series.

The northwest region selected Robert Schulman's production for KING-TV in Seattle, "Suspect." The program was a tribute to Schulman's theory that "the one-ton pencil" of television journalism must first yield to the ball-point pen. With a dogged reporter's instinct, a hate campaign in the state of Washington conducted by the John Birch society and other extremist groups — a campaign of smear and innuendo which led to the defeat of a liberal young state representative of fine reputation and unquestioned loyalty — was exposed by Schulman.

The range of these documentaries represented the best of the local station activity in a single year, 1962. All of them portend even greater use of the documentary as an instrument in dealing with community heritage, pride, and spirit, as well as social problems.

Other local efforts cut wide and deep. WNBQ-TV in Chicago has accepted, along with WBNS-TV in Columbus, Ohio, and many other local stations, the challenge of attempting a weekly half-hour News Documentary. WCCO-TV in Minneapolis has turned out a series with a local sting — News Documentary in the crusading tradition. At WSB-TV in Atlanta, George Page produced "Block-Busting, Atlanta Style," and at WBRZ-TV in Baton Rouge, Douglas Manship helped to pave the way for peaceful desegregation of that city's public schools by anticipating the crisis and then offering a series of programs in the documentary style which explained to teen-agers the need for pride in community and respect for law. These typify an emerging documentary journalism at the community level.

The Theme Documentary has also had widespread local application. In Chicago the ABC affiliate, WBKB-TV, brought the accomplished British documentarist, Denis Mitchell, to America to make a poetic study of the city — a documentary subsequently never seen in America after protest was raised over the resultant "image" of Chicago. Yet Mitchell's influence remained, and William Friedkin was moved from WGN-TV to WBKB-TV, where he has been allowed to create sensitive "experimental" documentaries. The *Group W* organization had also created an important 13-program documentary series in the late 1950's, using the Brady records of the Civil War. In New York, WNBC offered an impressionistic look at New York in "The Unquiet River," and Philadelphia's WFIL-TV presented a valuable program in the oldest tradition of documentary, "Land of Distelfink" (1962), which reported the lives of the Mennonites and the Amish in the Pennsylvania Dutch country.

Not all local documentaries, of course, have been effective. Such WGN-TV programs as "Tuf Guys" and "Friday's Children" have exhibited some tastelessness in visual execution and a badly overwritten "radio-style" narration. The same station's later "Ballad of Chicago," while saved by William Friedkin's magnificent color photography in its closing sequence, nevertheless holds the "sex and sock" of too primitive a kind of showmanship. Elsewhere, stations have allowed sports programs — generally sponsored by auto dealers — to slide into their program logs as significant achievements in "documentary." Too much, in too many stations, is still unoriginal — a pale imitation of what has already been done. And there is probably some direct relationship between the quality of documentary work and a station's professional pride coupled with concern for public conscience. Those who have been dragged along by what they called "the encroachment of government," instead of being spurred by their own sense of obligation, generally have produced only what is utterly banal. But these may still learn from the majority of stations which take their documentaries seriously. In the area of public affairs the excuse of providing a sound economic base for documentary programming can hardly be the concern of any commercially licensed VHF television station in the United States.

The matter of economics has, however, delayed the educational TV stations of America in their application of the documentary method. It is a case of a more-than-willing spirit, but an incapacity to develop expensive documentary units and make full use of film. Much of the best ETV work up to the 1960's was still confined to the live studio, as understaffed stations found it difficult to detach specialized personnel for documentary projects. As the number of educational stations on the air now moves toward 100, and as a growing public support seems imminent, the possibilities of important documentary work at these stations increase.

National Educational Television has developed rapidly in programming exceptional material by creating its own public-affairs series and by supporting the work of such network stations as KETC-TV, St. Louis, which produced *Forty-Five Years with Fitzpatrick* (1961), a still-in-motion series devoted to the work of the famed St. Louis *Post-Dispatch* editorial cartoonist. NET has also served the documentary movement with its "Lorentz on Film" (1961), which dealt with the work of the great film documentarist. Produced at WGBH-TV in Boston, this four-part treatment of the great films of Lorentz featured a commentary by film historian Charles Rockwell. And, of course, NET has offered to its member stations four of Robert Flaherty's greatest films.

Since 1963, NET, stimulated by the establishment of WNDT — a network "flagship" station — in New York City, has expanded documentary activities. David Susskind has occasionally entered the NET service as executive producer of such documentary projects as "Balance of Terror," a report on NATO produced by Jack L. Willis and directed by Canadian Douglas Leiterman. Ralph Tangney, who produced and directed the KETC-TV series on Fitzpatrick, has been given such special NET assignments as the semidocumentary "Of Time, Work and Leisure," a one-hour analysis of the misuse of free time in our society.

With its de-emphasis of radio service, NET has attempted to solve the problem of creating a wider audience for its significant TV programming by investing in one essential element — creative talent. It has begun to acquire fresh and talented documentarists who learned their craft with the best commercial units. Such men as James Karayn, who spent seven years as a documentary writer and director at KTLA in Los Angeles and earned additional research experience at NBC's *White Paper,* has now moved to NET, along with William Weston, who wrote, directed, and produced the 1963 ABC-TV special, "The Soviet Woman." Weston had previously worked under Irving Gitlin for six years during the latter's tenure at CBS. These appointments reflect NET's growth, and the future for documentary is now brighter than in all ETV history.

Finally, two unusual and important attempts to extend the scope of the television documentary deserve detailed attention, since they carry some future promise for bringing not only individual communities, but the community of nations itself, toward a new and greater understanding of common aims and purposes.

FOCUS ON AMERICA

In 1963 *Focus on America,* carried by the ABC network as a summer public-affairs series, featured documentaries produced by ABC owned and affiliated stations around the country. This series brought local station documentaries to a full national audience, proceeding toward the achievement of some broader social analysis and understanding in relation to the local point of view. The series offered such representative examples of documentary as WRVA-TV's "A Lincoln Legacy" and "Lee Memorial" — two half-hour programs which featured re-enactment of the lives of these famous Americans — combined as a single hour-long program by the network. The scripts were prepared from historical documents by John Collison and Al Tyler, and the productions directed by Dave Smally.

Station WXYZ-TV in Detroit was represented on *Focus on America* by "Emergency Room," an account of the details of treatment given a seriously injured victim of an auto accident at Detroit's receiving hospital. John Pival, Peter Strand, and Irving A. Mus collaborated in this effort, which was narrated by Dr. Alan P. Thal, Director of Surgery at the hospital. WJZ in Baltimore provided a document which sought increased knowledge of Hansen's disease (leprosy), "The Mark of Man." A production team led by Wallace Hamilton, Bill Weyse, and Bob Giuliana filmed this story with the co-operation of the World Health Organization, the United States Public Health Service, and the American Protestant Leprosy Association. WTVN-TV in Columbus, Ohio, was represented by "To the Moon and Beyond," which featured an interview with Wernher von Braun; WABC-TV in New York offered "Reported Missing — DD13," a study of the New York Police Department's missing persons' unit; KOCO-TV in Oklahoma City submitted "Flight to Yesterday," an exploration of the role played by Oklahoma and its people in the development of aviation; and KOMO-TV in Seattle produced "The Climb to the Summit," which traced the ascent of Mount Rainier by a group training for an assault on Everest.

Of the group, however, two productions were especially remarkable: "Synanon — So Fair a House" (WNHC-TV, New Haven, Conn.), and "Picture of a Cuban" (WLBW-TV, Miami). These were more meaningful than the others not only because they explained a local phenomenon of considerable social significance which was not common to other localities and regions, but because their conception and execution allowed once more for that complete and compelling study of people in an inward crisis. J. Arthur Stober's production for the New Haven station set out to explore the purpose and function of Connecticut's controversial narcotics rehabilitation center, Synanon, in terms of the expressions of the addicts who came there and found a cure. From a series of intense close-up encounters of Synanon's founder, Jack Hurst — and those addicts who hopefully followed him — Stober, photographer Jack Youngs, and editor Len Sanna created a documentary which carried all the urgency and drama of the best network offerings.

Similarly, "Picture of a Cuban" portrayed the plight of those who fled from Castro's Cuba to take up a new life in the Greater Miami area. The value of this work is in its reasoned statement of what life has come to mean for these unfortunates, and in the ways Miamians have responded with warmth and sympathy toward them. In the confusion of those first months after Castro's rise to power, our mass media gave Americans too hurried a picture of these new citizens, and this documentary of the hard-working and dignified Cuban community of Miami (where the juvenile delinquency rate is far lower than among the native Miami population) was a credit to the WLBW-TV "Project 10" staff, including writer Stanley H. Bloom, photographer-editor Ken Butcher, and News and Special Events director Jack Gregson.

The ABC experiment was a worthy one, deep in the tradition of the documentary commitment to "bring the empire alive." While the practice is growing, too few of these exchanges of local problems and institutions are yet in effect among America's TV stations. For it is in this area that the nation may realize the problems of the single, though diversified, American community. It is too easy for men of good will to make social and cultural judgments about the ways in which others should live, without feeling the peculiarities of circumstance which lead other communities or regions along life-patterns of their own. When these patterns do not conflict with the basic rights of men, or with a clear national interest, the exchange of documentaries may be a certain way to enlighten distant others — to make them sense the values of the past and the infinitely diverse ways in which men may organize their lives. Such exchange promises to enrich our culture and increase social understanding in new and subtle ways which the nationally produced documentary cannot often achieve.

INTERTEL

The same values can be attributed to *Intertel*, the most consequential project in TV documentary exchange yet conceived. *Intertel* came into being in late 1960 when five groups of broadcasters in the four major English-speaking nations formed the International Television Federation. The participants were: Associated Rediffusion, Ltd. of Great Britain; the Australian Broadcasting Commission; the Canadian Broadcasting Corporation; and, in America, the National Educational Television and Radio Center and the Westinghouse Broadcasting Company. These organizations created, in effect, an international TV production agency, producing hour-long documentaries on a bimonthly basis. Each member agency agreed to provide a means of national distribution in the nation it represented, as well as a source and facility for production. The *Intertel* participants agreed also to a number of conditions which favored a wide distribution for the individual programs, chief among which was the showing of these programs in prime time. In the United States the documentaries produced thus far have been aired over the five Group W stations and the growing number of NET affiliates. In addition, the series is now available for initial runs in markets not already covered, or for reruns in areas where further audiences are sought.

The 1960 commitment (renewed in each subsequent year) consisted of 12 programs to be broadcast in 1961 and 1962, of which four were produced by the British, four by the United States, and two each by the Australians and Canadians. Each group finances its own production, and the Americans have averaged from $50,000 to $60,000 for each episode

— a cost borne by WBC and NET, which also share the decision-making roles. NET president John F. White, NET vice president Robert Hudson, WBC president Donald McGannon, and WBC vice president Richard M. Pack co-operate closely in establishing policies and guidelines for the American productions. Aside from this hopeful example of the way in which America's educational and commercial telecasters can work with a common aim, the entire *Intertel* project carries great possibilities of a fresh and dynamic approach to international communication which such technological achievements as communication satellites can enhance, but hardly initiate.

The true prospect of what Goethe called a *Weltliteratur* is held forth in such innovations as *Intertel*, and the proof, quite naturally, lies not in good intentions, but in the actual productions of *Intertel*. We see in them a cogent effort to affect international understanding, the success of which depends upon an overriding policy that each member nation must not dwell upon its own social, economic, political, and human problems but upon those of other member nations. Thus, in the first programs, a British ARD unit headed by director Bill Morton and writer Elkan Allen examined "The Quiet War" in Viet-Nam, which included a rumination on the dictatorial rule of the now deposed Ngo Dinh Diem. The result was an illumination of the human factors in this conflict by an unimpassioned outside observer — and a revelation for Americans.

In "Postscript to Empire" a WBC-NET unit led by Michael Sklar journeyed to England to examine the social and industrial revolution there by contrasting the socio-economic structures of two communities. Focusing upon the typical residents of the Isle of Dogs, a drab and tradition-ridden shipping community, and Stevenage New Town, a modern and classless industrial community, Sklar and director Michael Alexander shaped a fascinating account of the change overtaking Britain. The Old Guard was here, represented by a conservative British couple on the Isle of Dogs who lamented the growth of labor unions and, as they would express it, the death of initiative. The New Guard was represented by a young Isle of Dogs couple who saw no hope in their future there, and moved to Stevenage New Town. There was relentless, and often humorous, contrast of the two outlooks upon life, brought to a subtle climax in a semi-interview scene between a miffed conservative (who so resented the invasion of the "common" worker at Stevenage New Town that he could barely keep his old-school manners intact) and a bristling Laborite from London who had become a community leader at Stevenage and carried on his shoulders some of the near-paternal responsibility for others which the wealthy lord had once reserved to himself. The "class-against-mass" attitudes were revealed in a devastating way. "Postscript to Empire," representing the American view of a changing England, also provided a source of discomfort to some Englishmen. Sklar commented that "half of the

"POSTSCRIPT TO EMPIRE"
Produced for Intertel by Michael Sklar, representing Westinghouse Broadcasting
and National Educational Television

Mr. and Mrs. Woodward Fisher, of the Isle of Dogs, London.

British press thought it good, one-quarter found it dull and the rest found it scandalous and full of lies."[5] In light of the planning for these documentaries, the reaction was perhaps typical, but it is precisely this look from the outside *in* which constitutes the highest value of the entire *Intertel* project.

There is some reason to believe, by way of further example, that a few Americans might find the British look at United States-Canadian relations less than amusing. "Living With a Giant" was an objective, albeit controversial, view of Canada subject to the economic dominance of its neighbor. Directed by Rollo Gamble for Associated Rediffusion, Ltd., this film did for Americans what "Postscript to Empire" did for Britons. If a United States citizen from the southwest who had never been in Canada were to see, without hearing the sound-track, lengthy sections of this film which portrayed general social conditions and customs in Guelph, Ontario, he might without question assume that he was witnessing a typical American small town. But it was when we heard Elkan Allen's narration and the arguments of Canadians among themselves about United States influence that the ironies of the situation were fully established. Perhaps the most significant technique of thematic revelation came when we heard voice-over debate about Canadian literature and the arts — as the camera slowly tracked an endless display of American magazines in a Canadian drugstore. The eavesdropping into Canadian bar-room conversations may have been disturbing to many Americans who fail to understand that people in foreign countries do not necessarily regard every aspect of our life and culture as ideal.

But "Living With a Giant" posed the questions to be asked — as do the very best of documentaries — and we were left wondering, at the close, which paths Canada must follow if it is to retain social and cultural, perhaps even political, independence.

The possibility that the "outside view" might have caused some resentment and friction was barely suggested in such programs as these. In

"LIVING WITH A GIANT"
Produced for Intertel by Rollo Gamble, representing Associated Rediffusion, Ltd.

a typical Canadian — American style.

future programs, however, the attitude of one nation toward a delicate issue on which another *Intertel* member has opposing views and policies may raise some awkward questions. There is, for example, the case of "Cuba, Si!" — a Canadian treatment of Castro's government which was to be shown early in *Intertel*'s first year of operation. The program has not yet been seen, or perhaps even completed.

Even more pertinent to this discussion is the program which was made on the American civil rights struggle, "One More River." Produced and directed by Douglas Leiterman as a CBC *Intertel* offering (although not originally commissioned by *Intertel*), the film was rejected for showing in the United States by both Westinghouse Broadcasting and NET, who arrived independently at their decisions. Analysis of "One More River," as well as Leiterman's other works for *Intertel* (including "40 Million Shoes," an examination of social, political, and economic conditions in Brazil, and "Don't Label Me," a report on Cheddi Jagan's "neutralism" in British Guiana), may lead us to appreciate why "Cuba, Si!" was first "delayed for revisions," and then quietly dropped from *Intertel* showings in the United States.

There is little doubt that Leiterman is a skilled film-maker. Yet he invaded the area of crucial public policy with a too private and often "art-for-art's-sake" attitude, exercising a style governed more by emotional effect than by journalistic resolve. In "One More River" the creator's hand was heavy and his taste indiscriminate. A great deal of the life and character of the American Negro was untouched, and such omission hopelessly distorted the total situation. Lengthy segments of the film portrayed only extremists, both white and Negro, and these were not always properly and honestly identified. There were incredible juxtapositions of voice and picture which tended merely to establish the standpoints of such extremists, and whole scenes in which music was emotionally dominant. Leiterman's preoccupation with only the most brutal and primitive aspects of the lives of a few whites and Negroes gave many scenes the same tone of cynicism and sensationalism seen in such banal theatrical "documentaries" as *Mondo Cane* and *Women of the World* — films which were combinations of the nudist movie, the travel film, and Ripley's "Believe It or Not."[6]

The very problem which "One More River" introduced points to the greatest inherent difficulty in all international exchange of documentaries. Just as there are Americans who might resent Leiterman's treatment of our integration problem, surely there must be many Britons who would disagree with Michael Sklar's selection of a single caricatured couple to represent the conservative view in England. In these programs the balance of control was shifted from life to art, and when creative approach is determined by the outsider's orientation, a new element of conservatism may not be amiss, while the need for added judgment and reserve becomes essential.

DOUGLAS LEITERMAN

. . . for Americans, too heavy a hand.

Despite these problems, *Intertel* remains the most far-reaching of the new directions in TV documentary. It has given Americans the opportunity to see first-hand the skills and achievements of great documentarists outside our nation. But this is only a small part of its significance.[7] The greatest value of *Intertel* lies in its potentiality for teaching us how to live together as neighbors in a world community. And this, in the final analysis, may be the greatest service which the television documentary can extend.

Part Five /
TELEVISION AND THE DOCUMENTARY QUEST

No EXPRESSION about television's role in relation to documentary is more germane than Hubbell Robinson's view that the medium is employed with greatest facility when it becomes "a channel to the minds and emotions of millions." Television, he believes, must always be measured by its success in penetrating *majorities*. This may be said of documentary in all media throughout the history of the form. Documentary still-photography attained maximum impact when it was incorporated into the widely circulated pictorial magazines; the documentary in radio flourished when attention was turned toward informing a broad public of wartime urgencies and obligations; documentary film became a truly meaningful instrument when it, too, sought to galvanize whole societies into supporting crucial national causes. Throughout this century the most effective documentary expression has reached outward to energize great masses of mankind.

In its documentary function television, the ultimate of the "dream machines" (as André Malraux has termed the electro-mechanical media), can no more avoid the implications of this history than escape its own powers. Television has given to the arts of social persuasion the final dimension which all documentarists of the past earnestly sought but could never summon: the control of the attention of an entire civilization. Not long ago I wrote that by the year 2000 a typical child born into this world may very well spend one-fifth of the waking hours of his life attending to messages emanating from a television receiver. This constancy of attention, utilized in the interests of admonishments for social change cast in an aural-visual, motion-in-time method, creates an essential precondition for what Sylvester Weaver has called "a mutation of man."

It is the *massness* of the television medium that dominates our hopeful applications of its potentials. But massness has its own terrors. Now that we possess this communicative means to control the course of civilization, the question all thinking men must ponder is what we will control it *for*. As we begin such inquiry in full view of television's influence, we see the need of further speculation upon that classic Griersonian use of documentary for promoting social interdependence — the energizing of a society into an acceptance of those immediate decisions which may lead to social betterment.

For those with a total commitment to social progress, the employment of a documentary method in television is only too obvious. Societal tensions must be reduced, and the political and economic complexities of a world faced by threats of atomic horror must be explained and reduced to soluble terms with all the speed and urgency we can summon. Documentary use of television seems the only logical implement for the achievement of these goals. There *is* need for a mutation in man, and none can gainsay the power of television for effecting it. Social propaganda on television screens — in large, repeated, and palatable doses — can reflect the highest aspirations for a working-out of practical and immediate solutions to incredibly involved and complex problems. For all who appreciate the difficulties and dangers of a truly democratic society, this is the challenge and the hope of documentary in television.

Yet we are aware that the argument has its paradoxes. In the ambitious rush to direct the television medium away from the merely titillating and entertaining, documentarists bent on social reform may find, with Rubashov, that while they have begun to create flower gardens they may end by building prisons. The world has changed since John Grierson initiated the tradition of "social analysis" in documentary film — that eager attempt to characterize man in relation to his institutions and thus help him to sense his social relationships with others. The tough and hard propaganda line for social betterment has run an unexpected course, and now we witness societies which are no better off than when they first began to convert their public media to social analysis, or to a private determination of how the media were to be used.

The example of Britain lies before us. In a nation where for nearly a quarter of a century the public media of communication were adapted to, or totally controlled by, the vision of a quantitative and qualitative "social good," and where in many instances a sharp limitation upon the nature and content of output in these media was operative policy, we are still confronted by a society in torment. Grierson's documentary vision is corrupted, as Dilys Powell has astutely observed, because "now we *have* the welfare state, and are no better off than before." For all of the value of Grierson's poetic propaganda is forever demeaned by the simple fact that while it helped Britain to reach such immediate decisions as would sustain social order in a paralyzing period, the ultimate results have made life no richer, no more enduring or endurable, than in any other industrial nation. If the goal is better *men* in a better *society*, then surely Grierson's vision has dimmed.

Certainly it must be recognized that without the help of compelling and widespread social communications, no nation might be able to survive the changes wrought during this century. The crisis of our age, Lippmann has argued, is a crisis in *journalism*, in the failure of the reporting media to show us the way. Decisions must be made with increasing rapidity in free societies, and documentary will always be useful in influencing the acceptance of such decisions among the electorates. Yet one may legitimately ask what is to be preserved if this onslaught of compelling communication stressing only problems of whole societies — the long Griersonian tradition of making us see ourselves exclusively as "socially interdependent" — goes on and on? Does the energizing of the masses pose greater dangers? Does the suggestion that television is a means for the mutation of man hold dreadful prospects of producing men who will no longer be men at all, but merely social components?

There is an alternative; and the alternative is clear to all who would return to the work of Robert Flaherty, a documentarist who gave Marxist critics little cause for cheer and who, while respected by Grierson, never shared the Griersonian ethic. If, as I have suggested in my summary of the evolution of documentary film, the efforts of Flaherty were "anachronistic" at a time when men were eagerly seeking new uses for this powerful interpretative force, they were also seminal. If the documentary film-maker did not move forward from Flaherty's position it may be because his work represented a state of human dignity, integrity, and understanding from which there is no movement other than regression.

Arthur Calder-Marshall stresses this quality in his recent biography of Flaherty. In describing *Industrial Britain,* Calder-Marshall notes that the visions of Flaherty and Grierson first crossed in the making of this "public-relations" film. "One sees," he writes, "at this single point . . . the fundamental division between the two men, Flaherty's individual quest for the long truth and Grierson's with the brief progressive one." There is no more basic point to be made. If the documentary in television is to attain its maximum potential as an agent for intelligent change in our civilization, it must continue to recognize and express the diverse philosophies and attitudes revealed in both the Flaherty and the Grierson approaches to the film of reality.

The lives and work of Robert Flaherty and John Grierson remind us again that there is little new under the sun; that all documentary efforts to help us "get on" in the world about us begin and end with their distinct ways of revealing life to us. In his own manner and style each expressed the ultimate needs of men and societies. Television's control of a civilization's attention places a broader responsibility upon those who follow in the paths of these two giants. The documentarists of television must nurture two ideals: of men as social agents, and of each man as a *person*.

Each man possesses, on the one hand, an awareness of that social necessity which impels him to order the world around him, to create social structures involving other men within which all may find justice and common welfare. Yet each man also holds firmly to a concept of self — that personal attunement with the cosmos which cannot end, he must believe, when his physical form has ceased to exist. Whatever uniqueness may be attributed to his condition of being more than animal and less than God, man alone is in conscious possession of the knowledge that while he must live with others, he will die alone. His sense of importance in the scheme of things may cause the gods (and not a few physical and behavioral scientists) to smile; but yet it is this sense that underlies all meaning, and is the very touchstone of reality and its representations.

Thus knowledge commits man not solely, then, to the immediate decision, to that necessary involvement with others which leads to control and direction of the quality of his existence. It also commits him to a search within himself — to a self-evolved ordering of experience. Upon social action depends his stability in the world; but upon his individual wonder and reflection depends the true progress of mankind. There are for each man realities which are his alone, and the strength with which he clings to them marks all that is prideful and noble about him. William James reminded us that "reality surrounds and overflows logic," and Nietzsche wrote that tragedy is the failure to learn from the experience of others. It is precisely that individual sense of wonder which makes the aware human question all that seems too narrowly logical and therefore insignificant in the long perspective — and finally come to look upon experience with the native and innocent eye.

The immediate decision, the innocent eye: these are the two great contradictory forces which underlie our confrontations with reality in all of its manifest forms. They succinctly characterize the work not only of Grierson and Flaherty, but of all who have since come to apply "creative treatment" to actuality. Of all those men of our century who must reflect a balance and wholeness between these two aspects of life, none may have more final effect upon our lives than the strange mixture of reporter and poet we call the documentarist. He, and the managers and editors who influence and control his work, may hopefully set the example by which all of us may not only survive, but prevail.

The possibilities are all but overwhelming. If we possess the technology by which to obliterate ourselves, we also have the capacities to harness technology in the responsible service of mankind — seeking not only an essential betterment and a new level of harmony among men and nations, but the individuation of man. Even the most skeptical detractors of the mass media will admit that television, in its greatest moments, has served both goals. For all can sense that the images on the TV screen help to create, for the first time in human history, *communicating man* — a creation which underlies both a social and an individual view of life. Through documentary, TV may show us that we are capable of identifying specific needs and issues of our world, and can adopt those intelligent plans of action which give us the positive security of a truly civilized social contract. And it can also apply its great force for individuation of the human spirit. This is what the American television documentary has attempted. If the function must be enlarged and made still more meaningful, the medium has at least engaged in the quest. And it is the *quest*, John Fitzgerald Kennedy once told us, that is the true adventure of this century.

REFERENCE NOTES

THE DOCUMENTARY IDEA: A FRAME OF REFERENCE
Pages 13-16

1. John Grierson, "The Story of the Documentary Film," *The Fortnightly Review,* August, 1939, 121-30.
2. Lewis Mumford, *Art and Technics,* New York, 1952, 21.
3. See *Grierson on Documentary,* Forsyth Hardy, (ed.), London, 1946. The earliest definitive statement of documentary purpose and function in the cinema is found in Part Two of this work, where Grierson laid down the basic principles which guided British documentary film in its formative years. "You photograph the natural life," he wrote, "but you also, by your juxtaposition of detail, create an interpretation of it.", 82.
4. Margaret R. Weiss, "Creative Vision — Six Decades of the Photographer's Art," *Saturday Review*, September 22, 1962, 51.

CHAPTER 1: PHOTOGRAPHY: THE FIXED MOMENT
Pages 17-31

1. Beaumont Newhall, *The History of Photography*, New York, 1949, 186.
2. Maya Deren, "Cinematography: The Creative Uses of Reality," *Daedalus,* Winter, 1960, 155.
3. Wilbur Schramm, "The Nature of News," *Journalism Quarterly*, September, 1949, 259.
4. Arthur Rothstein, *Photojournalism: Pictures for Magazines and Newspapers,* New York, 1956, 1.
5. *Ibid.,* 3.
6. Roy Stryker. *The Complete Photographer*, 1942, IV, 1364-74. Quoted in Newhall, *op. cit.,*180.
7. Newhall, *op. cit.*, 182-83.
8. *Loc. cit.*
9. Margaret R. Weiss, "In the Tradition of Joseph Costa," *Saturday Review*, January 12, 1963, 93.

246

CHAPTER 2: FILM: THE FLUID MOMENT
Pages 32-59

1. Rule Twelve, Section One: Special Rules for Documentary Awards, Academy of Motion Picture Arts and Sciences, Hollywood, California.
2. Erwin Panofsky, "Style and Medium in the Motion Pictures," *Critique,* New York, January-February, 1947, 5-28.
3. Andrew Buchanan, *The Art of Film Production,* London, 1936, 72.
4. In *Grierson on Documentary,* 78.
5. Quoted in Eugene Lyons, "Louis de Rochemont, Maverick of the Movies," *Reader's Digest,* July, 1949, 23.
6. Paul Rotha, *Documentary Film,* London, 1952, 248.
7. See Raymond Fielding's *The March of Time: 1935 1942,* unpublished M.A. thesis, The University of California, January, 1956, 17. Fielding provides a detailed analysis of production method throughout this valuable study.
8. *New York Times,* October 27, 1935.
9. Alistair Cooke, *The Listener,* November 20, 1935, 931.
10. Rotha, *op. cit.,* 117.
11. Raymond Spottiswoode, *A Grammar of the Film,* Berkeley and Los Angeles, 1959, 287.
12. Rotha, *loc. cit.*
13. It was in his review of *Moana* for the *New York Sun* that Grierson, writing as *The Moviegoer,* first employed the term "documentary."
14. Flaherty's cameraman for this film was Richard Leacock, whose influence in the television documentary is examined in Chapters 6 and 9.
15. Spottiswoode, *loc. cit.*
16. See Arthur Calder-Marshall's biography of Flaherty, based upon the notes of Paul Rotha and Basil Wright, *The Innocent Eye,* London, 1963, 140. Calder-Marshall writes: "Flaherty had nothing to do with the commentary of *Industrial Britain,* His vision made a direct contribution to the main sequence . . . But the idiom of the Commentary was Griersonian."
17. One of the greatest of documentary cinematographers, Crosby worked with Lorentz on later films, as well as with Flaherty.
18. The film was made by Willard Van Dyke, whose television work has been extensive. See Chapter 10 and Appendix 1.

CHAPTER 3: RADIO: THE FORGOTTEN ART
Pages 60-72

1. Martin Maloney, *The Radio Play,* Evanston, 1951, 196.
2. See Harrison B. Summers, *Radio Programs Carried on National Networks, 1926-1956,* Columbus, 1958. This authoritative study, including data on sponsorship, ratings and program classes, is the starting point for research in network program history.
3. See Milo Ryan, *History in Sound,* Seattle, 1963, for a valuable listing of World War II broadcasts by CBS preserved in the Phonoarchives of the University of Washington.
4. Reported in the published proceedings of the 1947 Institute for Education by Radio and Television, *Education on the Air,* Columbus, 1947, 377.
5. *Ibid.,* 374.
6. See Chapter 5.
7. Among the most interesting efforts dealing with the changing habits of the radio audience is KDKA's "vertical documentary" concept. Speaking before a meeting of the Group W 1963 *Cleveland Conference on Local Public Service Programming,* KDKA Program Manager Jack Williams described a series of regularly scheduled, five-minute capsules which pursue a common theme and story throughout a period ranging from one day to a week. Aired every hour on the half-hour, as few as 12 or as many as 48 of these may be included in a series. These are bulwarked by one or more hour-long documentaries on the subject

covered. Audience identification is sought by the playing of specially prepared songs prior to each five minute capsule.

CHAPTER 4: LIFE TO DRAMA: DOCUMENTARY'S LIMITS
Pages 73-88

1. Nicholas Vardac, "Documentary Film as an Art Form," *Sight and Sound,* April, 1951, 479.
2. John Gassner, (ed.), *A Treasury of the Theatre,* New York, 1950, 2-9.
3. See Morgan Y. Himelstein's *Drama Was a Weapon,* New Brunswick, 1963. Himelstein documents the full scope of theatrical activity in New York between 1929 and 1941.
4. Quoted in Himelstein, *op. cit.,* 87.
5. Mordecai Gorelik, *New Theatres for Old,* Binghamton, N.Y., 1949, 397.
6. Maya Deren, "The Creative Uses of Reality," 157.
7. Quoted by David Robinson, "Looking For Documentary: The Background to Production, Part I," *Sight and Sound,* Summer, 1957, 6.
8. Vardac, *loc. cit.*
9. "And indeed," wrote Maeterlinck, "the only words that count in the play are those that at first seem useless, for it is therein that the essence lies. Side by side with the necessary dialogue will you almost always find another dialogue that seems superfluous; but examine it carefully and it will be borne home to you that this is the only one that the soul can listen to profoundly, for here alone it is the soul that is being addressed." Quoted from his essay "*Le Tragique quotidien,*" in Barrett H. Clark (ed.), *European Theories of The Drama,* New York, 1947, 413. It is not coincidence that the scripts for the "golden age" works in TV seem slight to those who first examine them.

CONTROL OF SUBJECT: THE ESSENTIAL FRAMEWORK
Pages 89-92

1. René Wellek, *Concepts in Criticism*, New York and New Haven, 1963, 255.

CHAPTER 5: NEWS DOCUMENTARY: THE ONGOING CRISIS
Pages 93-120

1. I have been unable to locate the original source for this oft-quoted remark.
2. Edward R. Murrow and Fred W. Friendly, *See It Now,* New York, 1955. Quotations are taken from the Foreword to this anthology of scripts from the early history of the series. For a full listing of the "old team" see Appendix III.
3. *Loc. cit.*
4. *Loc. cit.*
5. *New York Times,* December 13, 1959.
6. Jacques Andrés, "Television Vérité," *Contrast,* Summer, 1963, 260-261.
7. From a speech before the CBS-TV Network affiliates, New York, May 5, 1961.
8. From "Dialogue: Reuven Frank and Don Hewitt," *Television Quarterly,* November, 1962, 15-16.
9. Arthur Knight, "The Decline of the Documentary," *Saturday Review,* March 30, 1963, 35. Lamenting the quality of the 1962 nominations for the Motion Picture Academy Awards, Knight echoes the ancient argument that "true" documentary cannot be attained when documentarists themselves have lost a sense of social protest.
10. Fred W. Friendly, "TV Can Open America's Eyes," *TV Guide,* December 10, 1960, 7.
11. Wasserman argued his position in this matter at the Group W *Cleveland Conference,* 1963. See also Appendix I.
12. Robert Rubin moved to CBS-TV as a producer in 1963, and was replaced by William Quinn at NBC News Creative Projects.

CHAPTER 6: NEWS DOCUMENTARY: THE CRISIS WITHIN
Pages 121-140

1. Quoted in *Broadcasting*, March 6, 1961, 82. Mr. Drew's remarks were elaborated upon in personal conversations held in early 1963. See Appendix I for a fuller statement of his philosophy.
2. Quoted from personal meetings held in New York City in early 1963. Additional remarks by Mr. Secondari are included in Appendix I.
3. Walter Lassally, "Communication and the Creative Process," *Film — Quarterly Magazine of the Federation of Film Societies*, Autumn, 1963, 19.
4. From the *Broadcasting* report cited in 1, above.
5. The name was coined in France by Jean Rouch and Edgar Morin, but the concepts of a *Cinema direct* probably existed in the earliest silent cinema, particularly in the work of the Russian director, Dziga Vertov, who sought to create a kind of unreconstructed film of reality which could be as revelatory of the human condition as the story film. See "Jean-Luc Goddard's Half-Truths" by Louis Marcorelles (*Film Quarterly, Spring, 1964*) for a discussion of Goddard and *Cinema direct*.
6. Drew insists upon a sharp distinction between the "unobtrusive" and the "hidden" camera. See Appendix I.
7. The irony of the presentation, perhaps, is that it was authorized by the Kennedy administration in response to a charge of "news management." It has been correctly pointed out that, for Wallace and the Kennedys, it was managed news in its essence.
8. The program's host and moderator was Stephen Scheuer, publisher of *TV Key*. Panelists included James Farmer, National Director of the Congress for Racial Equality; James Keogh, Assistant Managing Editor of *Time* Magazine; Frank S. Meyer, a Senior Editor of *National Review*; and Willard Van Dyke. Only documentarist Van Dyke felt that it was a worthwhile attempt; each of his colleagues objected to the purpose and method of his film.
9. Said James Farmer: "We didn't see the way decisions are really made; we didn't see the smoke-filled rooms, the agonizing soliloquies as the individual talks to himself . . . So it was play-acting in that sense." Said the conservative Mr. Meyer: "The end result, it seems to me, is that rather than electing officials whose function it is to consider their conscience and the Constitution of the United States, we're going to elect people to play for Oscars." Drew's answer is found in Appendix I.
10. From personal conversations held with Mr. Secondari in early 1963. See also Appendix I.

CONTROL OF THEME: ART AND RECORD
Pages 141-144

1. George Pierce Baker, *Dramatic Technique*, New York, 1919, 54.
2. Francis Fergusson, *The Idea of a Theatre*, Princeton, 1949, 36.
3. Jacques Maritain, *Creative Intuition in Art and Poetry*, New York, 1955, 255-56.
4. In a recapitulation of the history of this program delivered in an address before the Ohio State Institute for Education by Radio and Television, June, 1963, Frank observed: " . . . it is luck when you can get into a story and watch it unfold, when there is nothing left out, when there are very few questions to ask later, when you don't have to go chasing the story with eyewitnesses and experts, because you were there all the time. . . ."

CHAPTER 7: COMPILATION DOCUMENTARY
Pages 145-163

1. From remarks delivered at the 1957 University of Denver Seminar Workshop in Documentary. See also "Anatomy of a Documentary," *Journal of the University Film Producers Association*, Winter, 1962, 5-7, 20-21.

2. Bernard De Voto, "Easy Chair," *Harper's,* June, 1954. By permission.
3. The Denver Seminar, 1957.
5. Quoted by Clifford L. Jordan, Jr., "The World of Donald Hyatt," *Dartmouth Alumni Magazine*, January, 1961. Reprinted by NBC.

CHAPTER 8: COMPILATION: THE SUCCESSORS
Pages 164-179

1. Burton Benjamin, "The Documentary Heritage," *Television Quarterly*, February, 1962, 32.
2. Norman Swallow, "Ealing, 1961," *Journal: The Society of Film and Television Arts*, Summer, 1961, 4.
3. Gordon Hyatt, "Words *and* Pictures," *Television Quarterly*, Spring, 1963, 47.
4. Originally published in *The Listener*, reprinted in *Television Quarterly,* May, 1962, 73.
5. It has been said that in some of the earlier programs of this series actors were used to play eyewitnesses to events. If the charge is true — and I was not aware of the practice in the many films I saw — then the entire eyewitness concept is undermined. So long as the TV documentarist employs the technique in good faith, however, it remains as television's unique and most powerful contribution to documentary.
6. See Chapter 9.

CHAPTER 9: BIOGRAPHERS TO PLOT-FINDERS
Pages 180-206

1. Delivered in a regular evening TV newscast, CBS, May, 1964.
2. Burton Benjamin, "The Documentary Heritage," 33.
3. From a personal conversation held in New York City in early 1963.
4. Robert Lewis Shayon, "Biography's Backyard," *Saturday Review,* June 29, 1963.
5. An interesting account of corporate philosophy in the sponsorship of a network television series appears in Myron Berkely Shaw's Doctoral dissertation, written at the University of Michigan in 1962, *A Descriptive Analysis of the Documentary Drama Program, Armstrong Circle Theatre, 1955-1961.* Quotations are from a statement of policy issued by the Armstrong Company in the summer of 1955.
6. Quoted in Shaw, 64.
7. From promotional materials supplied by Robert Drew Associates.
8. Drew would insist that this approach destroys the "living camera" concept. See Appendix I.

CHAPTER 10: THE NETWORKS: VARIATIONS
Pages 207-220

1. Grierson, "The Story of the Documentary Film," 121.
2. In 1962 The Fund for Adult Education presented to University College of Syracuse University nearly every *Omnibus* program carried during the series' first two seasons (1951-1952, 1953-1954). The Film Library at Syracuse has made these kinescopes available for study.
3. The *Saga of Western Man* series probably represented Secondari's highest achievement in Television Documentary. The "1964" program, a summation of the entire series, displayed a different technique from its predecessors, as specially-shot film was employed throughout. The recurring sequences of waves pounding against the shore was matched by Secondari's brilliant poetic narrative at the close of "1964." The theme of man's insignificance in the endlessness of time was given a consummate expression.

4. While Van Dyke would argue in behalf of the social documentary which makes specific points (see Appendix I), his finest work has always reflected the "individualistic" style of Flaherty.
5. From material supplied by NBC Press Information.
6. "Dialogue: Reuven Frank and Don Hewitt," 19.
7. *Loc. cit.* See also Appendix II.

CHAPTER 11: LOCAL DOCUMENTARY: AN OVERVIEW
Pages 221-240

1. From an address before the Group W *Cleveland Conference*. Also published under title "Conscience and The Community," *Television Quarterly*, Winter, 1964.
2. See a statement prepared by Television Information Office director, Roy Danish, in *Sponsor*, December 30, 1963. By the end of 1963 the number of American commercial TV stations had increased by 11%, but the total number of stations responding to the *Sponsor* survey was 326 (compared to a 1960 total of 264). While 1,038 were listed for the 1960 TIO survey, over 1,500 were listed in the later survey. Heaviest emphasis in 1963 was given to programs in three areas: Community Affairs, Government and Politics, and Health and Social Problems. The rate of local sponsorship for such programs had increased from 10% to 27% in the three-year period between the surveys.
3. In a speech before the *Cleveland Conference*.
4. The 1964 regional award winners included WNBQ-TV's "Date-Line: Chicago," WCBS TV's "The Next Revolution," KSD-TV's "Operation Challenge — A Study in Hope," WMAL-TV's "Child-Beating," WBRZ-TV's "Without Violence," KPIX-TV's "The Case for the Limited Child," KNXT-TV's "Poison in the Air," WLW-TV's "The Last Prom," and KGW-TV's "Wednesday's Child." The National winner was KSD-TV.
5. *New York Times*, May 27, 1962.
6. On May 27, 1964, this program was honored by the CBC when it was given the first annual "Wilderness Award" for documentary. The program was shown again on that night. Leiterman himself appeared at the close to explain that what was shown did not fully represent the progress which had been made in race relations in the United States. Whether his appearance on the film was added after the WBC-NET decision not to permit showing in the United States is not known, but the result is still the same. Millions of Canadians might conclude from the film itself that Malcolm X and a handful of white supremacists represent the basic attitudes and opinions of all Americans in this sensitive question, and a tacked-on "message" can do little to overcome the heavy emotional thrust of the film itself.
7. It is sheer effrontery to set the remarkable evolution of the television documentary abroad within the limits of a footnote. There has been a continuing flow of important works from many nations over the past decade, and these deserve their own exhaustive analysis. Seen here in America have been some of the works of such British documentarists as Denis Mitchell, Richard Cawston and Tim Hewatt, representing the BBC as well as newer British commercial companies. In Toronto I was privileged to witness such films as "The Wilderness," a CBC-TV documentary almost beyond praise, and other works by Thom Benson's CBC units in the *Camera Canada* series. Such work deserves full and separate treatment of its own. Many Britons would, with great justification, protest the very idea of reviewing documentary evolution in radio and television without full attention to the fine and continuing work in England. The fault is mine. The excuse is the limitation of time and circumstance under which I have worked.

APPENDICES

I DOCUMENTARISTS ON DOCUMENTARY

II MEMORANDUM FROM A TELEVISION NEWSMAN

III TV DOCUMENTARIES FOR VIEWING AND ANALYSIS

For the material included in Appendix I, I owe thanks to the Forum Committee of the New York Chapter of the National Academy of Television Arts and Sciences; to Mr. Edmund Bert Gerard, producer of the panel discussion from which these materials were excerpted; and to the participants in the discussion.

Mr. Reuven Frank, executive producer of NBC News, has generously given me his permission to publish the materials included in Appendix II.

Data for each of the films listed in Appendix III are reported from the producing agency or organization, with approval of representatives of each.

Appendix I / DOCUMENTARISTS ON DOCUMENTARY

In December of 1963, the New York Chapter of the National Academy of Television Arts and Sciences sponsored the first of its regular Forum discussions to be devoted exclusively to the TV documentary. The opinions and reflections expressed by the participants in this discussion may serve to amplify and enlarge upon material in this volume.

The discussants were: Arthur Baron, Director of Creative Programs for the Metropolitan Broadcasting Company; Robert Collinson, Chief Film Editor for CBS's *The Twentieth Century;* Robert Drew of Drew Associates; Lou Hazam, NBC Staff Documentary Producer; David Lowe, Producer for *CBS Reports;* John Secondari, Executive Producer at ABC-TV; Willard Van Dyke, a free-lance documentary-maker; and Albert Wasserman, Producer for NBC News *Creative Projects.* The moderator was James F. Macandrew of WNDT, Channel 13, New York. What appears below is an abridged version of that discussion.

* * * *

MACANDREW:

Mr. Van Dyke, your career ranges from "pure" film-making, as in *The River* and *The City*, to the television documentary of 1963. What is the major difference between the TV documentary of today and the great film documentaries of the 30's and 40's?

VAN DYKE:

There are two or three significant differences. In the documentary film we took strong stands. It seems to me that the television documentaries don't often take strong stands; they take a "position," but one which is usually qualified by saying "on the other hand." We took uncompromising positions. We felt that soil erosion, for instance, was bad — that it was like sin and something needed to be done about it. We were indignant, and we brought poetry to bear on each issue we treated. We brought beautiful musical scores to bear on them, we were interested in composition in our photography. We were not so concerned about being journalistic as many documentaries are. I don't say that the change is necessarily good or bad, but that's the way it was.

Today, very often, nobody cares about the pictorial image. Nobody is very interested in whether or not the thing looks beautiful, or whether, indeed, the photography is even appropriate to the mood of the film. Nobody is very concerned about whether a great composer like Aaron Copland, or some hack, is doing the musical score. We used people like Copland, Mark Blitzstein, Alex North, and Virgil Thomson. We had the best composers in the world working for us, and we were concerned about every element that went into the film. We wanted to be sure that we expressed all that we could in relation to the thematic approach we had taken.

We had more time. We didn't have very much money, but we had a lot of time — and we had the feeling of a thing being brand-new, that nobody had done it before, and that there was a true form that it fell into. That kind of film disappeared to a large extent and perhaps it's just as well, because it reached a rather limited audience. Over the years *The River* reached a tremendous audience, as did *The City*, but for the most part the documentary film of that type never really reached great audiences.

MACANDREW:

I would like to pick up one point, because I think it interests all of us. I wonder if everyone in the panel would agree that the general tendency among documentarians today is to take a "softer" position than the position taken in the early documentary films?

HAZAM:

I would disagree with that. There are some men sitting at this table — Mr. Wasserman and Mr. Lowe, for instance — who have taken very firm positions with such shows as *CBS Reports* and at NBC. Further, I would like to take exception to the fact that we're not as careful in our shooting today, or as motherly about our music. I spend, as do a good many people I know, a considerable amount of money for good scores by very able composers. Pictorially, since we have more money than Mr. Van Dyke had in those days, our shooting proportions are something considerable; and this gives us a very wide selection of shots. We can be very fussy about the creativity of our shots. I think the problem arises when we fail to distinguish between a "news-type" show, which must often go along with what it can get in a hurry, and an "art-type" show, where the whole effort is premeditated.

WASSERMAN:

On this matter of taking "softer" positions, I think that television is, and has to be, more circumspect about it. Before television the documentary film was primarily a medium of editorializing. All of the technical and aesthetic resources of the film-maker — narration, music, editing, and the rest — were brought into play to communicate as powerfully as possible to an audience a predetermined point of view. This is not appropriate in television. A television documentary has to be more objective. But I do not think that "objectivity" means fear of taking a stand. If the investigations of the objective documentary reporter lead to definite conclusions, then I think such conclusions must be reflected in the finished program. It has been done in many television documentaries. What is crucial, though, is that the substance of the investigation must be communicated clearly and factually to the audience. The conclusions must grow out of what has been demonstrated in the body of the program, and not be the result of a personal orientation of the film-maker.

MACANDREW:

May we return to the point which Mr. Hazam made regarding the "news" and the "art" types of documentary? What would you say is the essential difference between those two?

SECONDARI:

I don't think that there is basically any difference between an "art" documentary and a "news" documentary. I think that they are directed toward the same audience. They use the same tools. They are put together by approximately the same people, who quite by accident happen to work on one or the other, and they basically have to subscribe to the same concept of what a documentary is. The concept of documentary cannot rest upon whether it is a "news" documentary or an "art" documentary. The documentarist can not set out by *saying* his work will fall into a certain class. What we are talking about here is a discipline. Or perhaps we are trying to discover if there is an entity called a documentary discipline. Within the maximum limits of the tools that are available a man can produce an honest work. This, I believe, is the limit of our definition.

HAZAM:

Many "news" documentaries are made with films that were never shot for the showing in which they were used.

SECONDARI:

This is possible. The greatest distinction, perhaps, between what Mr. Van Dyke used to do with *The River* and *The City* and what we try to do today rests upon the fact that we cannot always do the same type of subject. The largest problem confronting the television producer today is what subject can he handle — not what subject he's allowed to handle, not what subject he can sell, not what subject the sponsor will sit still for or what the audience will take. His problem is what subject can he *produce*. Because there is one essential requirement for any television documentary — the full co-operation on the part of the people who are being pictured. If you want to make a picture about a controversial subject, especially at a government agency where they will not talk, I don't think you can be successful.

LOWE:

I was going to suggest that perhaps we cannot draw analogies between the motion picture and television documentary at all. I think the television documentary is something that's unique. It's new, it has just been in the forming stage. I don't think there is any specific kind. Each man here makes a kind of documentary that nobody else could make. The documentary is born out of individual creative art. It seems to me that any effective documentary must come out of the inside of a man.

MACANDREW:

There is one other approach to TV documentary we should examine, and that is what has come to be known as the "actuality" documentary. Not too long ago ABC did one for which Robert Drew was responsible, and critics throughout the country became excited, in one way or another, about various aspects of it. I think we might turn to Mr. Drew.

DREW:

I said in the beginning I wasn't sure that what we were doing *was* documentary. Mr. Van Dyke's definition indicated that a documentary was a film in which the hero represented a social force or problem, and not just a man who was caught up in his own life. Now, I don't know what "actuality" means, and I wouldn't apply that name to my work, but the kind of reality film that I've been working on for some time is a film in which you *do* see a specific man caught up in his own specific problems. If these problems happen to relate to a great issue, then they shed light on it. If they don't relate to a great issue, then perhaps they shed light on human nature, or man, in the way that a drama would.

I think that everything that has been referred to as a documentary here thus far is what I would call a "word-logic" show — that is, the logic of the film is contained in the narration or in the words. The logic may also be contained in the picture, but the acid test between the kind of actuality that I'm working on and the kind represented on the shows we have been talking about might be established in this way: If a viewer can turn off the picture on his television set and still grasp the logic of the show from sound alone, then the program follows the conventional definition of documentary. If, on the other hand, he turns off the sound and can follow the logic — even the drama — of the show in what evolves *visually*, then we are confronted, perhaps, with a reality that was captured as it happened. It would not be something preconceived or directed.

I'm interested in one approach only, and that is to convey the excitement and drama and feeling of real life as it actually happens through film. I don't care whether it is thought of as "artistic." I hope it is not preconceived, because if it is, it probably isn't what really happened. I must admit I'm no author. I have to find a story that's actually happening with its own structure, its own dynamic. I seek people driven by their own forces — forces so strong that they can forget about me — and capture this action as it happens. I want to edit it, but not for information, not for size or weight, or time or space, but for feeling and character and a dramatic development of the story. Of course this is, in a sense, impossible to do. I haven't done it yet, and I don't know anyone who has, but I'm working with a group of people who are dedicated to breaking through on the technical as well as other fronts. Their work brought us to the film *Crisis: Behind a Presidential Commitment.*

All I can say of *Crisis* is that we tried, with four different cameras covering a two-day period, to capture what actually happened in an integration showdown which involved the Governor of the state of Alabama, the Attorney General, two Negro students, and, from time to time, the President. That's what we tried to do. There were many critical responses, but I think that much criticism implied that it was too bad that all these people took time out to "act" for the camera in the midst of a crisis. This happens to be the one criticism I could not have anticipated because I don't think any of these people *were* acting for our cameras.

SECONDARI:

The kind of documentary Mr. Drew describes is the purest documentary of all. When you can tell a story as it unfolds, with your camera and without very much need of words, you have documentary in the palm of your hands. But the presentation of truth as it happens is not the only concern. There must be a beginning, middle, and end — organization and a climax. Otherwise it can be truthful but dull.

WASSERMAN:

May I respond to that? There seem to be two major elements involved in documentary which sometimes conflict with each other. One element is social purpose, a classic function of the documentary films; the other is the effort to communicate aspects of the world as it really is, and as people in it are, to an audience through film. I think we find, in the kind of film Mr. Drew is talking about and also in some of the films we have made for the DuPont *Show of the Week*, a method which emphasizes the "life-as-it is" documentary. What is lacking, of course, is the social purpose. Now this complicates the matter of creating a definition of documentary. Still, as long as we know — functionally speaking — what we're talking about, I think we can say something more important than "Is this a documentary, or isn't it a documentary?" I feel that I am enough of a classic documentarian to want to assign a reason, a thematic purpose, to a film that I am doing. The purpose must extend above and beyond the communication of a glimpse of reality. I don't think that the two approaches are incompatible. It takes a little more work, perhaps, but when you can combine the kind of immediacy that flexible, synch-sound equipment can provide applied in some kind of dramatic situation that is unfolding — and when, at the same time, you're aware of the potentialities of a larger communication than this experience can express — then you have made documentary.

VAN DYKE:

Perhaps we are getting too involved in semantics here, but within my definition of the documentary film, and as much as I respect what Mr. Drew does, I think that he is doing *film documents*, not *documentary films*.

DREW:

I'd certainly agree with that.

HAZAM:

Pare Lorentz once defined the documentary as "the dramatic presentation of factual material." That's a pretty broad term. With that definition you could take Cary Grant into a Hollywood studio and, on an *ersatz* set, dramatically present factual material. I would like to try this one: "A documentary is a dramatic presentation of factual material made on location where the events are happening or have happened and the people concerned (or their equivalent) are doing what comes naturally." That might cover what each of us, in one way or another, is trying to do.

*   *   *   *

Question from the floor to Mr. Drew: Do you think that the importance or significance of an actuality might be heightened and crystallized in marriage with artistic creativity?

DREW:

To be perfectly frank I don't think it could be rendered at all without artistic creativity. I don't think it's possible to capture actuality without artistic creativity, or to edit it so that it works without applying creativity.

So far we haven't gotten the real thing, and all of our effort and creativity has to go into getting something that's basic and pure and straight, as it happened. The greatest danger we run is superimposing our brilliance on it and lousing it up.

* * * *

HAZAM (In response to a question regarding the legitimacy of the use of actors):
I think that any documentary that shows actors performing a scene corrupts the situation by introducing its own action into the scene. It is not a documentary at all. It's "made-up." In fact, I have a great kind of distaste for that kind of production.

* * * *

BARON (in response to an argument from the floor protesting "interpretation" of truth by a documentarist as lacking objectivity):
I do feel that documentary has to come, as Mr. Lowe pointed out, from individual passion — individual concern with the subject. And I don't see, given that passion and that concern, how you can do an "honest" documentary which does not, even with honest reporting of the facts, draw toward some positive point of view. I don't see how you can come out of an investigation of any social issue without a point of view. And it seems to me that, to the extent that a writer produces a point of view, he is not producing something bland, safe, and aimless.

SECONDARI:

I'll disagree with the argument that we are limited or controlled in our work. I've done the shows I've set out to do exactly as I wanted to do them. Secondly, I would disagree with the premise that we somehow lack "true" objectivity. There *is* no such thing as objectivity when we get 20,000 feet of film to work into a half hour. The very choice of what we put into that film is an expression of opinion.

COLLINSON:

I would like to enlarge upon that point by talking for a moment or two about the historical documentary, or document, and what I look for in that. If you are going to try to illustrate an event, or a series of events, it seems to me that what you have to look for is not an idea but *the feel of truth*. Somehow or other, you have to create a believability in the thing you are trying to tell about. I'm thinking of one show we did on the Battle of Cassino. When this subject first came up, my initial response was, "What do I know about the Battle of Cassino?" And all I could remember was that a monastery was there — and there was some fighting — and that was about all I could remember.

Now the amount of material that comes in on a historical show of this type amounts to some 60,000 feet of 35mm film. If you screened continuously it would take about eleven and a half hours just to look at it. All of that footage was shot by a number of different cameramen. It was put together by a number of different people, so the length of the shot is usually predetermined so far as you are concerned. Of course, you can extend scenes to a limited degree by optical devices like printing back and forth. The natural result of this is your own conviction that you don't want to make a battle show that's just another battle show. As you view this material you are impelled to find out the truth of that particular event. How do you create this feel of truth? How do you reconstruct a particular event which took place nearly 20 years ago?

First, of course, you read the research. If you can, you read at least one or two of the best books you can find about that event. And slowly it unfolds. You learn that the Battle of Cassino took five months, and was not one battle but four battles. You learn that while Germans were the constant enemy, several changes in Allied forces took place. Once you have an understanding of it, you begin to work out some proper sequence of events within the show. You try to structure the entire work so that you can make the best use of the film in hand. You have to arrange these sequences logically and interestingly, since many in the audience know little about World War II. You are trying to give an honest picture, but you cannot be dogmatic in saying you will or will not use a particular piece of film or a particular device. Now, I'm not going to make any public confessions about what I've done, as an editor, in the way of "honest cheating." My point is that *if* the end result is such that a person who lived through the event can say, "Gee, that's the way it was," then how I achieved it is my secret. The truth of the telling of the event must be as objective as possible. The truth must satisfy me and this is the only way that we can proceed.

The re-creating of an event out of the past is very difficult. It simply has to be put into a dramatic form whether one likes it or not. In the case of "The Battle of Cassino," the same old montage battle picture would have resulted if the story had not been properly structured in dramatic form.

WASSERMAN:

I think the idea of truth and how one communicates it is also a central issue in those films which deal with contemporary affairs. Just as in the historical films, there must occur some taking of liberties with literal truth in order to get at a deeper truth. We run into similar kinds of choices and similar kinds of conflicts. We have to acknowledge the dirty word "staging," which is something we are not supposed to do, and which we can not do (in the sense of causing things to happen which would not otherwise happen). We can not manipulate content, or people, to further our own ideas. Yet we are producing in a medium which does require editing and continuity. There are always choices to be made. To what extent, for example, do we film transitional material which will help smooth out a story, help make it more interesting, and which, for example, may require having people do something again that might have happened only once? Certainly the question of the extent to which we can manipulate the environment in a documentary film for television is one that we must be concerned with all the time. And I think there are no absolute answers.

LOWE:

I think that any re-enactment which tries to let the audience know what happened does a great dis-service to the entire field of documentary. A single re-enactment, a single record which is not actually so, will mar all documentary efforts. Yet an interview in which you ask a person to tell you what happened seems valid. But when you introduce an element, for whatever purpose, which is not true and honest, the effort has been demeaned.

DREW:

I would agree entirely with the idea that re-enactment is a bad thing. Not just in the interest of honesty, but because I think that when you ask a person to do something, you ruin the chances that it will be true and natural. I can recall shooting in a situation where a character was in shadow, one inch away from proper light, and we were rolling and I knew we wouldn't get anything in that light. Yet I'd rather lose the whole scene and everything that was said than to ask that man to move an inch. Because if I did tell him what to do, an hour later, two hours later, in some other situation, he would begin to wonder in back of his mind: "What does he want me to do now?" I think even interviewing can establish a control over the subject, or can introduce your propulsion into the subject to such an extent that from then on you won't get what that character would have done without the interview.

HAZAM:

I think the key to this matter of re-enactment is whether the device is employed to a substantial degree within the whole context. We were doing a medical show in which a doctor in one room was operating on a girl who was about to donate a kidney, while in another room another doctor was operating on the recipient. The camera's action was fairly limited. The cameraman got a shot of this fellow coming down the hall with the pan holding the kidney, and he was able to get him as he entered the operating room and delivering it. But we needed a shot of this person turning the corner. I can't see any harm in asking that fellow to repeat that action later.

WASSERMAN:

The problem must be dealt with as best you can. Even in doing an interview, if you take reaction shots of your interviewer after the interview is over (so that you can cut it) you're injecting an artificial element into the situation. But it's done all the time. I think the word "substitute" is a useful distinction from "re-enact" in cases like this.

I would like to add something in relation to what Bob Drew said regarding following reality. Of course if something real is happening in front of the camera, you'd be a damned fool if you interfered with it. On the other hand, often you have to do something beyond simply keeping your crew in pursuit of what is really happening in the hope that something dramatic will occur. I think that what one does in certain kinds of documentaries is trying to create, beforehand, a reality which will happen in front of the camera; something which would not have happened without your intervention. An example is a film I did some years ago for CBS, which followed a psychotic mental patient in therapy over a period of three months. Now this was an event which would not have occurred if we had not made a film about it. We arranged for the doctor, we selected a particular patient, we asked this doctor to treat this patient individually. We set up a room in which therapy was conducted, and then we let it happen. But without this kind of process taking place we would not have had a reality.

DREW:

Could I say something at this point? When Al Wasserman made that film I was on a Neiman fellowship at Harvard, and I was basically a correspondent and print editor at that time. I was wondering how journalism could become more effective in television. I saw that film, and to this moment I don't think I was aware that Al had exercised this creative beginning on the story. I know damn well . . . I hope you won't say I'm wrong . . . that what you shot was absolutely as it happened, without any intrusion at all.

First of all, certainly anyone who has a camera in his presence *knows* it. And I'm not interested in hidden cameras spying on defenseless people. I would not regard what Mr. Wasserman did as that at all. I do regard a certain ashcan school of Bowery photography as being that. Spying on helpless people, without their knowledge or even with it, does not appeal to me. What I think has been happening in the past ten years, however, is that equipment and journalists have become better able to exist in situations without disturbing them. The level at which they have been able to capture reality has been getting less and less public. I think that the level of publicness has now been reduced to such a point that it is quite possible, under the right circumstances and with people who are highly motivated by their own affairs in the midst of a pressing situation, for cameras to be present without influencing human actions or reactions. In *Crisis* I am quite convinced that the cameras did not, in anything that was seen in the film, influence people's actions. I think that when the Attorney General picked up the telephone and talked to his operative in the South he was unaware of the camera. First of all, the camera had been with the Attorney General for more than a week and he didn't know when it was running and when it wasn't. The experts who were running the camera had become adept at handling people in a way that may seem almost unbelievable unless you've seen it happen. I saw this happen, and you probably have, too, in the 35mm still-picture reporting business. At *Life* Magazine it has been possible for the tiny 35mm still-camera to capture real events in people's lives without really disturbing them. I think we could agree on that. Now somewhere in between that and the kind of disturbance caused by a camera set up on a tripod, we arrived at something. I think what we achieved was quite true, and really happened, and these people really did what they did for their own reasons without reference to us. I am quite convinced of that.

VAN DYKE:

It seems to me that we have been skirting an issue here, an issue which involves the central difference between the film documentary and the television documentary. The television documentary is most successful when it manages to make the audience feel that they are participating in an event as it is happening. It gives them the feeling of actuality, of immediacy, of being present in the situation, which the documentary film never tried to achieve and indeed never could attempt. I think that in order to achieve this, the film-maker must not express himself in the "artist's" way. He must remain, in the best sense, an artist, in that he lets the work talk for itself rather than impose upon it any of those elements that I ascribed to the documentary film. We brought our own egos, in a sense, to the film.

WASSERMAN:

I agree. Questions were raised referring to two films that I have been involved in; let me take them up one at a time. I think the questions referred, basically, to the privacy of individuals and to matters of taste in what one communicates to an audience. The film *Out of Darkness* was about a mental patient, and the therapy was filmed through a one-way glass. This was a psychotic patient, and nothing was done without her knowledge, at least to the extent that she was capable of understanding. Our interest was explained to her, we took her into the room where we had our set-up, showed her the camera, tried to explain to her what we were doing, and then filmed. In addition to this, part of the filming was done, not behind one-way glass but in the open, where the patient was aware of what was happening. So it wasn't a question of spying. And of course, as in all films, we had to get a release, both from the patient and her nearest relative. We did this with all patients who were filmed for that program. The project was discussed beforehand with the American Psychiatric Association and had their approval. After it was finished there was no complaint from anybody who had appeared in the film, which is a fairly good empirical test.

In the Newburgh film for NBC's *White Paper* there was a scene in which a man who had been denied welfare broke down and wept in front of the camera. This was unquestionably an emotional scene, and, as with the case of the mental patient, the question of propriety arises when you try to get inside people — allowing them to reveal themselves emotionally. To me the object is not the emotion itself. What is important is the reason you are seeking it. It is the difference between sensationalism and the responsible use of emotion to make a point. In the Newburgh program we filmed this man not because we knew he was going to cry, but because there was a very definite reportorial point that he could make. The City Manager had made a statement to the effect that nobody in the city who needed welfare assistance had been denied it. We found a man who was in need of aid and who had been denied it, and that's why we filmed him. The fact that he broke down and cried was really incidental.

*   *   *   *

Appendix II /
MEMORANDUM FROM A TELEVISION NEWSMAN

As the television networks made ready for the half-hour daily news programs in mid-1963, news producers engaged in some deeper reflection upon the challenges and difficulties which the expanded time would present. Of particular import in this framework is a lengthy memorandum prepared and circulated to the staff of NBC News by executive producer Reuven Frank, as the entire organization contemplated its new functions and responsibilities. Mr. Frank's comments are of significance for that area of television programming where the journalist's and the documentarist's functions draw near to each other.

THERE MUST BE more to this news program than that it is 30 minutes long. From the first announcement, the first rumor, its mere 30-minuteness brought out a varied host of subjective pictures, horizons and limitations, fears and ambitions, prejudices, preconceptions, hopes and plans. It has been a kind of game. So many different people with so many differing jobs and responsibilities have felt they wandered into the presence of a large blank canvas stretched over an easel, theirs to fill. But the canvas is not blank. And none of us may fill it alone.

The problem is given. The conditions for the most part are given. The problem is to present the best television news program ever known. Audiences of the magnitude of 20 million Americans a night must be retained and expanded without relaxation of standards or lapses of taste. We built this audience slowly and painfully without ever once patronizing a person in it or insulting the intelligence of its most intelligent member. Now we must hold the interest of all of them. To do that, we must be interesting. Nor may we forget that the competitive pressure will be greater than anything one of us has known, greater than it was during the coverage of the conventions and elections, classically the arena of bitterest competition among the news divisions of television networks.

Given this problem, one can be grateful that the canvas is not in fact entirely blank.

It is my purpose to set down as much as I can of the structure, procedures and philosophy by which I shall try to operate the program. Some of what follows has been conveyed to me as stated instruction; some I have assumed as unstated mandate; some I have proposed to my superiors and colleagues and obtained their agreement; and some, finally, I state myself as operating rules. None of it is changeless. But this is where we start.

*   *   *   *

It is a news program. Its purposes are journalistic. Its postulate is an audience no less intelligent than we, but necessarily (because professionally) less well informed. Its methods are the methods of television journalism. The highest power of television journalism is not in the transmission of information but in the transmission of experience.

Another of its high powers is that it is now accepted as authoritative, and its authority sustains it where it cannot rely on the impact of pictures and cannot shirk the mandate to inform comprehensively. This second power, this authority, is delicate and can easily be destroyed because it is essentially the result of a trust. The television journalist is received trustingly. He cannot with impunity abuse that trust for long by glibness, irresponsibility, or — his greatest danger — assuming that it exists for his personal advantage. The first, the power to transmit experience, is intrinsic in the physical existence of television and cannot be damaged so long as there is television. There are events which exist in the American mind and recollection primarily because they were reported on regular television news programs. We have found a dimension of information which is not contained in words alone.

Not all of the major stories of the past dozen years were created by television. The Supreme Court nine-to-nothing decision in Brown vs. Board of Education worked a major permanent change in American society; but television could not report the decision itself as well as newspapers could. The failure of any Communist country to feed itself may be the climactic fact of this century. It is primarily a story for magazines and books.

Yet, because of television's ability to transmit experience, established during the Korean War and the Berlin airlift, television news has an audience and a responsibility to that audience. It has developed its own authority to do this, and its own loyalties among its followers, who comprise most Americans. Any new form for television news reporting must be founded on television's power in transmitting experience and its authority in presenting information. (I differentiate here between regularly scheduled programs and live coverage. Live television coverage has a quality of its own which is incomparable, but outside this discussion. Our concern here is with disciplined journalism as applied to this medium; with the gathering, editing, and dissemination of news.)

We did not plan the growth of the authority of television news in presenting information. Nor did we anticipate the unique power of television news to transmit experience; we do not take enough advantage of it even yet. For several years the patterns of news programs have been changing, but the change has been haphazard instead of growing out of these two unique powers of television news reporting.

Most of the talk about expanded programs, ours and others', has centered around length. There has been too little talk about the implications of greater length: if a half-hour is twice as good as a quarter-hour, which I believe is true, then an hour is four times as good, which I believe is ridiculous. Something has obviously been left out. It has been argued, and I think well argued, that the audience has been brought to where it might accept the right half-hour as a daily news diet. Extending existing programs to double their length is no answer. The fact that existing programs cannot encompass all the news their editors would like is specious argument. No vehicle of journalism in any medium ever encompassed all the news its editors would like, not even the Sunday edition of the *New York Times*. A successful half-hour program would be one which rejected or wasted almost as much material as it used. No newspaper publishes the full Associated Press report and no reader would read it if it did. And broadcasting does not have the newspaper's luxury of letting its audience choose what it wants and what to skip. If the half-hour is aimed at giving the viewer more of the same it will not only drive him away, it will stifle for a long time this fully logical movement toward a new and expanded form.

The half-hour nightly news program must be not more but different.

A half-hour nightly television news program should retain the present half-hour program's function of transmitting information while better and more fully utilizing television reporting's unique capacity to transmit experience. The *Washington Post* can explain that the mainland Chinese are living on 1,200 calories a day. Television can show hunger. The *Kansas City Star* can feature a study of the trend toward larger farms in the Midwest; we can watch a farmer and his family while his farm is being auctioned.

There is no need to prove the point again. But my argument, admittedly largely subjective, is clearly heading to the conclusion that the proper formula for a half-hour news program is not doubling the length of the quarter-hour program but adding to it the functions, subjects and techniques of the half-hour once-weekly programs. This would build on the established authority of the regular television news report and exploit its unique capacity to transmit experience.

The Function of Interviews

An interview too often can be a crutch. Getting a picture of an event as it happens takes effort and luck, sometimes a lot of both. Neither is needed to back some hapless eye-witness, or even participant, against a wall and let him tell what happened. It is too easy to consider this an adequate substitute.

Most people are dull. That is, they communicate ineptly. If they are dull, their description of interesting events will be dull. Sometimes they are interesting, but for the wrong reasons. They suffer from speech defects, tic, or strabismus, and what may make them interesting is precisely what interferes with their contribution to information. Those who communicate aptly — politicians, actors, and the like — tend to be self-serving.

It is natural and human and in many ways commendable that most of us recoil at being personally unpleasant to our fellow men. In conversation we take answers on faith, and even when that is not possible we do not express incredulity rudely or press our partners into confessions of dissimulation. This is part of good manners. But an interviewer is not an individual human in conversation. He is the representative of the curiosity of an audience, presumably its legitimate curiosity. His supposed good manners are often the means of denying information to his fellow citizens. An interview which is not more than a conversation is less than an interview. You are wasting our time, and we are invading the dullness and superficiality of your privacy.

Some interviews are devices for putting a reporter's notes on the air. Every beginning journalist is trained to talk to as many people as he can at the scene of a fire or a murder and note what they say — usually in thick copy pencil on newsprint cut into copy paper or on the backs of envelopes. He would have been bemused if, when he returned to the city room, his city editor had sent his smudged copy paper or envelope to photo-engraving instead of letting him write his story from his notes. Most spot interviews of eye-witnesses are in this category.

To be sententious about it, the essence of professionalism is discipline. Interviews too often are broadcast before they are edited, before they are disciplined. This is embarrassingly true of live interviews, but even filmed interviews are not innocent. It is relevant here to recall an audience of up to 20 million Americans. A two-minute interview commands an aggregate attention of more than 600,000 man-hours. What effort must we make to justify this! So, of course, does a two-minute silent film story. In my experience, interviews betray this attention more often.

Interesting questions do not guarantee interesting answers, nor important questions useful answers. There is nothing more awkward than an interview in which the interviewer is more interesting than the subject. This sometimes happens by itself, but also at other times when the reporter is too busy framing the next question ιo listen to the previous answer. Just as some interviews are self-serving, so are some interviewers. Too many of the best interviews are achieved at the expense of integrity. An interesting, important, articulate subject can often command his own ground rules as the price of granting the interview. And if we don't pay the price, the competition will.

All of you, I am sure, have your own reservations about television interviews. These are some of mine. They are, however, reservations, not prohibitions. The interview is a basic tool of our business and we could not survive without it.

Let there be a reason for every interview, a reasoned reason, not a reflex. Every subject must be chosen because he can contribute something no reporter can say better and shorter and more interestingly and more grammatically. This unique contribution may be the subject's personality, or his exalted position, or his matchless experience. Or he may be such a person as would by his instantly recognizable stature make larger what he says by the very fact that he is saying it. What he says must also reflect what he feels. There should be an emotional involvement of some kind to justify all those man-hours of attention. If what he says is an interesting fact which belongs on the film caption sheet, enter it there — the sound camera is better occupied recording street noises.

The best interviews are of people reacting — not people expounding. Joy, sorrow, shock, fear — these are the stuff of news. No important story is without them. They can be recorded and transmitted tastefully. Integration, Algeria, the Skybolt, nuclear disarmament, unemployment, floods, automation — name me a recent major story without its human involvement. It is easier to cover such stories through statistics, intergovernmental arrangements, the language of diplomacy, and the quoting of self-aggrandizing officials. Easier, but duller. At the core of journalism is reporting, if not yours, then someone else's. And no qualified reporter can afford revulsion at random contact with other humans.

One thing more needs saying: the orientation to print, which is so difficult to lose, persisted nowhere more stubbornly than in the making of filmed interviews. The best of these, by the standards we grew up with, mean nothing here. And for this reason you could well follow all the rules I have set down and, within one context, fail.

Let us consider the ultimate: Khrushchev, in an exclusive interview with NBC News, threatens nuclear war against the United States if Hollywood persists in making a movie out of *Fail-Safe*. Any reporter would give up drink and women for his by-line on this story. Across the country, the eight-column banner would be set in Second Coming type: K THREATENS H-WAR — and in quotes arranged to play maximum hob with the American spinal column the exclusive story would run on from there.

We have no eight-column banners. Khrushchev banging his shoe is the unforgettable picture which made no eight-column banner; Khrushchev showing how Russian peasants choke cats and bang their heads made no eight-column banner. He *said* nothing immortal either time. But think of the impact of *seeing* him read in unemphatic Russian, with those gold-rimmed glasses down on the end of his nose, a threat of war. Or consider any one of half the crowned heads and the mighty of your experience making some equally momentous statement, even in direct conversation, even in English.

It takes a professional journalist to knew what sentence in a speech or in his own interview should be pulled to the top, set in large type, quoted in the headline and the banner-line. In our business we cannot pull that sentence out and up. The audience must pick its own sentence and set its own front page around it and do it before we have passed that story and gone on to the next. Television interviews have value, but it is not the same value that printed interviews have.

The best illustration I can think of is this: we have evolved so far in television that the Sunday afternoon interviews of the famous and frightening are much more useful to the Washington bureaus of the wire services and the *New York Times* than they are to the television audience. They still make news, if what appears on front pages is the criterion for news. But unless he is waiting for a lead sentence to be spoken, even a professional is likely, as he listens, to miss the one big news story of the program. Certainly the audience is not sure what it heard until it reads the Monday morning newspapers.

Interviewing Technique

Let us begin by agreeing that in any interview the subject is more important than the interviewer. This means that questions should be short.

It also means that an interview should be filmed with the camera full on the subject. The interviewer should sit with his back to the camera. Perhaps somewhere between the back of his head and his quarter profile to the camera, a shoulder should be visible for the wider shot only. The other shots should be in closer from the same angle, so that we have the feeling the camera has moved in.

Where possible, questions should be repeated with the camera moved around to face the interviewer, but not really head on. Imagine a line joining the interviewer and his subject. All camera positions must be on the same side of this line — for the interview; when moved around for the interviewer's questions; for silent pictures of the interviewer's face and of the subject's face, hands, characteristic actions, etc.; and for establishing cutaway wide shots.

A cutaway is a picture which covers a compression of action. A man walks a block. It takes him one minute. We show him starting his walk.

We show a *cutaway* of a policeman watching. We show the man ending his walk. Total edited film time: eight seconds. If we had cut the walk without using the cutaway, he would have appeared after four seconds to cover miraculously most of the block by ectoplasmic transference. This is known as a jump cut. The same applies to sound film. A man makes a speech. We want the first sentence and the last. We cut them out and join them. His head suddenly moves from facing right to facing left at the point of the splice. We cover the splice with a *cutaway* shot of his audience listening. Cutaways must always be germane and they must also appear to be germane. These are not the same thing. Certain angles of the crowd may, because of background or other peculiarities, seem to be in different places. Consider, for example, an interview in a garden. The subject is seated with his back to the stuccoed wall of a house. The interviewer is seated with a hedge visible behind him. Our cutaway, as is usual in interviews, is of the interviewer in sound film asking his question or in silent film listening — please, not nodding, grimacing, smiling, or doing anything but listening! But the man against a white wall is intercut with another man against a hedge. They were in fact in the same garden. They seemed not to be.

It is hard to explain the rule about keeping the camera on the same side of the line except by another example. Think back to live football coverage in television's early days. Team A was charging down the field. The press-box camera showed the action moving from right to left across the screen. The director saw a shot on his camera across the field. He took the shot. Team A suddenly was moving from left to right. Still another example: I once received an interview done in a cramped leatherette corner of a cheap restaurant. After the interview was finished the subject was allowed to leave, and the cameraman started to move his camera and lights around to get the interviewer repeating his questions. But there was no room. So he left his camera and lights where they were and moved the interviewer to the other side of the booth. At every cutaway we seemed to be flipping to a mirror image. It was disturbing.

It is rarely wise to interview more than one person at a time. If you must, pick one who is the chief subject. Let the interviewer stay where he is for only one subject, with the additional subject or subjects on the side of the principal subject away from the interviewer. (There is one advantage to interviewing more than one person simultaneously. You can film each listening to the other, or others, as silent cutaways.) Once a reporter interviewed four subjects at once. All five men sat facing the camera, the reporter in the middle. He became the center of interest. All speech was in profile, as they turned away from the camera to speak to each other. Out of a half-hour of film, there was one useful sentence. It was spoken by a man at one end of the picture. Most of him had been cut off by the television frame. The one important sentence was broadcast without a body to utter it.

A cameraman who cannot light is not a cameraman. A reporter who underestimates the importance of light is a fool. Film is not reality but illusion, at best an imitation of reality. Film is a strip of plastic overlaid with arrangements of finely divided silver. The camera cannot always see what the eye can see. To bring the film into an approximation of the reality that we are seeking takes light, often artificial light. Film is an arrangement of light and shadow. Lights disturb subjects more than cameras. Unlit, they are unseen. Current experiments in the use of available light in soft focus, achieving intimacy through pebbly grain, seemingly unprofessional standards, and a violation of rules can mislead the unwary into concluding that the time, effort, and requirements of making film professionally are unnecessary. These new techniques are valid only as dramatic or dramatizing devices; they are useful and effective only in the hands of the most highly skilled cameramen. Khrushchev says Picasso paints "like my son." Perhaps. But first he taught himself to be the most accomplished draftsman alive and then he began to paint like Khrushchev's son. Experiment must be relevant to the purpose. It is not a denial of technique; it is a step beyond technique. Or, to re-establish some relevancy myself, the kind of interview you are likely to do will not be enhanced but destroyed by a face without features. (By the way, when shooting dark faces, be particularly careful with light enough to fill each face, and, if possible, shoot against dark or medium dark backgrounds.)

All that applies to any film we are likely to need. It is especially relevant to the problems of interviewing. By definition, an interview is at least somewhat controllable. It must be arranged; it must be agreed to. It is not a picture of a building being blown down. Try not to interview in harsh sunlight. Try not to interview in so noisy a setting that words cannot be heard. Let subjects be lit. If lights bother your subject, talk to him, discuss the weather, gentle him, involve his interest and his emotions so that he forgets or ignores the lights. It takes longer, but speed is poor justification for a piece of scrapped film. Film takes time.

News as Film

The aim of newsfilm should be less to record an event than to bring the audience into its presence. The techniques I was so scornful about a few paragraphs ago can be invaluable in the proper hands because this is what they do. Here, indeed, lie the opportunities of transmitting experience. By this I do not mean that we transmit to the viewer one participant's impression of what it was like to undergo the experience, but that we ourselves transmit to him the essence of the experience itself. Ideally we should make him smile and sweat, fear, and exult. We want him to feel that he is crossing the Vietnamese marsh under fire, that it is he who has just been elected, that it is he who faces the problem of learning a new trade and moving his family to a new city. It is an ideal we shall rarely achieve, but it is not absolute. It can be approached by degrees.

In practical terms there are two important elements, indispensable to such aims, which are oftenest forgotten. The first is that hearing is a part of seeing. The second is that the setting is a part of the story. The picture is not a fact but a symbol. Its symbolic truth, its power of evocation, is enhanced by the supposed reality which the sounds which surround it stimulate.

Natural sound is where you find it. It always enhances a story, but perhaps it does not enhance some stories enough to justify the effort. And the effort, too, must vary not only with the story but with the equipment available. One day every cameraman will come with a portable camera synchronized by remote control to a high-fidelity portable tape recorder. That day has not yet come. If it came tomorrow, it would catch us with highly competent crews not quite certain how to use it, or why. We must use the equipment we have while cameramen and soundmen start thinking their way to an appreciation of the difference sound can make.

Anyone can handle a portable tape recorder. Where union commitments do not prohibit it a correspondent can record sound while the cameraman is making his pictures. Or you can hire a small boy. Sound should be slated. That is, for each sound there should be — on that same tape — a brief, spoken slug-line telling us what the following sound will be. As far as possible, the sounds recorded should correspond with the films being shot. But don't do as one man did and fill the tape with a running commentary of the event as it is unfolding. That's not natural sound; that's you talking. If there is a professional soundman available, use him. He can get more out of even a portable tape recorder than the reporter can. If not, he is not a soundman.

A sound camera, especially a portable sound camera, is better. It can record natural sound in synch with the picture. A sound camera has uses beyond recording talking heads. (Hint to cameramen: when filming natural sound in synch let your scenes run a little longer than you would if you were shooting silent film.) This is not a general rule, but it is my experience with natural sound, whether shot wild or in synch, that the microphone should be farther back than the camera for wide shots, closer than the camera for close-ups. This makes for problems, especially if you are recording sound simultaneously with picture. As always in such cases, compromise is called for. I do not need pictures of sound being recorded.

Sound can establish the environment of your event. So can pictures. Very few events we trouble to cover are not enhanced by including a feeling of where they took place. This is not the tired newsreel cliché called the establishing shot — a wide picture usually of the exterior of a building inside which what interests us is taking place. It would include shots of the inside walls, the spectators, the minor actors, pictures of the scene from high up, from far away. In a Congressional hearing we should see the table of legislators, the crowd in its seats, even the cameras banked together. Recently a Chicago alderman was murdered in his office. We had good pictures of the corpse under a blanket on the floor, the desk at which he was working when he was shot, the chair in which he was sitting. Another network had a walking shot through the door of his office as it opened, past the phalanx of policemen, the lights of the film man — our lights, presumably — the scurrying, and the tension. It looked like a crime in Chicago. It told you much more than a blanket-covered corpse on the floor.

Even more basic, there are in most locations small pictures of signs and artifacts and the like which, while having no relevancy to the event itself, hint interestingly at where it happened. A street sign in a foreign language, a store selling strange goods, the clothes of bystanders, a main street with cars parked down the center — these can take the viewer to the place of the event. Cameramen usually film these little scenes. Reporters sometimes get testy at the time it takes, but they submit. Here editors and film editors are usually at fault. They are in New York, dealing not with one story at a time but many stories all at once, and they face the ineffable problem of irreducible total time. It is understandable that they should lose these little pictures, but it is not wise, not responsive to what television is and does.

Every news story should, without sacrifice of probity or responsibility, display the attributes of fiction, of drama. It should have structure and conflict, problem and denouement, rising and falling action, a beginning, a middle, and an end. These are not only the essentials of drama; they are the essentials of narrative. We are in the business of narrative because we are in the business of communication. The rules for short films apply to larger films. It is intriguing that so many do not find this obvious, or do not act as if they did.

The expansion of our news program to double its length will be accomplished by the use of longer film stories. There have been times when the material we have had to cut down or the stories we have had to throw out would have filled most of the gap and still be interesting. There were days when one story, properly anticipated and adequately covered, could have used twice our time and more, and held the attention of our audience and ministered to its needs. But those were rare days. At a half-hour they will be rarer. Each of us and each member of our audience has felt, when his favorite subject failed to get encyclopedic treatment, that we could have done so much more with a little more time. Such treatment of the favorite subjects of others would bore us. The picture of the producer, frustrated at what he has had to leave out, is less accurate than the picture of the producer canvassing the nooks and crannies of his cutting room for 45 seconds more.

We cannot do the same thing for 15 more minutes. We must do something else which is at least as interesting. Except for those days when other material becomes available, the gap will be filled by planned and prepared film stories, and we are assuming the availability of two each night.

For awhile, among ourselves, we referred to these as features, and to the people we would hire to do them as a feature department. Please do not use these terms. They get in the way. They conjure up nostalgic trifles, twins' conventions, contrived humor, and all the attitudes of a city room on a hot, newsless summer's day. We are expected to be a news program for 30 minutes. Our longer pieces will be planned, executed over a longer period of time than the spot news, usable and relevant at any time within, say, two weeks rather than confined to one day, and receptive to the more sophisticated techniques of production and editing — but journalism withal. (Nostalgia has no dynamics. It is a still picture. If you find a village blacksmith somewhere, what is there to say about him after you have said he exists?) Our longer pieces — our planned pieces — are not fillers.

APPENDIX III /
TV DOCUMENTARIES FOR REVIEW AND ANALYSIS

IN THIS SECTION ARE listed 100 important TV documentaries produced both in America and abroad since the early 1950's. All works chosen reflect my own opinion of their value, significance, or quality. Basic information about each program is provided, including initial air date, length and production credits. For some entries complete information is not available, and in others I may have erred when recording details. Errors of both commission and omission are mine. I have also attempted to indicate whether the entries are available for screening by individuals or groups who may wish to study them in detail. A number of programs are already circulated by film-distribution companies. Many of those listed as "restricted" may be secured by applying directly to the producing organization.

NETWORK DOCUMENTARY

WALK IN MY SHOES   ABC-TV (*Close-up!*)
September 19, 1961   60 minutes

Credits: Executive producer, *John Secondari;* Producer-Director, *Nicholas Webster;* Associate producer, *Louis E. Lomax*; Writer, *Arthur Holch*; Cameramen, *William B. Hartigan, Stanley Meredith, Al Stacey, Douglas Dare;* Film editors, *Nils Rasmussen, Samuel Cohen, Edward Lempa*; Research, *Lucy Geringer*; Production coordinator, *William Starkey*; Program coordinator, *John Lynch.*

Rental or purchase: McGraw-Hill Book Company, Text-Film Department, 330 West 42d Street, New York, N. Y. 10036.

BRITAIN: ALLY ON THE VERGE   ABC-TV (*Close-Up!*)
April 24, 1962   60 minutes

Credits: Executive producer, *John Secondari*; Producer-Writer, *Helen Jean Rogers*; Cameraman, *William Hartigan;* Second cameramen, *Edmondo Ricci, Adrian Console*; Assistant producer, *Lucy Geringer*; Sound, *Dudley Plummer, Joseph Charman*; Film editors, *Walter Essenfeld, Edward Lempa, Samuel Cohen, Edward Shea, Edward Powick*; Research, *Mona Kahn, Judith Weintraub, Jonathen Donald*; Production coordinator, *William Starkey*; Program coordinator, *John Lynch*.

Restricted screening: Write ABC-TV Special Projects, 7 West 66th Street, New York, N.Y. 10023.

MEET COMRADE STUDENT   ABC-TV (*Close-Up!*)
September 28, 1962   60 minutes

Credits: Executive producer, *John Secondari*; Producer-Director, *Nicholas Webster*; Writer, *Robert Lewis Shayon*; Cameraman, *William Hartigan*; Research, *Michael Campus*; Sound, *Dudley Plummer*; Film editors, *Alexander Hamilton, Hans Dudelheim, Samuel Cohen, Edward Lempa, Stewart Wilensky*; Production manager, *William Starkey*; Program coordinator, *John Lynch*.

Rental or purchase: McGraw-Hill.

THE MINERS' LAMENT   ABC-TV (*Close-Up!*)
April 9, 1963   30 minutes

Credits: Executive producer, *John Secondari*; Producer-director, *William Weston*; Cameraman, *George Silano*; Assistant producer, *Catherine Clarke*; Second cameraman, *Sid Dobish*; Sound, *Stan Kasper*; Film editors, *Nils Rasmussen, Robert Sandbo*; Production manager, *William Starkey*; Program manager, *John Lynch*.

Restricted screening: Write ABC-TV Special Projects.

THE VATICAN   ABC-TV (*Close-Up!*)
April 14, 1963   60 minutes

Credits: Executive producer-Writer, *John Secondari*; Unit Manager, *Franco Bucarelli*; Cameramen, *William Hartigan, Edmondo Ricci*; Film editors, *Walter Essenfeld, Stewart Wilensky, Samuel Cohen, John Roberts, Edward Shea, Edward Lempa, Walter Morun*; Program manager, *John Lynch*; Music composed and conducted by *Joseph Moon*; Music orchestrated by *Rayburn Wright*; Research, *Patricia Breckir*; Production assistant, *Mona Kahn*. Narrator, *John Secondari*.

Rental or purchase: McGraw-Hill.

A VANISHING BREED: PORTRAIT OF A COUNTRY EDITOR
                                           ABC-TV (*Close-Up!*)
April 23, 1963   30 minutes

Credits: Executive producer, *John Secondari*; Producer-director, *Sam Rosenberg*; Cameraman, *Henry Javorsky*; Assistant producer, *Mike Campus*; Film editors, *Alexander Hamilton, Ed Shea;* Production manager, *William Starkey;* Program manager, *John Lynch*.

Restricted screening: Write ABC-TV Special Projects.

1492   ABC-TV
                                                         (*The Saga of Western Man*)
          October 16, 1963   60 minutes

Credits: Producers, *Helen Jean Rogers, John Secondari*; Writer-Narrator, *John Sec-ondari*; Director, *Helen Jean Rogers*; Associate producer, *Patricia Sides;* Cameraman, *William B. Hartigan*; Assistant cameraman, *Sidney Dobish*; Film editors, *Nils Rasmussen, Walter Essenfeld, Edward Shea, Hans Dudelheim, John Roberts*; Music, *Joseph Moon, Rayburn Wright*; Lighting, *Gregorio Gomez*; Associated in production, *Patricia Breckir, Mona Kahn*; Production coordinator, *William Starkey*. For a second unit in Spain: Associate director, *Samuel Rosenberg*; Cameraman, *Henry Javorsky*; Unit manager, *Fernando Vidal*. (Executive producer, entire *Saga* series, *John Secondari*; Associate producer; *Lucy Geringer.*)

Rental or purchase: McGraw-Hill.

1776   ABC-TV
                                                         (*The Saga of Western Man*)
          December 8, 1963   60 minutes

Credits: Producers, *Helen Jean Rogers, John Secondari*; Writer-Narrator, *John Sec-ondari*; Director, *Helen Jean Rogers*; Co-directors, *Harry Rasky, Ray Garner, Warren Wallace*; Associate producer, *Michael Campus*; Cameramen, *William B. Hartigan, George Silano, Henry Javorsky, Richard Shore*; Film editors, *Walter Essenfeld, Nils Rasmussen, Edward Shea, Hans Dudelheim, Robert Sandbo;* Assistant cameraman, *Sidney Dobish;* Music composed by *Ulpio Minucci*; Music arranged and conducted by *Richard Hayman*; Research, *Bernard Hassan, Edward Hingers, Lenore Gilbey*; Assistant to producer, *Margot Winchester*; Production manager, *Paul Wilson*; Production coordinator, *William Starkey.*

Rental or purchase: McGraw-Hill.

1898   ABC-TV
                                                         (*The Saga of Western Man*)
          February 16, 1964   60 minutes

Credits: Producers: *Helen Jean Rogers, John Secondari*; Writer-Narrator, *John Sec-ondari*; Director, *Helen Jean Rogers*; Co-directors, *Ray Garner, Harry Rasky, Warren Wallace*; Associate producer, *Patricia Sides*; Associates in production, *Arch Lustberg, Eugene W. McGarr, Margot Winchester*; Film editors, *Edward Shea, Walter Essenfeld, Nils Rasmussen, James Algie, Samuel Cohen, Alexander Hamilton, Edward Lempa, Walter Moran, Robert Sandbo*; Cameramen, *William Hartigan, Robert Kuhne, George Silano;* Assistant cameraman, *Sidney Dobish*; Music composed by *Ulpio Minucci, Joseph Moon*; Musical director, *Rayburn Wright*; Research, *Larry Pickard, Dennis Azzarella, Lenore Gilbey, Bernard Hassan, Edward Hingers*; Production coordinators, *John F. Hughes, William H. Starkey, Paul E. Wilson.*

Rental or purchase: McGraw-Hill.

1964   ABC-TV
                                                         (*The Saga of Western Man*)
          March 29, 1964   60 minutes

Credits: Producers, *John Secondari, Helen Jean Rogers*; Writer, *John Secondari*; Director, *John F. Hughes*; Director of Photography, *George Silano*; Cameramen, *George Silano, William Hartigan, William Birch*; Assistant cameramen, *Louis McMahon, Sidney Dobish*; Film editors, *Walter Essenfeld, Nils Rasmussen,*

Edward Shea, Samuel Cohen, James Algie, Alexander Hamilton, Edward Lempa, Walter Moran, Robert Sandbo; Music composed by *Ulpio Minucci, Joseph Moon*; Musical director, *Rayburn Wright*; Research, *Patricia Breckir, Bernard Hassen, Dennis Azzarella, Joe Scanlan, Alice Delman, Arch Lustberg*; Production coordinators, *John F. Hughes, William H. Starkey, Paul E. Wilson.*

Rental or purchase: McGraw-Hill.

CRISIS: *BEHIND A PRESIDENTIAL COMMITMENT*

For ABC-TV by Robert Drew Associates
(Special)

October 28, 1963 — 60 minutes

Credits: Executive producer, *Robert L. Drew*; Producer, *Gregory Shuker*; Film-makers, *Richard Leacock, D. A. Pennebaker, James Lipscomb, Hope Ryden*; Narrator, *James Lipscomb*; Editing Assistants, *Nicholas Proferes, Eileen Nesworthy.*

Restricted screening: Write Robert Drew Associates, 107 West 43rd Street, New York, N.Y., 10036.

YANQUI NO!

For ABC-TV by Robert Drew Associates
(*Close-Up!*)

November, 1960 — 60 minutes

Credits: Executive producer, *Robert L. Drew;* Film-makers, *Richard Leacock* with *Albert Maysles, D. A. Pennebaker;* Narrator, *Joseph Julian;* Translator, *Patricia Powell;* Reporters, *William Worthy, Quinera King;* Edited by *Robert Farren, Stephen Schmidt, Zina Voynow.*

Restricted screening: Write Robert Drew Associates.

THE CHILDREN WERE WATCHING

For ABC-TV by Robert Drew Associates
— Co-produced by Time, Inc.
(*Close-Up!*)

November, 1960 — 30 minutes

Credits: Executive producer, *Robert L. Drew*; Film-maker-Producer, *Richard Leacock*; Film-maker, *Kenneth Snelson*; Correspondents, *Lee Hall, Gregory Shuker*; Editors, *Zina Voynow, Stephen Schmidt*; Narrator, *Joseph Julian.*

Restricted screening: Write Robert Drew Associates.

THE MAKING OF THE PRESIDENT, 1960

For ABC-TV By David Wolper Productions
(Special)

December 29, 1963 — 90 minutes

Credits: Executive producer, *David L. Wolper*; Producer, *Mel Stuart*; Writer, *Theodore H. White*; Music by *Elmer Bernstein*; Film editor, *William Cartwright*; Narrator, *Martin Gabel.*
No information on screening.

CHRISTMAS IN KOREA   CBS-TV (*See It Now*)
December 29, 1953

EDWARD R. MURROW TALKS ON SENATOR McCARTHY
March 9, 1954

ANNIE LEE MOSS BEFORE THE McCARTHY COMMITTEE
    March 16, 1954
SENATOR McCARTHY'S ANSWER TO MR. MURROW
    April 6, 1954
A VISIT TO FLAT ROCK — CARL SANDBURG
    October 5, 1954

Credits: Production credits are not available for individual programs. The entire *See It Now* series was produced and edited by *Edward R. Murrow* and *Fred W. Friendly.* The members of the *See It Now* unit, as listed in 1955, were as follows: Cameramen, *Martin Barnett, Charles Mack, William McClure, Leo Rossi;* Reporters, *Joseph Wershba, John Beck, Gene DePoris, Edward Jones, Edmund Scott;* Film editors, *Mili Lerner, F. H. O'Neill, William Thompson;* Soundmen, *David Blumgart, Lawrence Gianneschi, Robert Huttenloch, Maurice Reitberger;* Studio director, *Don Hewitt;* Associate producer, *Palmer Williams;* Staff assistants *Robert Clemens, Joseph Fackovec, Natalie Foster, H. E. Gille, Leo Levy, Vera Marsh, Jane Thornbury, Earl Toliver.*

Some *See It Now* programs are available for rental or purchase from Contemporary Films, Inc., 267 W. 25th Street, New York, N.Y. Screening of other programs listed above is restricted. Write CBS Program Information, 485 Madison Avenue, New York, N.Y. 10022.

THE POPULATION EXPLOSION	CBS-TV
	(CBS Reports)
December 11, 1959	60 minutes

Credits: Executive producer, *Fred W. Friendly;* Producer-Director, *Av Westin;* Operations director, *Palmer Williams;* Narrator, *Howard K. Smith;* Chief Cameraman, *Martin Barnett;* Assistant Cameraman, *John Eisinbach;* Sound, *Lawrence Gianneschi.*

Rental or purchase: Carousel Films, Inc., 1501 Broadway, Suite 1503, New York, N.Y. 10036.

LIPPMANN ON LEADERSHIP	CBS-TV
	(CBS Reports)
July 7, 1960	60 minutes

Credits: Executive producer, *Fred W. Friendly;* Associate producer, *Gene DePoris;* Cameramen, *Leo Rossi, Martin Barnett;* Film editor, *F. H. O'Neill;* Interviewer, *Howard K. Smith.*

Purchase only: CBS Films, Inc., 485 Madison Avenue, New York, N.Y. 10022.

HARVEST OF SHAME	CBS-TV
	(CBS Reports)
November 25, 1960	60 minutes

Credits: Executive producer, *Fred W. Friendly;* Producer, *David Lowe;* Reporter, *Edward R. Murrow;* Cameramen, *Martin Barnett, Charles Mack;* Film editor, *Charles Schultz;* Operations manager, *Palmer Williams;* Production manager, *David Buksbaum.*

Rental or purchase: McGraw-Hill.

THE BUSINESS OF HEALTH: MEDICINE, MONEY AND POLITICS	
	CBS-TV
	(CBS Reports)
February 2, 1961	60 minutes

Credits: Executive producer, *Fred W. Friendly;* Producer, *Stephen Fleischman;* Reporter, *Howard K. Smith;* Cameramen, *Martin Barnett, Charles Mack, Leo*

Rossi, *Robert Downey*; Film editor, *Mili Lerner*; Operations director, *Palmer Williams*.
Restricted screening.

BIOGRAPHY OF A BOOKIE JOINT

CBS-TV
(*CBS Reports*)

November 30, 1961 — 60 minutes

Credits: Executive producer, *Fred W. Friendly*; Producer-writer, *Jay McMullen*; Cameramen, *Robert J. Clemens, Martin Barnett, Charles Mack, Peter Garbarinia, Robert Downey*; Film editor, *John Schultz*; Narrator, *Walter Cronkite*.
Restricted screening.

STORM OVER THE SUPREME COURT

(Three parts)

CBS-TV
(*CBS Reports*)

February 20, March 13 and June 19, 1963 — 60 minutes each

Credits: Executive producer, *Fred W. Friendly*; Producer, Part I, *Gene DePoris*; Producer, Parts II and III, *William Peters*; Cameramen, *Charles Mack, Leo Rossi, Robert Clemens*; Film editors, *Mili Lerner, Jules Laventhol*; Operations director, *Palmer Williams;* Narrator, *Eric Sevareid*.
Rental or purchase: Carousel Films, Inc., or CBS Films, Inc.

TRIAL AT NUREMBERG

CBS-TV
(*The Twentieth Century*)

March 2, 1958 — 30 minutes

Credits: Producer, *Burton Benjamin*; Associate producer, *Isaac Kleinerman*; Narrator, *Walter Cronkite*; Writer, *Andy Logan*; Film editor, *Aram Boyajian*; Production manager, *Robert Asman*; Film research, *James McDonough*; Research, *Judith Rathvon*.
Rental or purchase: McGraw-Hill.

FROM KAISER TO FUEHRER

CBS-TV
(*The Twentieth Century*)

April 5, 1959 — 30 minutes

Credits: Producer, *Burton Benjamin*; Associate producer, *Isaac Kleinerman*; Narrator, *Walter Cronkite*; Writer, *James Benjamin*; Music composed by *George Kleinsinger*; Music conducted by *Alfredo Antonini*; Film editor, *Robert Collinson*; Film research, *Mel Stuart*; Story editor, *Marshall Flaum*; Production manager, *Robert Asman*.
Rental or purchase: McGraw-Hill.

PARIS IN THE TWENTIES

CBS-TV
(*The Twentieth Century*)

April 17, 1960 — 30 minutes

Credits: Producer, *Burton Benjamin*; Associate producer, *Isaac Kleinerman*; Narrator, *Walter Cronkite*; Narration written by *Marvin Barrett*; Music composed by *George Kleinsinger*; Conducted by *Alfredo Antonini*; Film editor, *Lora Hays*; Research, *Mel Stuart, William Novik*; Story editor, *Marshall Flaum*; Production manager, *Robert Asman*; Sound, *Richard Vorisek, Jack Higgins*.
Rental or purchase: CBS Films, Inc.

IRELAND: THE TEAR AND THE SMILE   CBS-TV
  (Two Parts)   *(The Twentieth Century)*
      January 29 and   30 minutes each
      February 5, 1961

Credits: Producer, *Burton Benjamin*; Associate producer, *Isaac Kleinerman*; Narrator-Reporter, *Walter Cronkite*; Writer, *Elizabeth Bowen*; Director, *Willard Van Dyke*; Music composed by *Clinton Elliott*; Photographer, *James Allen*; Assistant director, *Robert Monks*; Film editor, *Lora Hays*; Story editor, *Marshall Flaum*; Reporter, *Alexander Kendrick*; Assistant to Producer, *Barbara Sapinsley.*

Rental or purchase: McGraw-Hill.

THE BURMA SURGEON TODAY   CBS-TV
                               (The Twentieth Century)
      March 5, 1961   30 minutes

Credits: Producer, *Burton Benjamin*; Writer, *Peter Kalischer*; Associate producer, *Isaac Kleinerman*; Directed and photographed by *Wade Bingham*; Edited by *Aram Boyajian*; Story editor, *Marshall Flaum*; Production manager, *Robert Asman*; Sound, *David Scott, Richard Vorisek.*

Rental or purchase: CBS Films, Inc.

NEW YORK IN THE TWENTIES   CBS-TV
                               (The Twentieth Century)
      April 22, 1961   30 minutes

Credits: Producer, *Burton Benjamin*; Narration written by *Marvin Barrett*; Associate producer, *Isaac Kleinerman*; Narrator, *Walter Cronkite*; Music composed by *George Kleinsinger*; Music conducted by *Alfredo Antonini*; Film editor, *Lora Hays*; Story editor, *Marshall Flaum*; Production manager, *Robert Asman*; Research, *Cynthis Coulson*; Sound, *Richard Vorisek, Roy Friedman.*

Rental or purchase: CBS Films, Inc.

SO THAT MEN ARE FREE   CBS-TV
                               (The Twentieth Century)
      November 25, 1962   30 minutes

Credits: Executive producer, *Burton Benjamin*; Producer, *Isaac Kleinerman*; Director, *Willard Van Dyke*; Narration written by *Earle Luby*; Narrator, *Walter Cronkite*; Reporter, *Charles Kuralt*; Associate producer, *Peter Poor*; Story editor, *Earle Luby*; Music composed by *Carlos Surinach*; Music conducted by *Alfred Antonini*; Film editor, *Lora Hays*; Photographer, *Jorge Ruiz*; Sound, *David Scott*; Production manager, *James Jackson*; Research director, *John Gilligan.*

Rental or purchase: McGraw-Hill.

THE PLOTS AGAINST HITLER   CBS-TV
  (Two parts)   *(The Twentieth Century)*
      November 24 and   30 minutes each
      December 1, 1963

Credits: Executive Producer-Writer, *Burton Benjamin*; Producer, *Isaac Kleinerman*; Reporters, *Walter Cronkite, Daniel Schorr*; Associate producer *Peter Poor*; Story editor, *Earle Luby*; Photography, *Gerhard Schwartzkopff*; Sound, *Maurice Reitberger*; Film editor, *Leo Zochling*; Production manager, *James Jackson*; Research, *Richard Slote*; Film research, *Lee Reichenthal*; Recorded by *Richard Vorisek.*

Rental or purchase: CBS Films, Inc.

OUT OF DARKNESS   CBS-TV
    March 18, 1956   (*The Search*)

Credits: Executive producer, *Irving Gitlin*; Producer-writer, *Albert Wasserman*; Associate Producer, *Lewis Jacobs*; Production Managers, *Harry Robin, Arthur
Swerdloff*.

Rental or purchase: McGraw-Hill.

PEARL HARBOR: UNFORGOTTEN   CBS-TV
                                (*Accent*)
    September 6, 1962   30 minutes

Credits: Producer, *Don Kellerman*; Associate producer, *James Perrin*; Writer, *Joseph
Hurley*; Narrator, *John Ciardi*.

Rental or purchase: CBS Films, Inc.

THE DIALOGUES OF ARCHIBALD MACLEISH AND MARK VAN DOREN
                                                       CBS-TV
                                                       (*Special*)
    August 2, 1962   60 minutes

Credits: Producer, *Warren V. Bush*; Director, *Hilary Harris*; Narrator, *Lee Richard-
son;* Music composed and conducted by *Kenyon Hopkins*; Research, *Leon
Rice*; Assistant to producer, *Roger Smith*.

Rental or purchase: CBS Films, Inc.

ON THE ROAD TO BUTTON BAY   For CBS-TV by Robert
                                           Drew Associates —
                                           (*Special*)
    1962   60 minutes

Credits: Executive producer, *Robert L. Drew*; Film-makers, *Stanley Flink, Abbot
Mills, Hope Ryden, James Lipscomb, Richard Leacock, D. A. Pennebaker;*
Assistants, *Peter Eco, Alfred Wertheimer*; Editors, *Leon Prochnik, Saul
Lunoa, Mike Jackson, Nancy Sen*; Assistant Editors, *Mara Janson, Tom By-
waters*; Narrator, *Garry Moore*.

Available for screening at minimum charge from Girl Scouts of the U.S.A., 830 Third
Avenue, New York, N.Y. 10022.

THE TURKEY SHOOT
DESIGN FOR WAR
THE BLUE ROUTE   NBC-TV
                                       (*Victory at Sea*)
                                       30 minutes each

    Entire *Victory at Sea* series (26 segments), was first aired on the NBC-TV
network in the 1952-53 season. A 90-minute version has also been made
from the entire series.

Credits: (Entire series): Producer, *Henry Salomon*; Music, *Richard Rodgers*; Music
arranged by *Robert Russell Bennett*; Narrator, *Leonard Graves*; Written by
Henry Salomon with *Richard Hanser*; Edited by *Isaac Kleinerman*; Executive
producer, *Robert W. Sarnoff*.

In mid-1964, Encyclopaedia Britannica Films contracted for the distribution of over
500 NBC-TV films. Many of those listed below as unavailable or restricted may therefore now be obtained from Encyclopaedia Britannica Films, Inc., 202 East 44th Street,
New York, N.Y. 10017.

FIRE RESCUE   NBC-TV
                                                   (*DuPont Show of the Week*)
            September 30, 1962   60 minutes

Credits: Executive producer, *Irving Gitlin*; Producer, *Fred Freed*; Writer-director, *John G. Fuller*; Cameramen, *Michael Clark, Douglas Downes*; Film editor, *David Roland*; Sound, *Jerome Gold*; Production supervision, *Robert Rubin*; Narrator, *Walter Mathau*.

Restricted screening: Write Program Information, NBC-TV, 30 Rockefeller Plaza, New York, N.Y. 10020.

PRISONER AT LARGE   NBC-TV
                                                   (*DuPont Show of the Week*)
            April 21, 1963   60 minutes

Credits: Executive producer, *Irving Gitlin*; Producer-Director-Writer, *William Jersey*; Associate director, *Walter Millis*; Film editor, *Robert Farren*; Assistant film editor, *Joanne McGarrity*; Cameraman, *Joseph Vadala*; Assistant cameraman, *Thomas Landi*; Sound, *Jerome Gold*; Research, *JoAnn Goldberg*; Production supervisor, *Robert Rubin*.

Restricted screening: Write Program Information, NBC-TV.

MANHATTAN BATTLEGROUND   NBC-TV
                                                   (*DuPont Show of the Week*)
            October 20, 1963   60 minutes

Credits: Executive producer, *Irving Gitlin*; Producer-Director-Writer, *William Jersey*; Associate producer, *Philip Burton, Jr.*; Film editors, *Robert Farren, Darold Murray, Joanne McGarrity*; Cameramen, *Joseph Vadala, Michael Clark, Morton Heilig*; Sound, *Harold Bieben, Jerome Gold*; Research, *JoAnn Goldberg;* Production supervision, *William Quinn*.

Restricted screening: Write Program Information, NBC-TV.

HIGH WIRE: THE GREAT WALLENDAS   NBC-TV
                                                   (*DuPont Show of the Week*)
            March 22, 1964   60 minutes

Credits: Executive producer, *Irving Gitlin*; Producer-Writer, *Albert Wasserman*; Director, *George Freeland*; Cameraman, *Robin Still*; Film editor, *Angelo Farina*; Sound, *David Scott, Emil Kolisch, Charle Hipszer*; Research, *JoAnn Goldberg*; Production supervision, *William Quinn*.

Restricted screening: Write Program Information NBC-TV.

THE U-2 AFFAIR   NBC-TV
                                                   (*White Paper*)
            November 29, 1960   60 minutes

Credits: Executive producer, *Irving Gitlin*; Producer-Director, *Albert Wasserman*; Writers, *Albert Wasserman, Arthur Baron*; Cameraman, *Thomas Priestly*; Associate producer, *Arthur Baron*; Editorial chief, *Jerome Jacobs*; Film editor, *Luke Bennett*; Production supervision, *Norton Bloom*.

Rental or purchase: McGraw-Hill.

ANGOLA: JOURNEY TO A WAR   NBC-TV
                                                   (*White Paper*)
            September 19, 1961   54 minutes

Credits: Executive producer, *Irving Gitlin*; Producer, *Albert Wasserman*; Director-Cameraman, *Robert Young*; Associate director-Cameraman, *Charles Dorkins*;

Cameraman, *Louis Hepp*; Film editor, *Luke Bennett*; Special correspondent, *Robert McCormick*; Production supervision, *Robert Rubin*.
Rental or purchase: McGraw-Hill.

THE BATTLE OF NEWBURGH

NBC-TV
(*White Paper*)
January 28, 1962   60 minutes

Credits: Executive producer, *Irving Gitlin*; Producer, *Albert Wasserman*; Director, *Arthur Zegart*; Writers, *Albert Wasserman, Arthur Zegart*; Cameraman, *Joseph Vadala*; Assistant cameraman, *Thomas Landi*; Film editor, *Eleanor Hamerow*; Sound, *Jerome Gold*; Research, *Walter Millis, Jr., Penny Bernstein*; Production supervision, *Robert Rubin*.
Restricted screening: Write Program Information, NBC-TV.

THE DEATH OF STALIN

NBC-TV
(*White Paper*)
January 27, 1963   60 minutes

Credits: Executive producer, *Irving Gitlin*; Producer-Writer, *Fred Freed*; Associate producer-Director, *Len Giovannitti*; Research, *Morris Calden*; Film editor, *Jack Kaufman*; Production supervision, *Robert Rubin*.
Restricted screening: Write Program Information, NBC-TV.

THE BUSINESS OF GAMBLING

NBC-TV
(*White Paper*)
April 28, 1963   60 minutes

Credits: Executive producer, *Irving Gitlin*; Producer-Writer-Director, *Arthur Zegart*; Associate producer-Film editor, *Luke Bennett*; Cameraman, *Joseph Vadala*; Assistant cameraman, *Thomas Landi*; Sound, *Jerome Gold*; Film research, *Robyn Mendelsohn*; Production manager, *William Quinn*; Production supervision, *Robert Rubin*.
Restricted screening: Write Program Information, NBC-TV.

CUBA: BAY OF PIGS

NBC-TV
(*White Paper*)
February 2, 1964   60 minutes

Credits: Executive producer, *Irving Gitlin*; Producer-Writer, *Fred Freed*; Associate producer-Director, *Len Giovannitti*; Research, *Morris Calden, Doris Frye, Joan Cummings, Helmut Sontag*; Film editor, *John Teple*; Cameramen, *Robert Anderson, Irving Smith*; Production supervision, *William Quinn*.
Restricted screening: Write Program Information, NBC-TV.

CUBA: THE MISSILE CRISIS

NBC-TV
(*White Paper*)
February 9, 1964   60 minutes

Credits: Executive producer, *Irving Gitlin*; Producer-Writer, *Fred Freed*; Associate Producer-Director, *Len Giovannitti*; Research, *Morris Calden, Joan Cummings*; Cameramen, *Irving Smith, Joseph Vadala*; Film editor, *Peter Punzi*; Production supervision, *William Quinn*.
Restricted screening: Write Program Information, NBC-TV.

NIGHTMARE IN RED   NBC-TV
                                                        (*Project XX*)
              December 27, 1955   60 minutes

Credits: Producer, *Henry Salomon*; Written by *Henry Salomon* with *Richard Hanser*;
         Editor, *Isaac Kleinerman*; Music, *Robert Russell Bennett*; Narrator, *Alex-
         ander Scourby*; Assistant Film editor, *Silvio D'Alisera*; Research, *Daniel Jones,
         Mel Stuart, S. W. Little*; Production supervision, *Donald E. Hyatt*.

Rental or purchase: McGraw-Hill or Contemporary Films, Inc.

THE TWISTED CROSS   NBC-TV
                                                        (*Project XX*)
              March 14, 1956   60 minutes

Credits: Producer, *Henry Salomon*; Written by *Henry Salomon* with *Richard Hanser*;
         Assistant producer, *Donald Hyatt*; Editor, *Isaac Kleinerman*; Music, *Robert
         Russell Bennett*; Narrator, *Alexander Scourby*; Assistant film editor, *Silvio
         D'Alisera*; Research, *Daniel Jones, Mel Stuart, Judith Greene*.

Rental or purchase: McGraw-Hill or Contemporary Films, Inc.

CALL TO FREEDOM   NBC-TV
                                                        (*Project XX*)
              January 7, 1957   90 minutes

Credits: Producer, *Henry Salomon*; Written by *Henry Salomon* with *Richard Hanser*;
         Assistant producer, *Donald B. Hyatt*; Editor, *Isaac Kleinerman*; Assistant edi-
         tor, *Silvio D'Alisera*; Writer, *Phil Riesman, Jr.*; Music, *Robert Russell Bennett*;
         Narrator, *Alexander Scourby*; Research, *Daniel Jones, Mel Stuart, Judith
         Greene*.

Available for screening: Write NBC-TV Program Information.

THE INNOCENT YEARS   NBC-TV
                                                        (*Project XX*)
              November 21, 1957   60 minutes

Credits: Producer, *Henry Salomon*; Written by *Henry Salomon* with *Richard Hanser*;
         Director, *Donald B. Hyatt*; Editor, *Silvio D'Alisera*; Music, *Robert Russell
         Bennett*; Narrator, *Alexander Scourby*; Research, *Daniel Jones*.

Available for screening: Write NBC-TV Program Information.

MEET MR. LINCOLN   NBC-TV
                                                        (*Project XX*)
                                                        30 minutes
              February 11, 1959

Credits: Producer-director, *Donald B. Hyatt*; Writer, *Richard Hanser*; Music, *Robert
         Russell Bennett*; Narrator, *Alexander Scourby*; Assistant producer, *Robert
         Garthwaite*; Film editor, *Silvio D'Alisera*; Assistant editor, *John Christophel*;
         Research, *Daniel Jones, Rhoda Grady, Charles Osborn*.

Available for screening: Write NBC-TV Program Information.

THE STORY OF WILL ROGERS   NBC-TV
                                                        (*Project XX*)
              March 28, 1961   60 minutes

Credits: Producer-director, *Donald B. Hyatt*; Writers, *Richard Hanser, Rod Reed*;
         Narrator, *Bob Hope*; Music, *Robert Russell Bennett*; Associate producer,
         Robert L. Garthwaite; Film editor, *Silvio D'Alisera*; Assistant film editor,
         James Pallan; Research, *Daniel Jones, Peretz Johnnes*.

Available for screening: Write NBC-TV Program Information.

THE REAL WEST   NBC-TV
                                                (*Project XX*)
March 29, 1961   60 minutes

Credits: Producer-director, *Donald B. Hyatt*; Narrator, *Gary Cooper*; Writer, *Philip Reisman, Jr.*; Music, *Robert Russell Bennett*; Associate producer, *Robert L. Garthwaite*; Research, *Daniel Jones, Rhoda C. Grady, Claire Rosenstein, Robert M. Doty*; Film editor, *Silvio D'Alisera*; Assistant editor, *James Pallan*.

Rental or purchase: McGraw-Hill.

THAT WAR IN KOREA   NBC-TV
                                                (*Project XX*)
November 20, 1963   90 minutes

Credits: Producer-director, *Donald B. Hyatt*; Writer, *Richard Hanser*; Music, *Robert Russell Bennett*; Associate producer, *Robert Garthwaite*; Research director, *Daniel W. Jones*; Research assistants, *James Sage, Claire Rosenstein, Rhoda Grady, Barbara Monks*; Film editor, *Silvio D'Alisera*; Assistant editor, *James Pallan*; Narrator, *Richard Boone*.

Restricted screening: Write NBC-TV Program Information.

THE WORLD OF BOB HOPE   NBC-TV
                                                (*The World of —*)
October 29, 1961   60 minutes

Credits: Executive producer, *Donald B. Hyatt*; Producer-Director, *Eugene S. Jones*; Associate producer, *James L. Reina*; Writer, *Joseph Liss*; Music, *Skitch Henderson*; Narrator, *Alexander Scourby*; Film editor, *John Christophel*; Assistant editor, *Ron Ciccolini*; Filmed by *Haskell Wexler, Joseph F. Coffey, Sanford Greenwald, Jack Leppert, Lawrence Pal, Andy Werner, Joseph Bush*; Research coordinator, *Charles Grinker*; Production associate, *Shirley A. Chabot*.

Restricted screening: Write NBC-TV Program Information.

THE WORLD OF BILLY GRAHAM   NBC-TV
                                                (*The World of —*)
November 29, 1961   60 minutes

Credits: Executive producer, *Donald B. Hyatt*; Producer-Director, *Eugene S. Jones*; Associate producer, *James L. Reina*; Writer, *Joseph Liss*; Narrator, *Alexander Scourby*; Music by *Robert Emmett Dolan*; Filmed by *Cy Avnet*; Assistant cameramen, *John Peters, Christopher Gallery, Felix Lazarus, Bernard Dresner, Robert Blair, Michael Dresner*; Film editor, *John Christophel*; Assistant editor, *Ron Ciccolini*; Unit manager, *Robin Bursch*; Research supervisor, *Charles Grinker*; Production associates, *Virginia Shanley, Shirley A. Chabot*.

Restricted screening: Write NBC-TV Program Information.

THE WORLD OF JACQUELINE KENNEDY   NBC-TV
                                                (*The World of —*)
November 30, 1962   60 minutes

Credits: Executive producer, *Donald B. Hyatt*; Producer-Director, *Eugene S. Jones*; Writer, *Joseph Liss*; Associate producer, *James L. Reina*; Narrator, *Alexander Scourby*; Music by *Robert Emmett Dolan*; Filmed by *Cy Avnet*; Assistant cameraman, *Herman Vandevender*; Sound, *Edward Fenton*; Film editor, *John Christophel*; Assistant editor, *Ron Ciccolini*; Unit manager, *Robin Bursch*; Program coordinator, *Charles Grinker*; Production associates, *Virginia Shanley, Shirley A. Chabot*.

Restricted screening: Write NBC-TV Program Information.

VINCENT VAN GOGH: A SELF PORTRAIT   NBC-TV
                                             (Special)
          November 17, 1961   60 minutes

Credits: Producer-Writer, *Lou Hazam*; Director, *Ray Garner*; Photography, *Guy Blanchard*; Music by *Jacques Belasco*; Film editors, *Constantine S. Gochis, Fred Flamenhaft, Ray Fincke*; Production associates, *Rodney H. Clurman, Barry Bingham, Jr., Barbara Muller*; Unit managers, *Dan O'Connor, John Kennedy*.

Available for screening: Write NBC-TV Program Information.

SHAKESPEARE: SOUL OF AN AGE   NBC-TV
                                             (Special)
          November 30, 1962   60 minutes

Credits: Producer-Writer, *Lou Hazam*; Director-Photographer, *Guy Blanchard*; Assistant to producer, *Daniel Karasik*; Music by *George Kleinsinger*; Supervising film editor, *Constantine S. Gochis*; Film editor, *Loftus McDonough*; Unit manager, *Ray Marsh*; Research, *Robert Butman*; Production associates, *Patricia Erickson, Dorothy Buckner*.

Available for screening: Write NBC-TV Program Information.

GREECE: THE GOLDEN AGE   NBC-TV
                                             (Special)
          November 19, 1963   60 minutes

Credits: Producer-Writer, *Lou Hazam*; Director, *Ray Garner*; Photographer, *Brad Kress*; Supervising film editor, *Constantine S. Gochis*; Additional photography, *Paul Bruck*; Sound, *Albert Gramaglia*; Film editors, *P. F. Young, III, Loftus McDonough, Russell Moore*; Music, *George Kleinsinger*; Production coordinator, *Louis Hepp*; Unit manager, *Bill Bard*; Production associates, *Patricia Erickson, Dorothy Buckner*.

Available for screening: Write NBC-TV Program Information.

ORIENT EXPRESS   NBC-TV
                                             (Special)
          January 7, 1964   60 minutes

Credits: Producer, *Lou Hazam*; Director, *Thomas Priestley*; Photography, *Paul Bruck*; Cameramen, *Joseph Oexle, Harry Thoess, Claude Favier*; Music by *Jacques Belasco*; Supervising film editor, *Constantine S. Gochis*; Film editor, *Loftus McDonough*; Assistant films editors, *Russell Moore, P. F. Young, III*; Sound, *Andres Lebaut*; Unit manager, *William Lynch*; Associated in production, *Patricia Erickson, Dorothy Buckner*; Correspondent, *Edwin Newman*.

Available for screening: Write NBC-TV Program Information.

THE TUNNEL   NBC-TV
                                             (NBC-TV News Special)
          December 10, 1962   90 minutes

Credits: Executive producer, *Reuven Frank*; Produced and written by *Reuven Frank* and *Piers Anderton*; Cameramen, *Peter Dehmel, Klaus Dehmel*; Film editor, *Gerald Polikoff*; Music composed and conducted by *Eddie Safranski*; Production supervisor, *Garry Stindt*.

Restricted screening: Write NBC-TV Program Information.

REPORT ON HAITI   NBC-TV
  (Two parts)   (*David Brinkley's Journal*)
    May 6 and May 13, 1963   30 minutes each

Credits: Reporter-Narrator, *David Brinkley*; Producers, *Stuart Schulberg, Ted Yates*; Cameramen, *Fred Montague, James Norling.*

Restricted screening: Write NBC-TV Program Information.

LOCAL, REGIONAL AND NATIONALLY SYNDICATED DOCUMENTARY

SYNANON   WNHC-TV
  (Two parts)   New Haven, Connecticut
    June 17 and June 25, 1963   30 minutes each

Credits: Producer-Director-Writer, *J. Arthur Stober*; Cameraman, *Jack Youngs*; Film editor, *Len Sanna*; Narrator, *Stelio Salmona.*

Available on loan: Write J. Arthur Stober, WNHC-TV, New Haven, Conn.

OPERATION CHALLENGE — A STUDY IN HOPE
     KSD-TV
     St. Louis, Missouri
    December 10, 1963   30 minutes

Credits: Producer-Writer, *Mary Spencer;* Director, *Patricia Williamson;* Cameraman, *Richard Hardcastle, Jr.*

Available on loan: Write Mr. Keith Gunther, Program Manager, KSD-TV, St. Louis, Mo.

THE LAST PROM   WLW-T
     Cincinnati, Ohio
    May 26, 1963   60 minutes

Credits: Producer-Director-Writer, *Gene McPherson*; Cameraman, *Lou Phillips*; Unit manager, *Joe Lewin*; Narrator, *Jack Gwynn.*

Available on loan within coverage area of WLW stations. Prints may also be purchased. Write WLW-T, Cincinnati, Ohio.

CONFORMITY   WCAU-TV
     Philadelphia, Pennsylvania
    December 26, 1962   60 minutes

Credits: Executive producer, *Alvin L. Hollander, Jr.*; Producer, *George Dessart*; Writer, *John Keats*; Director, *David E. Wilson*; Film director, *Phil Galligan*; Film editor, *Don Matticks*; Sound, *Bill Ludes*; Narrator, *Harry Reasoner.*

Available on loan: Write WCAU-TV, Philadelphia, Pa.

JUNKYARD BY THE SEA   WCBS-TV
     New York City
    January 12, 1961   60 minutes

Credits: Producer-Writer-Reporter, *Warren Wallace*; Director, *Robert Goodman*; Assistant to producer, *Paul Melton*; Cameraman, *Edmund Bert Gerard*; Music composed and conducted by *Michael Colicchio*; Supervisory film editor, *Herman Kroll*; Film editor, *Bernadette Sauve*; Production supervisor, *William Bard*; Narrator, *Bill Leonard.*

Available on loan: Write Director of Public Affairs, WCBS-TV, New York, N.Y.

LA VIE ÉLÉGANTE   WCBS-TV
                                                 New York City
May 31, 1962   30 minutes

Credits: Executive producer, *Ned Cramer*; Producer, *Gordon Hyatt*; Director of photography, *Karl Malkames*; Film editor, *John Carter*; Music supervisor, *Ronald W. Noll*; Reporter, *Robert Trout*.

Available on loan: Write Director of Public Affairs, WCBS-TV.

THE NEXT REVOLUTION   WCBS-TV
                                                 New York City
December 20, 1963   60 minutes

Credits: Producer-Director-Writer-Reporter, *Warren Wallace*; Cameraman, *Karl Malkames*; Associate producer, *Herbert Krosney*; Production supervisor, *William Turque*; Music composed and conducted by *Michael Colicchio*; Supervisory film editor, *John McManus*; Narrator, *Bill Leonard*.

Available on loan: Write Director of Public Affairs, WCBS-TV.

SUPERFLUOUS PEOPLE   WCBS-TV
                                                 New York City
July 26, 1962   60 minutes

Credits: Producer-Director-Reporter, *Warren Wallace*; Cameraman, *Edmund Bert Gerard*; Assistant to producer, *Marc Brugoni*; Music composed and conducted by *Michael Colicchio*; Supervisory film editor, *John McManus*; Film editor, *David Donovan*; Production supervisor, *Sheldon Lubow*; Narrator, *Bill Leonard*.

Available on loan: Write Director of Public Affairs, WCBS-TV.

THE WASTED YEARS   WBBM-TV
                                                 Chicago, Illinois
February 21, 1962   30 minutes

Credits: Producer-Writer-Narrator, *Hugh Hill*; Cameraman, *Irv Heberg*; Sound, *Mike Kesmar*.

Available on loan: Write Reference Library, WBBM-TV, Chicago, Ill.

THE RUN   WKY-TV
                                                 Oklahoma City, Oklahoma
April 21, 1961   30 minutes

Credits: Producers, *Gene Allen, Scott Berner*; Writer, *Gene Allen*; Cameraman and Film editor, *Scott Berner*; Music, *The Wayfarers*.

Available on loan: Write WKY-TV, Oklahoma City, Okla.

TIME'S MAN   WKY-TV
                                                 Oklahoma City, Oklahoma
April 2, 1962   30 minutes

Credits: Writer-Director, *Gene Allen*; Cameraman, *Huston Hall*.

Available on loan: Write WKY-TV.

PIONEER PAINTER   WKY-TV
                                                    Oklahoma City, Oklahoma
January 15, 1963   30 minutes

Credits: Executive producer, *Joe Jerkins*; Writer-Director, *Gene Allen*; Cameraman, *Cliff Adkins*; Audio, *Gale Thorsen*; Research, *Cliff Warren*.

Available on loan: Write WKY-TV.

PICTURE OF A CUBAN   WLBW-TV
                                                    Miami, Florida
July 26, 1962   30 minutes

Credits: Producer-Writer, *Stanley H. Bloom;* Directors, *Stanley H. Bloom, Bill Dunstall*; Cameraman-Film editor, *Ken Butcher*; Sound, *Ralph Faber, Ken Butcher*; Research, *Raul Armand, Stanley H. Bloom*.

Available on loan: Write WLBW-TV, Channel 10, Miami, Fla.

WEDNESDAY'S CHILD   KGW-TV
                                                    Portland, Oregon
July 17, 1963   30 minutes

Credits: Producer-Narrator, *Thomas R. Dargan*; Script supervision, *Robert H. Schulman*; Writer, *Robert McBride*; Director, *Ralph McGraw*; Cameraman, *Richard Althoff*; Sound-Film editor, *Ralph McGraw*; Research, *Robert McBride*; Assistants to the producer, *LeRoy Smith, Ken Yandle*.

Available on loan: Write Helen Platt, Educational and Public Service Department, KGW-TV, Portland, Ore.

WITHOUT VIOLENCE   WBRZ-TV
                                                    Baton Rouge, Louisiana
1963   60 minutes

Credits: Writer-Narrator, *Al Crouch*; Cameraman, *Robert Durham*; Film editor, *Harold White*; Sound, *William Benedetto*.

Available on loan: Write WBRZ-TV, Channel 2, Baton Rouge, La.

CHILD BEATING   WMAL-TV
                                                    Washington, D.C.
December 1, 1963   30 minutes

Credits: Executive producer, *Matthew Warren*; Co-producers, *Jerome K. Johnson, Ronald Van Nostrand*.

For information, write WMAL-TV, Washington, D.C.

SUSPECT   KING-TV
                                                    Seattle, Washington
October 19, 1962   30 minutes

Credits: Executive producer, *Lee Schulman*; Producer-Director, *Kit Spier*; Writer-Narrator, *Robert Schulman*; Cameraman-Film editor, *Ralph Umbarger*.

Available on loan: Write Mr. Jack Fearey, KING-TV Seattle, Wash.

A VOLCANO NAMED WHITE   KING-TV
                                                Seattle, Washington
        November 29, 1961   60 minutes

Credits: Executive producer, *Lee Schulman*; Producer-Director, *Kit Spier*; Writer-narrator, *Robert Schulman*; Cameraman-Film editor, *Merle Severn*; Music, *Meyer Slivka*.

Available on loan: Write Mr. Jack Fearey, KING-TV, Seattle, Wash.

THE THREE WAY STREET   WBZ-TV
                                                Boston, Massachusetts
        February 28, 1962   30 minutes

Credits: Producer, *Jeff Kalil*; Film director-Cameraman, *Robert Cirace*; Narrator, *Jack Borden*; Writer, *Ira Lurvey*; Executive producer, *George Moynihan*.

Available on loan: Write WBZ-TV Program Manager, Boston, Mass.

THE UNQUIET RIVER   WNBC-TV
                                                New York City
        November 8, 1962   30 minutes

Credits: Producer, *Ray Weiss*; Narrator, *Chet Huntley*; Writer, *Morton Silverstein*; Director, *Anthony Messuri*; Cameraman, *Nathan Cohen*; Film editors, *Howard Ginser, Dave Weixel*; Unit Manager, *Dick French*.

Restricted screening: Write Jack Reynolds, Manager, Public Affairs, WNBC-TV, New York, N.Y.

THE CASE FOR THE LIMITED CHILD   KPIX-TV
                                                San Francisco, California
        December 4, 1963   30 minutes

Credits: Executive producer, *Ray Hubbard*; Producer, *Caryl Coleman*; Writer-Director, *Brad Wright*; Photographer-Film editor, *Dick Williams*.

Loaned upon request. May also be purchased. Write KPIX-TV Public Affairs.

THE CHAIR   Robert Drew Associates with
                                                Time-Life Broadcast, Inc.
        1963   60 minutes

Credits: Executive producer, *Robert L. Drew*; Producers, *Gregory Shuker, Richard L. Leacock, Donn Alan Pennebaker*.

Restricted screening: Write Robert Drew Associates.

INTERNATIONAL DOCUMENTARY

MORNING IN THE STREETS   BBC-TV
        First aired in England,   36 minutes
        March, 1959

Credits: Directors, *Denis Mitchell* and *Roy Harris*; Photographers, *Roy Harris, Gerry Pullen, Graham Turner, Ted Wallbank*; Editor, *Donald James*; Research, *Frank Shaw*; Musical score, *Thomas Henderson*.

Available for screening at approximately $20.00 per rental. Write BBC-TV, 630 Fifth Avenue, New York, N.Y. 10020.

TELEVISION AND THE WORLD   BBC-TV
    First aired in England,   87 minutes
    October 31, 1961. U. S. premiere,
    September 16, 1962

Credits: Producer-Director-Writer, *Richard Cawston*; Photographer, *Kenneth West-bury*; Sound, *Michael Colomb, Robert Saunders*; Film editor, *Harry Hastings*; Narrator, *Michael Flanders*.

Available for screening or purchase. Rental, approximately $25.00. Write BBC-TV New York.

THE WINDS OF CHANGE   BBC-TV
    (In three parts: "Main Street Africa," "A View from the Farm," and
    "Between Two Worlds.")
    First aired in England, April 10, 11, 12, 1960. U. S. premiere,
    December, 1960.

Credits: Producer, *Denis Mitchell*; Cameraman, *Kenneth Westbury*; Sound, *Maurice Everitt*; Film editor, *Leonard Trumm*.

Available for screening at $10.00 per segment. Write BBC-TV, New York.

THE TITANS   BBC-TV
    (In two parts: "The Rise of Russian Power" and
    "The Rise of American Power.")
    First aired in England, January 9 and 16, 1962. U. S. Premiere
    October 30, 1962

Credits: Producer, *Therese Denny*; Writer-Narrator, *Malcolm Muggeridge*; Music composed and conducted by *Robert Farnon*; Music director (Part II), *Ron Grainer*; Sound mixer, *Robert Saunders*; Film editor, *Ian Callaway*.

Part I only available for U. S. screening. McGraw-Hill.

ONE MORE RIVER   CBC-TV
    First aired in Canada, April 24, 1963   (Intertel)
    (Not aired in U. S.)   60 minutes

Credits: Producer-Director, *Douglas Leiterman*; Co-director, *Beryl Fox*; Cameraman, *Richard Leiterman*; Film editor, *Don Haig*.

Screening restricted. Write CBC-TV, P. O. Box 500, Terminal "A," Toronto, Canada.

WILDERNESS   CBC-TV
                                               (*Camera Canada*)
    First aired in Canada, May 27, 1963   60 minutes

Credits: Executive producer, *Thom Benson*; Producer, *Norman Caton*;* Cameramen, *Len Macdonald, Charles Reigler*;* Writer, *Len Peterson*; Music composed by *Doctor W. MacCauley*; Narrator, *Esse W. Ljungh*.

*(The producer and two cameramen were killed in a plane crash during the last days of shooting for this production. In their honor the "Wilderness Award", for outstanding film achievement at CBC-TV, was established.)

For information regarding screening, write CBC-TV.

THE LOOKING GLASS PEOPLE   CBC-TV
                                              (*Camera Canada*)
    First aired in Canada, July 28, 1963   60 minutes

Credits: Executive producer, *Thom Benson*; Producer, *Norman Campbell*; Writer, *George Salverson*; Cameramen, *Jack Long, John Foster, Graham Woods*; Film editor, *David Knight*; Musical direction, *Louis Applebaum, George Crum*; Narrator, *Bud Knapp*.

For information regarding screening, write CBC-TV.

FORTY MILLION SHOES   CBC-TV
                                              (Intertel)
    First aired in Canada, November 28, 1961   52 minutes

Credits: Producer-director, *Douglas Leiterman*; Cameraman, *Grahame Woods*; Music composed by *Harry Freedman*; Executive producer, *Cliff Solway*.

Rental or purchase: N.E.T. Film Service, Indiana University, Bloomington, Indiana.

POSTSCRIPT TO EMPIRE   Westinghouse Broadcasting —
                                              N.E.T. (Intertel)
    First aired in U. S., November 20, 1961   52 minutes

Credits: Executive producer-Writer, *Michael Sklar*; Producer-Director, *Michael Alexander*; Narrator, *Joseph Julian*; Reporter, *Roderick MacLeish*; Cameramen, *Harry Hart, Ricky Briggs*; Sound, *Basil Rootes, Don Alton*; Film editor, *Angelo Ross*; Research, *J. Charrott-Lowidge*; Unit manager, *Tom Hawkins*; Continuity, *Marjorie Lavelly, Trix Wilkin*.

Rental or purchase: N.E.T. Film Service, Indiana University.

LIVING WITH A GIANT   Associated-Rediffusion, Ltd.
                                              (Intertel)
    First aired in U. S., May 14, 1962   52 minutes

Credits: Director, *Rollo Gamble*; Writer, *Elkan Allan*; Narrator, *Lord Boothby*; Film editor, *David Gill*; Chief cameraman, *Adrian Cooper*; Research, *Nona MacDonald*.

Rental or purchase: N.E.T. Film Service, Indiana University.

Selected Bibliography

"A Real Pro," *The Reporter*, XXIV (February 16, 1961), 16-20.

"Accent on Today," *Newsweek*, LVI (August 22, 1960), 84.

Adler, Mortimer. *Art and Prudence.* New York: Longmans, Green and Co., 1937.

Allan Elkan. "Scripting Actuality Television," *Sight and Sound*, XXVII (Winter, 1957-58), 120-1.

Andrès, Jacques. "Television Vérité," *Contrast*, II (Summer, 1963), 260-1.

———. *Film as Art.* Berkeley and Los Angeles: University of California Press, 1958.

———. *Radio.* London: Faber and Faber, Ltd., 1936.

Baddeley, Hugh. *The Technique of Documentary Film Production.* London: Focal Press Ltd. New York: Hastings House, Publishers, 1963.

Baker, George Pierce. *Dramatic Technique.* New York: Houghton Mifflin Co., 1919.

Belson, William A. "Selective Perception in Viewing a TV Broadcast," *Audio-Visual Communication Review*, VI (Spring, 1958), 13-19.

Benjamin, Burton. "The Documentary Heritage," *Television Quarterly*, I (February, 1962), 29-34.

———. "TV Documentarian's Dream in a Challenging World," *Variety* (January 4, 1961), 91.

"Best: *CBS Reports*," *Newsweek*, LII (January 8, 1962), 42.

Black, Peter. "Round The World," *Contrast*, I (Spring, 1962), 169.

Bluem, A. William, John F. Cox and Gene McPherson. *Television in the Public Interest.* New York: Hastings House, Publishers, 1961.

Bluestone, George. *Novels into Film.* Berkeley and Los Angeles: University of California Press, 1961.

Bogart, Leo. *The Age of Television.* New York: Frederick Ungar Publishing Company, 1956.

Bretz, Rudolph. "TV as an Art Form," *Hollywood Quarterly*, V (1950-51), 153-63.

Bryson, Lyman and Edward R. Murrow. "You and Television," *Hollywood Quarterly*, IV (1949-50), 178-81.

Buchanan, Andrew. *The Art of Film Production.* London: Sir Isaac Pitman & Sons, 1936.

Calder-Marshall, Arthur. *The Innocent Eye.* London: W. H.. Allen & Co., 1963.

Capa, Robert. *Images of War*. New York: Grossman Publishers, 1964.
Cass, James. "Face of Soviet Youth," *Saturday Review,* XLV (October 27, 1962), 28.
Chayefsky, Paddy. *Television Plays*. New York: Simon and Schuster, 1955.
Ciardi, John. "Improve Your Mind Between Commercials," *Saturday Review,* XLV (September 1, 1962), 17.
Clair, Renè. "Renè Clair Embattled," *Contrast,* III (Autumn, 1963), 65.
Clark, Barrett H. (ed.). *European Theories of the Drama* (Revised Edition). New York: Crown Publishers, 1947.
Cleveland Conference on Local Public Service Programming. Group W, 1963.
Cooke, Alistair. *The Listener* (November 20, 1935), 931.
"Creme De La Kremlin," *Time,* LXXXV (May 31, 1963), 48.
Cronkite, Walter. "Television and the News," *The Eighth Art,* ed. Robert Lewis Shayon. New York: Holt, Rinehart and Winston, 1962, 227-40.
de Antonio, Emile and Daniel Talbot. *Point of Order!* New York: W. W. Norton & Co., 1964.
De Voto, Bernard. "The Easy Chair," *Harpers,* CCVIII (June 1954), 8-11.
"Denis Mitchell," *Film.* No. 35 (Spring ,1963), 18-20.
Deren, Maya. "Cinematography: The Creative Use of Reality," *Daedalus, Journal of the American Academy of Arts and Sciences*: "The Visual Arts Today," LXXXIX (Winter, 1960), 150-67.
Fergusson, Francis. *The Idea of a Theatre*. Princeton: Princeton University Press, 1949.
Fielding, Raymond. *The March of Time, 1935-1942.* unpublished masters thesis, University of California, Los Angeles, January, 1956.
———. "Time Flickers Out: Notes on the Passing of the *March of Time,*" *Quarterly of Film, Radio and Television,* XI (Summer, 1957), 354-61.
Frank, Reuven. "The Making of The Tunnel," *Television Quarterly,* II (Fall, 1963), 8-23.
———. and Don Hewitt. "Dialogue," *Television Quarterly,* I (November, 1962), 6-20.
Friendly, Fred W. "Television Can Open America's Eyes," *TV guide,* VIII (December 10, 1960), 7-11.
"From the Work of the Masters," *Time,* LXXVI (December 26, 1960), 39.
Gallez, Douglas W. "Patterns in Wartime Documentaries," *The Quarterly of Film, Radio and Television,* X (Winter, 1955), 125-35.
Gassner, John (ed.). *A Treasury of the Theatre* (revised edition for colleges) New York: Simon and Schuster, 1950.
Gilligan, John. "TV Documentaries Use Amateur Footage," *Popular Photography,* XLII (January, 1958), 120-2.
Gordon, George N., Irving Falk and William Hodapp. *The Idea Invaders*. New York: Hastings House, Publishers, 1963.
Gorelik, Mordecai. *New Theatres for Old*. Binghamton, New York: Samuel French, 1949.
"Grace of Graustark: A Look at Monaco," *Time,* LXXXI (February, 1963), 34.
Grierson, John. *Grierson on Documentary*, ed. Forsyth Hardy. London: Collins, 1946.
———. "Grierson on Television," *Contrast* II (Summer 1963), 220-4.
———."The Story of Documentary Film," *The Fortnightly Review* CLII (August, 1939), 121-30.
Griffith, Richard. *The World of Robert Flaherty*. New York: Duell, Sloan and Pearce, 1953.
———. Gilbert Seldes and Jac Venza. *Television U.S.A.: 13 Seasons*. New York: The Museum of Modern Art Film Library, 1963.
Guthrie, Tyrone. "Theatre and Television," *The Eighth Art,* ed. Robert Lewis Shayon. New York: Holt, Rinehart and Winston, 1962, 91-9.
Hamburger, Phillip. "Victory at Sea," *New Yorker* XXIX (April 4, 1953), 77-9.
Hazam, Lou. "Dollars and Documentaries — 'This Fair Conjunction'," *Television Quarterly,* II (Winter, 1963), 33-9.
Hazard, Patrick. "Instant History," *Contrast* II (Winter 1962), 92-97.

"Here We Go Again — Cancellation of *Spy Next Door,"* *National Review,* X (February 11, 1961), 71.

Hill, Derek. "The Short Film Situation," *Sight and Sound,* XXXI (Summer, 1962), 108-12.

Himelstein, Morgan Y. *Drama Was a Weapon — The Left Wing Theatre in New York, 1929-1941.* New Brunswick, New Jersey: Rutgers University Press, 1963.

Houston, Penelope. "Captive or Free," *Sight and Sound,* XXVII (Winter, 1957-58), 116-20.

————. *The Contemporary Cinema.* Middlesex, England: Penguin Books, Ltd., 1963.

"How To Get Involved," *Newsweek,* LVII (May 8, 1961), 64.

Hyatt, Gordon, "A Form for Television," *Television Quarterly,* I (February, 1962), 24-8.

————."Words *and* Pictures," *Television Quarterly,* II (Spring, 1963), 46-50.

"Indians Protest Film on Caste System," *Christian Century,* LXXX (April 24, 1963), 515.

"Insecurity in Numbers," *New Republic,* CXLI (November 30, 1959), 7.

Institute for Education by Radio and Television. *Education on the Air-1947.* Columbus: Ohio State University, 1947.

Jenkins, Peter. "The Political Screen," *Contrast,* III (Autumn, 1963), 25-9.

Kaplan, Abraham. "Realism in the Film: A Philosopher's Viewpoint," *Quarterly of Film, Radio and Television,* VII (1952-53), 370-84.

Katz, Robert and Nancy. "Documentary in Transition, Part II: The International Scene and the American Documentary," *Hollywood Quarterly,* IV (1949-50), 51-64.

Knight, Arthur. "The Decline of the Documentary," *Saturday Review,* (March 30, 1963), 35.

Lassally, Walter, "Communication and the Creative Process," *Film,* No. 37 (Autumn, 1963), 18-24.

Littell, Robert. "A Glance at Newsreels," *American Mercury,* XXX (November, 1933), 263-71.

Luft, Herbert G. "Rotha and the World," *Quarterly of Film, Radio and Television,* X (Fall, 1955), 89-99.

Lyons, Eugene. "Louis de Rochemont, Maverick of the Movies," *Reader's Digest,* LV (July, 1949), 23-7.

Knight, Arthur. *The Liveliest Art.* New York: The Macmillan Company, 1959.

Lindgren, Ernest, *The Art of the Film.* London: Allen and Unwin, 1948.

Maddison, John. "What Is a Television Film?," *Contrast,* III (Autumn, 1963), 6-9, 71-5.

Maloney, Martin. *The Radio Play.* Evanston, Illinois: School of Speech, Northwestern Student Book Exchange, 1950.

Mannes, Marya. "Just Looking," *The Reporter,* XXIV (March 16, 1961), 49-50.

————. "The Lost Tribe of Television," *The Eighth Art,* ed. Robert Lewis Shayon. New York: Holt, Rinehart and Winston, 1962, 23-9.

Manvell, Roger. *Film* (Revised and Enlarged Edition). London and Aylesbury: Hazell, Watson and Viney, Ltd., 1946.

————. *Film and the Public.* Middlesex, England: Penguin Books Ltd., 1950.

————. *The Crowded Air.* New York: The Channel Press, 1953.

Marcorelles, Louis. "Jean-Luc Goddard's Half Truths," *Film Quarterly,* (Spring, 1964), 4-7.

————. "The Nazi Cinema 1933-1945," *Sight and Sound,* XXV (Autumn, 1955), 65-9.

Maritain, Jacques. *Creative Intuition in Art and Poetry.* New York: Meridian Books, 1950.

Martin, Pete. "I Call On Edward R. Murrow," *Saturday Evening Post,* CCXXX (January 18, 1958), 32-3.

Mayer, Martin, "How Good is TV at Its Best?," *Harpers,* CCXXI (August, 1960), 82-90.

————. "TV's Lords of Creation," *Harpers*, CCXIII (November and December, 1963), 25-32; 45-52.

Mickelson, Sig. "TV Accepts Its Greatest Challenge," *Television*, XV (May, 1958), 82, 84.

————. "Growth of Television News," *Journalism Quarterly*, XXIV:3 (Summer, 1957), 304-310.

Montagu, Ivor. *The Political Censorship of Films*. London: Victor Gollancz, 1929.

Morgan, Thomas B. "Crisis, Conflict and Change in TV News," *Look*, XXV (November 7, 1961), 48-62.

Moshkin, J. Robert. "Newton Minow — A New Look at TV," *Look*, XXVI (October 9, 1962), 98-100.

Mumford, Lewis. *Art and Technics*. New York: Columbia University Press, 1960.

Murrow, Edward R. and Fred W. Friendly. *See It Now*. New York: Simon and Schuster, 1955.

Newhall, Beaumont. *The History of Photography from 1839 to the Present Day*. New York: Museum of Modern Art, 1949.

Nicoll, Allardyce. *Film and Theatre*. New York: Thomas Y. Crowell Co., 1936.

"Oasis in a Wasteland," Commonweal, LXXV (September 29, 1961), 30.

O'Gara, James. "Battle of Newburgh: NBC's *White Paper*," Commonweal, LXXV (February 16, 1962), 532.

Panofsky, Erwin. "Style and Medium in the Motion Picture," *Critique*, I (January-February, 1947), 5-28.

Pedell, Kathy. "This is Murrow," *TV Guide*, III (February 5, 1955), 4-7.

Pichel, Irving. "Films for Television," *Hollywood Quarterly*, V (1950-51), 363-72.

Project XX, The Staff of. "Anatomy of a Documentary," *Journal of the University Film Producer's Association*, XIV (Winter, 1962), 5-7, 20-21.

Purser, Phillip. "Think-Tape — A Profile of Denis Mitchell," *Contrast*, I (Winter, 1961), 108-14.

"Reactions to Third Reich," Commonweal, LXXIII (February 10, 1961), 497.

Robinson, David. "Looking for Documentary: The Background to Production," *Sight and Sound*, XXVII (Summer, 1957), 6-11.

————. "Looking for Documentary: The Ones That Got Away," *Sight and Sound*, XXVII (Autumn, 1957), 70-5.

————. "News Story," *Contrast*, I (Spring, 1962), 185-95.

————. "Shooting on Tape," *Contrast*, III (Autumn, 1963), 30-3.

Rose, Ernest D. "In Search of Documentary," *Arts in Society*, Part I (Fall, 1960), Part II (Spring-Summer, 1962). University of Wisconsin. (reprint).

Rosten, Leo. "The Intellectual and the Mass Media: Some Rigorously Random Remarks," *Daedalus*, XXIX (Spring, 1960), 33-46.

Rotha, Paul. *Celluloid — The Film Today*. London, New York and Toronto: Longmans, Green and Co., 1933.

————. *Documentary Film* (Third Edition). London: Faber and Faber, Ltd., 1952. New York: Hastings House, Publishers.

————. "Television and the Future of Documentary," *Quarterly of Film, Radio and Television*, IX (Summer, 1955), 366-73.

————. *Television in the Making*. London: Focal Press, Ltd., 1956.

———— and Richard Griffith. *The Film Till Now*. New York: Twayne Publishers, Inc., 1963.

Rothstein, Arthur. *Photojournalism: Pictures for Magazines and Newspapers*, New York: American Photographic Book Publishers ,1956.

Ryan, Milo. *History in Sound*. Seattle: University of Washington Press, 1963.

Schramm, Wilbur. "The Nature of News," *Journalism Quarterly*, XXVI (September, 1949), 259-69.

Schreiber, Flora Rheta. "Television: A New Idiom," *Hollywood Quarterly*, IV (1949-50), 189-91.

————. "TV in Public Affairs," *Hollywood Quarterly*, V (1950-51), 144-52.

Seldes, Gilbert. *The Public Arts*. New York: Simon and Schuster, 1956.

Severin, Werner J. "Cameras with a Purpose: The Photojournalists of F.S.A.," *Jour-

nalism Quarterly, XLII:2 (Spring, 1964), 191-200.

Shayon, Robert Lewis. "Biography's Back Yard," *Saturday Review,* XLVI, (June 29, 1963), 22.

———. "Fuse in the Documentary," *Saturday Review,* XLIII (December 17, 1960), 29.

———. "Gift of Value," *Saturday Review,* XLVI (January 19, 1963), 57.

———. "Intertel and Grass Roots," *Saturday Review,* XLIII (December 24, 1960), 32.

Shils, Edward. "Mass Society and Its Culture," *Daedalus,* LIIIIX (Spring, 1960), 288-314.

Siepmann, Charles A. "Documentary Redefined," *Ideas on Film.* New York: Funk and Wagnalls Company, 1951.

Slesinger, Donald. "The Film and Public Opinion," *Print, Radio and Film in a Democracy,* Chicago: University of Chicago Press, 1942, 79-98.

Spiegel, Irwin, O. "The Hidden Persuaders in the Garden," *Telefilm,* I (Fall, 1961), 13, 47.

———. "The Importance of Other People," *Telefilm,* II (Fall, 1962), 3, 25.

Spottiswoode, Raymond. *A Grammar of the Film.* Berkeley and Los Angeles: University of California Press, 1959.

Sugrue, Thomas. "The Newsreels," *Scribner's Magazine,* CI (April, 1937), 9-18.

Summers, Harrison B. *Radio Programs Carried on National Networks, 1926-1956.* Columbus: The Ohio State University, 1958.

Swallow, Norman, "Ealing, 1961," *Journal: The Society of Film and Television Arts,* V (Summer, 1961), 2-6.

———. "Instant Truth," *Contrast,* II (Summer, 1954), 225-29.

Swing, Raymond. *"Good Evening!"* New York: Harcourt, Brace & World, Inc., 1964.

"Through a Lens Clearly," *America,* CVII (August 4, 1962), 583.

"Too Hot To Handle," *Newsweek,* LXII (August 5, 1963), 67.

"TV in the Holy Land: *Way of the Cross," Newsweek,* LV (April 18, 1960), 79.

"Two-Pronged Attack," *Newsweek,* LXI (June 3, 1963), 82.

"Two Men and a Camera in Cuba," *Time,* LXXVI (December 19, 1960), 54.

Waldron, Gloria. *The Information Film.* New York: Columbia University Press, 1949.

Weiss, Margaret R. "Creative Vision — Six Decades of the Photographer's Art," *Saturday Review,* XLV (September 22, 1962), 45-51.

———. "In the Tradition of Joseph Costa," *Saturday Review,* XLVI (January 12, 1963), 92-3.

Wellek, René. *Concepts in Criticism.* New York and New Haven: Yale University Press, 1963.

"Where Real Drama Is: *CBS Reports," Newsweek,* LVI (December 12, 1960), 88.

Whiteside, Thomas. "The One-Ton Pencil," *New Yorker,* XXVII (February 17, 1962), 41-2.

"World of Donald Hyatt," reprinted from the *Dartmouth Alumni Magazine* (January, 1961). Distributed by the National Broadcasting Company.

Vandermeulen, Howard. "Now What, McGee?," *Electronic Age,* XXI (Summer, 1962), 22-5.

Vardac, Nicholas. "Documentary Film as an Art Form," *Sight and Sound,* XIX (April, 1951), 477-80.

"Victory Still Going Strong," *Broadcasting,* LIV (January 13, 1958), 52.

"Whole Truth Someday," *New Republic,* CXLIII (December 12, 1960), 8.

Yeager, Murray. *An Analysis of Edward R. Murrow's See It Now Program.* Unpublished doctoral dissertation, University of Iowa, August, 1956.

INDEX